The WOODS family

The 300 year history of the GRIFFITHS, LOWE, and WOODS families plus Mary Ann Lowe and John Woods and their 10 children in New Zealand.

by **Trevor N Price**

Mary Ann Lowe Woods 1880 aged 45

Other family history books by Trevor N Price

MORGAN PRICE & family … Wales & Southland, NZ.
The THOMAS family (John & Uncle George) Devon, England & NZ.
WILLIAM THOMAS & family … Devon, England & NZ.
The STEVENS family … Devon, England & Canterbury, NZ.

First published 2020 by:
Starting Gun Books, Auckland, New Zealand

National Library of New Zealand Cataloguing-in-Publication Data

Price, Trevor N. (Trevor Nelson), 1937-
The WOODS family: The 300 year history of the GRIFFITHS, LOWE and WOODS families of Wales, England and New Zealand. / T.N. Price.
Includes bibliographical references and index. (v2)

ISBN 978-0-473-53108-9

Cover by Mary-Ann Attree
Printed by Lightning Source

This book is dedicated to the four descendants of
Mary Ann and John Woods' children, who met often,
sharing their research, & providing much of these family facts …
Peggy D Meikle .. Jessie: **A Christine Woods** .. Edward:
Gwyneth I Broadbent .. Harry: **Trevor N Price** .. Phebe:

"To be ignorant of what occurred before you were born,
is to remain a child" …… *Marcus Tullius Cicero*
Roman Statesman 106BC – 43 BC

CONTENTS and PAGE FINDER

children from these 2 families married in New Zealand in 1853

MARY ANN LOWE born 1835

married in 1853, in Auckland, NZ

JOHN WOODS born 1828

page 180

they had 10 children ....

The GRIFFITHS and LOWE families

Of Wales ..... Brief Tree

EDWARD GRIFFITHS b est 1780-85
married 1803
JANE EVANS b est 1777-80

2 children were born in Flintshire, Wales.
JOHN GRIFFITHS b 1803
ANN GRIFFITHS b 1805 (continues below)

ANN GRIFFITHS b 1805
married 1830
GRIFFITH LOWE bc1798

5 children were all born in Flintshire, Wales
EDWARD LOWE b 1829
JOSEPH LOWE b 1831
MARY LOWE b 1833
JOHN LOWE b 1835
WILLIAM LOWE b 1838

The LOWE FAMILY HISTORY

WALES.

It was general knowledge within the family in New Zealand, that Ann and Griffith Lowe were from Wales and research has provided us with the following facts gained from the northern area of Wales' parish church registers and general history of the Parish of Flintshire, Wales.

Griffith Lowe and Ann nee Griffiths and 5 children, came to New Zealand and settled at Wellington in 1840.

GRIFFITH LOWE was born about 1798. He may have been born in the Flintshire area but his baptism has not been found. Some Lowe families were recorded at Worthenbury but that Griffith Lowe was too old and married Mary in Shropshire.

ANN GRIFFITHS. To find Ann's baptism and parent's names, we hired a Welsh professional researcher. We strongly felt the age Ann recorded in the Bolton ship's passenger register was accurate at 35, which gave her a birth in 1805. We proved there were no Ann Griffiths baptism's at Overton Parish Church between 1798 and 1809. She married at Flint town in 1830 so we moved the search there. He found 2 Ann Griffith's baptisms, with one dying young. The other baptised at Flint Parish Church Sept 8, 1805 to an Edward and Jane Griffiths. Our researcher then perused the indexes for marriage registers for Flintshire and the parishes adjoining it, for the marriage of Edward and Jane. In all those parishes there was only one found... at Ysceifiog Church, a few months before Ann's brother John was born in 1803. (T)

EDWARD and JANE GRIFFITHS

1780/5 EDWARD GRIFFITHS was born in the early 1780s in Flintshire County, Wales.

1803 Edward Griffiths married **JANE EVANS** at the St Mary's Ysceifiog Parish Church, Flintshire, on 14 May 1803. Banns were called and the Curate was also named Edward Griffiths. Edward signed and Jane gave her X mark. The witnesses were John Parry and the X mark of John Griffiths. (father?) They lived in Ysceifiog Village where Edward was a 'Joiner'. (cert T)

St Mary's Church was in such a state of dilapidation in 1835 that services had to be discontinued. That building was demolished and the present church opened in 1837. (Topographical Dic-L)

YSCEIFIOG PARISH CHURCH in 1837

YSCEIFIOG is a small village and Parish, in Flintshire, 4 mile SE of Holywell, 8 mile W of Flint. It lies on a back road just north of the A541 highway between Nannerch and Caerwys. The name translates roughly as ...... *"a place where Elder trees grow."* (Wikipedea)

The metal, lead, abounds in the Ysceifiog Parish and several mines, which had been worked for many years with great advantage, have recently been discontinued due to the low price of the metal. On the high ground in this parish are the remains of a Roman encampment. (Topographical Dictionary 1834)

1803 Edward and Jane's son **JOHN GRIFFITHS** was baptised at the Flint Parish Church 31 July 1803.

1805 Edward and Jane's daughter **ANN GRIFFITHS** was baptised at Flint Parish Church on 8 Sept 1805. We have not found any more children for Edward and Jane, and Flintshire records are not available for easy researching over the internet.

We do not know why people living in Ysceifiog which had its own Anglican Church, needed to travel 8 mile to Flint town to baptise their two children. Perhaps their Church was without a Vicar for those two to three years. Perhaps they felt it unsafe to enter the building. Perhaps Flint Church was the Griffiths family's original Church.

Flint Parish Register's Ann Griffiths entry, 8 Sept 1805

The vicar has written Anne but she was known in NZ as Ann ... without the e on the end.

1841, 7 June census. We have no knowledge of what happened after these children's births, but we found Edward and Jane in the Wales 1841 census. Living at Ysceifiog Village in Flintshire, were Edward Griffiths, a joiner, aged 55-59, with wife Jane aged 60-64, and their female servant Leah Jones aged 15-19. All three noted they were of this parish of Ysceifiog.

There were only 9 houses in the township with 25 people, the large Church (no Vicar living in the town) and the 'Rose and Crown', which sounds like a pub but no Landlord mentioned living there or nearby.

Son John at 38, had left home by this date and daughter Ann 36 was now married, had 5 children and was living at Wellington in New Zealand.

FLINT. *"The county town in the shire of that name is beautifully situated on the estuary on the River Dee, about 5 miles E.S.E. of Holywell and about 203 miles distant from London. It was formerly a place of considerable importance, on account of its maritime situation and its extensive fortress."*

(Gleanings of the Histories of Flint (etc) by J Poole 1831)

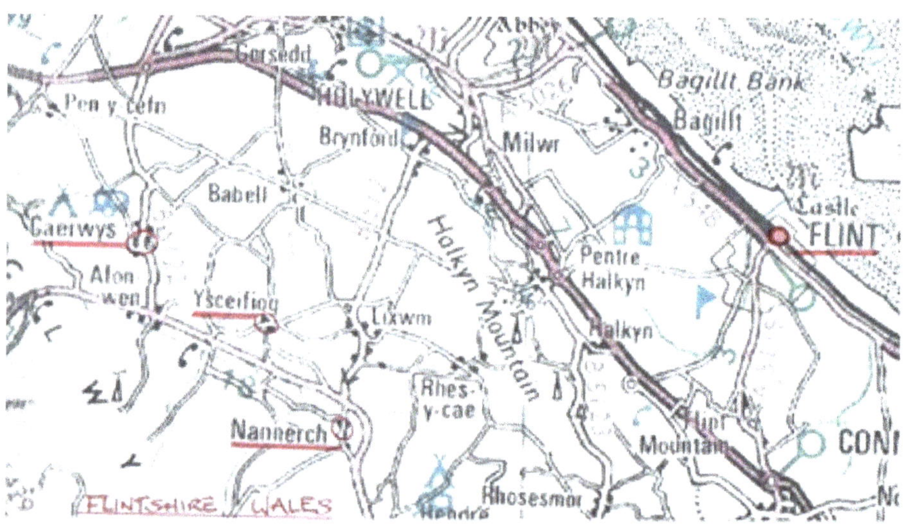

YSCEIFIOG location in Flintshire:

1841-1851 Between these censuses Jane Griffiths died ….. and Edward remarried.

1847 JANE DIED: On February 15, 1847 at Llan-Ysceifiog Jane died of a Bronchial disease aged 70 years. Her niece Jane Biddy notified the authorities. Husband Edward was noted as 'Farmer'. (I do not think Jane Biddy got this right as in all other records we have found Edward was a Joiner) (T cert)
The Welsh word LLan in English means Glebe described in my dictionary as *'land granted to a clergyman as part of his benefice; land especially with regard to growing things'*. From all this it seems Jane may have died while weeding the Vicar's vegetable patch.

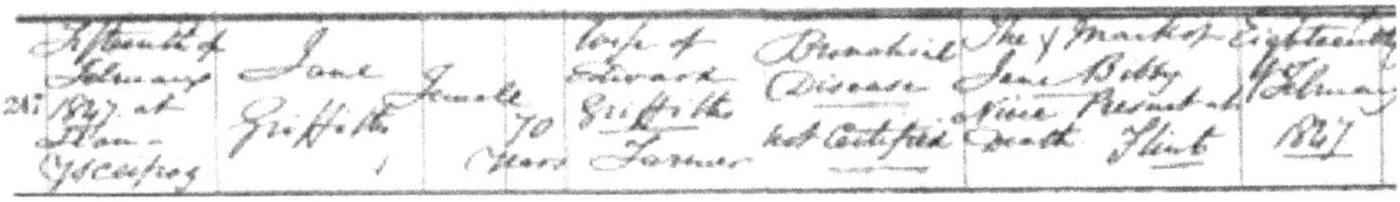

24	Fifteenth of February 1847 at Llan-Ysceifiog	Jane Griffiths	Female	70 Years	Wife of Edward Griffiths Farmer	Bronchial Disease not Certified	The X Mark of Jane Biddy Niece Present at death Flint	Eighteenth of February 1847

1848. Edward Griffiths (63) married Leah Williams (24) during the Apr - June quarter 1848 in the Holywell Registration District, which included the Ysceifiog Parish Church. (JT)

Leah, was christened on 12 Sept 1824 at Cilcain in Flintshire. The records mention her father John Williams and mother Dorothy Jones. Leah joined Edward and his wife Jane as a house servant before the 1841 census using her mother's surname. Maybe she was raised only by her mother. We guess that by law she needed her father's surname to marry. (T)

1851, 31 March census. Living in the same village … at 3 Northgate St, Ysceifiog, were Edward Griffiths aged 66 a Joiner, his wife Leah Griffiths 27, and son John 2.
Seems Edward married his servant.

1851-1861 Between these censuses Edward Griffiths died. Leah remained living in that house.

1860 EDWARD DIED: On June 16, 1860 in the Village of Ysceifiog, Edward, a Joiner, died suddenly aged 80.
Peter Parry the Flintshire Coroner held an Inquest 2 days later and Edward's cause of death as written on the certificate was ...
"Died suddenly by the visitation of God in a natural way." (T)

39	Sixteenth Day of June 1860 in the Village of Ysceifiog	Edward Griffiths	Male	80 years	Joiner	Died suddenly by the visitation of God in a natural way	Information received from Peter Parry Coroner for Flintshire Inquest held 18 June 1860	Twenty fourth June 1860

1861, 7 April census. Living at 3 Northgate St, Ysceifiog Village were Leah Griffiths, widow 34, (37 ?), a Laundry Maid and her son John aged 12 (born 1848) a scholar.
We have not searched for Leah and her son beyond this date.

Ann named 3 of her children... Edward, Jane and John.... with other children probably named after their father's families. (T)

ANN GRIFFITHS in WALES

Ann Griffiths born 1805, probably lived with her parents in Ysceifiog Village, until she was old enough to go out to work. There were no schools in those days and Ann remained illiterate all her life. At an early age Ann may have been employed by friends of the family and later she may have attended a 'labour market' held at Caerwys, or Mold or Flint town where employment was found. She may have been offered work as a Domestic Servant in the Parish of Overton, in Flintshire, some 27 miles south of her family home ... as we found her there in 1829.

OVERTON was the main town in the Overton Parish on the southern border of Flintshire.

"Overton was granted Borough status by Edward 1st in 1292. Overton, a small village, lies about 1 mile south east of the bridge over the River Dee, and situated on a lofty ridge. On one side an extensive flat consisting of rich meadows, varied, enlivened by the windings of the river and bounded in front with fertile well wooded slopes, while the naked rusty coloured mountains soar above in the distance. On the other side, a grand contrast by the vale of Cheshire and the plain of Salop."

(Beauties of England & Wales by Rev. J Evans 1812)

OVERTON: *A parish, and town, with railway station, and sometimes referred to as Overton-on-Dee, situated in the detached part of Flintshire, near the River Dee, and 6 mile SE of Wrexham.*

(Gazetteer 1887)

--oo0oo--

1829 We found Ann Griffiths (single, aged 23) at the Overton St Mary's Parish Church where she baptised her son ....

................**EDWARD GRIFFITHS**, described as illegitimate, on 11 January 1829. Ann's 'abode' was noted as "The Overton Workhouse". (also known as Poorhouse) (Cert CW)

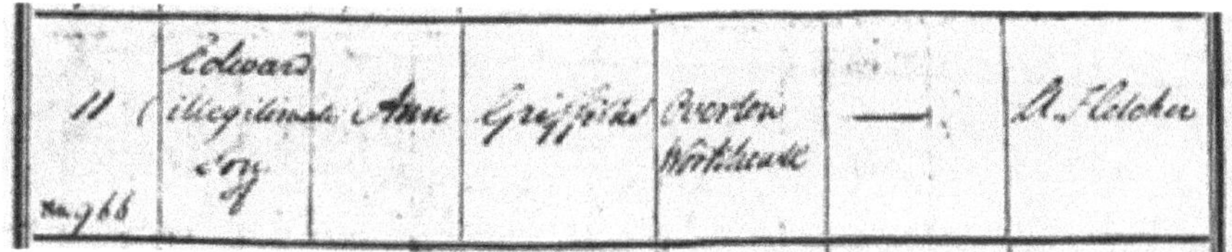

11 No. 966	Edward illegitimate son	Ann	Griffiths	Overton Workhouse	—	A. Fletcher

We think the employment she enjoyed within the parish was terminated, maybe because the people died or maybe because she became pregnant and, if she had parents, siblings or even cousins in the area, we feel sure she would have approached them for temporary accommodation. When the employment ceased she would then be alone, jobless and homeless, and having lived in the parish for a number of years, the 'fathers' of the town would have given her a room at the local workhouse until she found a more permanent residence.

The OVERTON POORHOUSE: *"The Poor Law act and Poor houses were created to provide a place where people who were unable to support themselves could live and work. Most parishes provided relief in the form of money, food, clothing, goods and housing or allowed recipients to continue living independently. There were 5 towns in the Overton Parish and each paid an annual sum for the privilege to send their poor to the Overton Poorhouse, which was very small ... little else than a brick cottage. Each pauper was farmed out at 2 shillings a week to a contractor, who was entitled to all the labour he could extract from the inmates.*

(extracts from House of Commons reports on the Poor Laws 1834)

St Mary the Virgin's Church, Overton. (CW)

1830 We have no way of proving this, but it is probable Griffith Lowe was working as a farm labourer in the Overton area at the start of the year 1830, and he met Ann. Then, during the year of 1830 Griffith seems to have moved (probably for available work) up to the northern edge of Flintshire ... some 27 miles. We think soon after he left, Ann found herself pregnant and immediately travelled north to meet Griffith and to introduce baby Edward to her parents in Ysceifiog. We imagine after some discussion between the four of them, Griffith and Ann decided to marry and Banns were called at St Mary's Anglican Church in Flint town. (T)

1830 MARRIAGE. The wedding register of St Mary's & St David's Flint Parish Church in Wales, advises ....

ANN GRIFFITHS and GRIFFITH LOWE
were married there on 6 December 1830.

Griffith was <u>of this parish</u> and Ann, was of the parish of Overton, Flintshire. They were married after Banns were called 14 Nov, 21 Nov, 28 Nov, and with consent by William Maddock Williams, the Flint parish Curate. Both Ann and Griffith signed with their mark 'X'. Their witnesses were Edward Griffiths and Mary Jones. Edward, actually signed his name and we believe he was Ann's father. (cert CW,T)

Above is a sketch of St Mary's Flint Parish Church,
which was erected in the 13th Century, made of timber boards, and demolished in 1847 … 17 years after Griffith and Ann married.

Griffith Lowe of this Parish
Bachelor
and Ann Griffiths of The Parifh
of Overton
were married in this Church by Banns with Confent of
this sixth Day of
December in the Year One thoufand eight hundred and thirty
By me Wm Maddock Williams Per: Curate
This Marriage was folemnized between us { The mark X of Griffith Lowe
The mark X of Ann Griffiths
In the Prefence of { Edward Griffiths
The mark of + Mary Jones
No. 171.

(Two minor points of interest..........
Griffith Lowe stated he was "of this Parish" (Flint) but this does not mean he was born there... it means that he had been living there for at least 3 weeks before he married. He may have been born there, or anywhere in Wales or even anywhere in England.
Griffith or Griffiths. In Wales a name can be used as either a given or surname .... But a surname generally has an s on the end and where the name is a given name, it doesn't.)

1831. Son **JOSEPH LOWE** arrived on March 27, 1831, nearly 4 months after they married. He was baptised at Overton St Mary's Church.

(Maybe he was named after Griffith Lowe's father ?
We have not been able to locate his parents.)

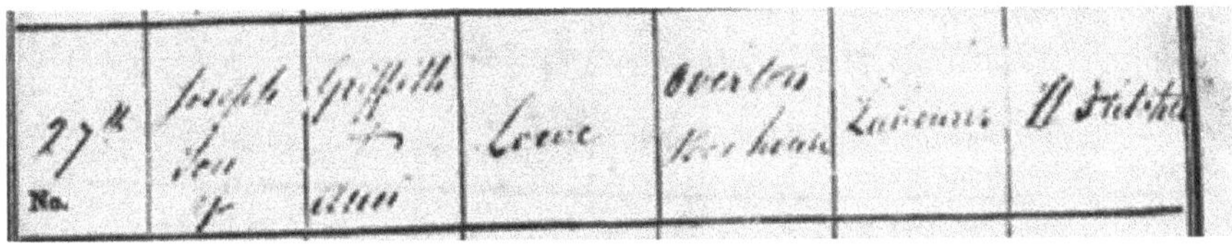

27th No.	Joseph Son of	Griffith & Ann	Lowe	Overton Poor house	Labourer	D Griffith

1830. It seems that soon after their 1830 marriage Ann and Griffith Lowe returned to the Overton township in Wales, as the baptismal record shows the four of them living at the 'Overton Poorhouse'.

Initially, Ann was given shelter in the Overton Poorhouse when she was pregnant with Edward and as a single mum the Poorhouse trustees would have recognised her need and allowed her to stay on and tend to Edward's needs. When Ann married and gave birth to Joseph the Poorhouse trustees have continued to help this family now of four.

The House of Commons Reports of 1834, also stated......
Of the 13 in the poorhouse at the beginning of September 1832, only one was between the ages of 12 and 60 years."

This means, Ann and Griffith Lowe and their two children had moved on before Sept 1832. (T)

The OVERTON FONT where Edward and Joseph Lowe would have been christened.
(photo by CW)

1832 to 1839

Over the following years Ann and Griffith probably moved about within the immediate district, as they did not own land and had to move to wherever Griffith found farm work. Most farm labouring jobs came with accommodation and we think Griffith must have found such a place at Sarn, a general farming area in Wales near Threapwood.

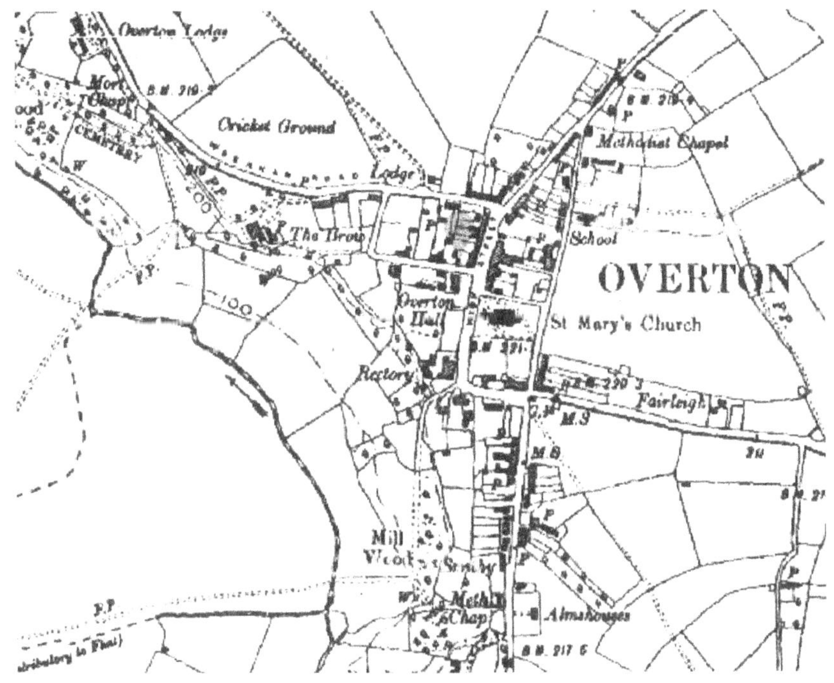

MAP: This map of the **Town of Overton** was dated 1900 but the oldest map we could find dated 1878 still showed the location of the Overton Poorhouses (Almshouses) on the southern border of the town. This must be where Ann lived for at least four years, during the birth of her first two children. The road running past St Mary's Church and off to the right is the road Ann and Griffith would have taken when they moved to the Sarn and Threapwood area.

GENERAL .... Daughter Mary Ann's NZ death certificate shows she was born in Liverpool. Sons John and William's NZ death certificates show they were born at Bolton in Greater Manchester. (?) (This information (probably given to the NZ funeral company by their children) was confused as they came to New Zealand on the ship 'Bolton', and we have found their baptism records in Flintshire, Wales and in Cheshire, England, just a step or two over the Wales / England border. (more details later)

1832 THREAPWOOD:

From 1832 until 1839, our Lowe family were living near the town of Threapwood, (more probably on a farm in the Hamlet of Sarn, in Wales, nearby) where Griffith would have been employed as a farm labourer. Late in 1839 they left Wales for life in New Zealand.

Threapwood was almost a no man's land, being near the border of Cheshire in England and the borders of Flintshire and Denbighshire, both in Wales. Over the years the border shifted regularly and Threapwood's history was quite chequered.

THREAPWOOD'S St John the Evangelist's Church in England.

In the book .... *"A Topographical Dictionary of Wales" by S. Lewis in 1834,* we find it *'An extra-parochial district containing 477 inhabitants and until of late years*

formed a tract of waste common, (an area of open public land) *which, on account of its extra-parochial exemption from all local jurisdiction, was long the resort of abandoned characters of every description, and especially of women of loose or blemished morals, who made a transient abode here, to be freed clandestinely from consequences of illicit amours.... The inhabitants considering themselves beyond the reach of all legal authority opposed, even with force, the execution of the assizes and other laws within their precinct. Some years ago, however, a chapel was erected here...'*
Another book "*Tours of Wales" by T Pennant 1778,* records that the *'Threapwood name is from the Anglo-Saxon Threapian, to threap means to persist in an argument whether it be right or wrong. Threapwood was a common in an ancient oak forest.* It states that Threapwood *'...was for hundreds of years not actually part of any parish and the residents considered themselves beyond the law and it became a refuge for vagabonds and fugitives.*

We do not think our family was raised under these conditions but this gives some history to the district where Griffith and Ann moved to work and live, about 1832.

CHILDREN. Ann and Griffith Lowe are known to have brought up five children ....

EDWARD	born	1829.	**JOSEPH**	born	1831
MARY ANN	born	1833.	**JOHN**	born	1835
WILLIAM	born	1838.			

BAPTISMS. The records show 3 baptisms of children of ***'Griffith Lowe, labourer and wife Ann, of Threapwood',*** were performed by the Rev John Frederick Churton at the St John's Parish Church at Threapwood, Cheshire, England ....

1833 Griffith and Ann Lowe baptised their daughter **MARY LOWE** on 10 February 1833. Used the name Mary Ann in NZ.

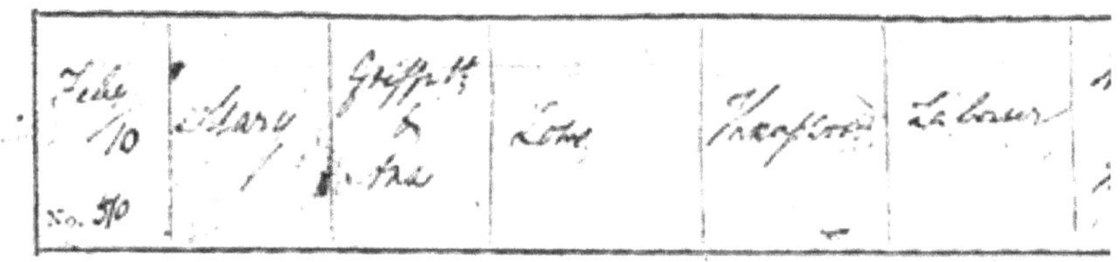

Feb 10 No. 510	Mary	Griffith & Ann	Lowe	Threapwood	Labourer

1835 Griffith and Ann's third son named **JOHN LOWE** was born about 1835 at Sarn, but seems to have been missed when it was time to baptise him.

1837/9 Fourth son, & 5th child **WILLIAM LOWE** was baptised at Threapwood by Rev Churton on 16 June 1839. (more later)

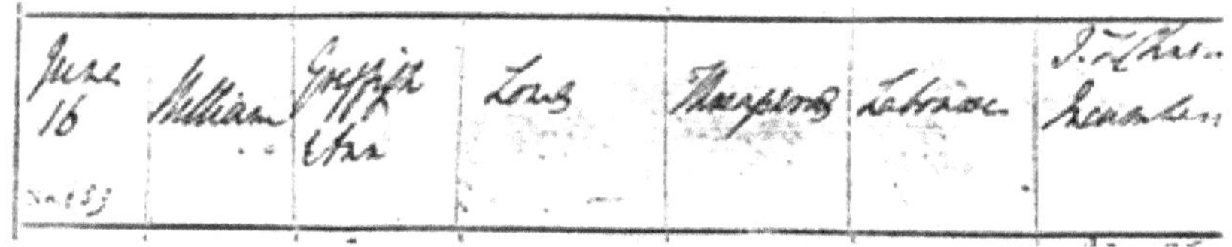

June 16	William	Griffith & Ann	Lowe	Threapwood	Labourer

JOSEPH LOWE baptised Sept 28, 1833 was also baptised at Overton March 27, 1831) Joseph was baptised twice.

We do not know where son **JOHN LOWE** born in 1835 was baptised and he may not have been. In New Zealand he must have needed a birth certificate or at least knowledge of a baptism, as enquiries were made from NZ in 1870.

A LETTER dated May 1870, from Edward Davies of Ruabon, Wales to The Parish Clerk of Tallarn Green, asks .. *"Will you kindly search your register for the christening of John Lowe son of Griffith and Ann Lowe, The Sarn, Worthenbury, about* *the year 1835."* He noted *"Mr Churton, Vicar, took them over to New Zealand."* He added *"If you can furnish the certificate I will remit your claim."* We have no idea if the certificate was forwarded. We think the comments in the letter give **the address** of Griffith and Ann in 1835 at least.

The Tallarn Green, Church in Wales church was built in 1874... too late for our family's use.

We found no record of baptisms for John at the Threapwood, the Worthenbury and the Wrexham parish churches, for John Lowe born any year around 1835 ....

Son Joseph baptised in 1833....(?) His emigration records imply he was born 1831.

Son William's emigration entry would suggest he was born in the middle of 1837.

Rev J. F. Churton seems to have ignored the boundary between England and Wales.

He described himself as Rector of Threapwood (England) when registering the only marriage we could find of his at the parish church at Worthenbury (about two miles from Threapwood, in Wales) on 29 October 1832. We found two baptisms and lots of burials performed by him, the earliest being 24 June 1832 and the last being on 8 April 1839. The last activity recorded in the Threapwood parish records by Rev Churton was a baptism on 29 Sept 1839. During Sept 1839 a farewell gathering was held at Wrexham (Wales) for the Rev Churton. Soon after this Rev Churton and his family, and our Lowe family of seven, travelled to London (probably with other people from the Threapwood district) where they boarded the ship *'Bolton'* on 19 November 1839 for the long trip to New Zealand.

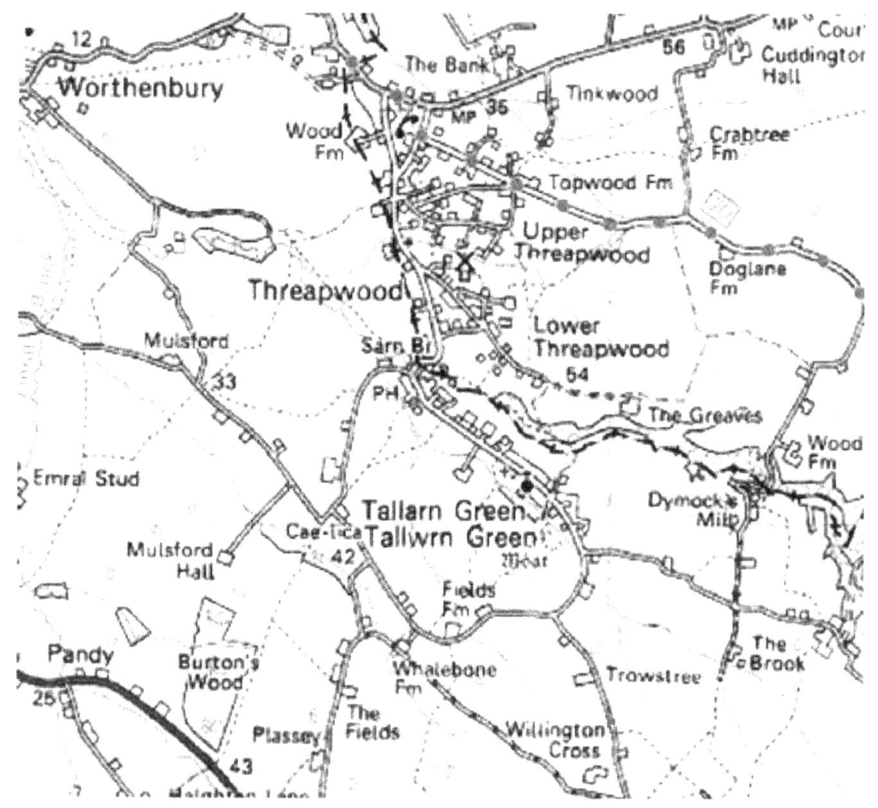

This MAP shows Worthenbury, Threapwood, the SARN BRIDGE & Tallarn Green.

The line of dashes starting on the right edge of the map locates the boundary between England and Wales, running north westerly down the Wych Brook to Sarn Bridge, then north across land to the west of Threapwood village, and on the join the River Dee. So, Wales was on one side and England on the other side of Sarn Bridge.

The Sarn area was basically a rural area with a few farms around the bridge. There were 3 or 4 cottages with one housing a small grocery shop, plus The Queen's Head Hotel, The Sarn Mill, and the Well House where many local people drew water for domestic use.

The QUEENS HEAD HOTEL and The SARN BRIDGE 2011 The Hotel in England and across the bridge is Wales.

The QUEEN'S HEAD and the SARN BRIDGE in 2011

The Hotel is in England and the house seen over the bridge is in Wales.

--oo00oo--

GRIFFITH LOWE:

In our search of the baptismal registers of the Threapwood Extra-Parochial Chapelry we found only two Lowe families (Thomas and Griffith) active in this church around 1758 to 1798 ... but our Griffith Lowe not mentioned.

In the Worthenbury Church and the Hanmer Church registers, we noticed two Lowe families ... John bc1735 and his son Joseph b1757 involved in baptisms, marriages and burials... but our Griffith Lowe was not mentioned.

John's son Griffith Lowe was born 1762 died 1763, and Joseph's son Griffith Lowe born 1778 baptised Griffy, married Mary Pountney at Broseley, Shropshire 1 July 1805 and had a son named John baptised in 1809.

No other Griffith Lowe seems to match our fellow. (T)

1839. EMIGRATION.

The New Zealand Land Company was formed by the British Government early in 1939 for the purpose of sending British settlers to NZ on a planned basis.

An *"EMIGRATION TO NEW ZEALAND"* advertising bill of 1839, invited applications from UK residents to move and live in New Zealand, with the offer of a FREE boat trip.

EMIGRATION

TO

NEW ZEALAND.

The Directors of the New Zealand Company, do hereby give notice that they are ready to receive Applications for a FREE PASSAGE to the

TOWN OF WELLINGTON,

AT LAMBTON HARBOUR,

PORT NICHOLSON, COOK'S STRAITS,

NEW ZEALAND,

From Agricultural Laborers, Shepherds, Miners, Gardeners, Brickmakers, Mechanics, Handicraftsmen, and Domestic Servants, BEING MARRIED, and not exceeding Forty years of age; also from SINGLE FEMALES, under the care of near relatives, and SINGLE MEN, accompanied by one or more ADULT SISTERS, not exceeding, in either case, the age of Thirty years. Strict inquiry will be made as to qualifications and character.

Apply on Mondays, Thursdays, and Saturdays, to Mr. JOSEPH PHIPSON, 11, Union Passage, Birmingham,

AGENT TO THE COMPANY.

TOWN and COUNTRY SECTIONS of LAND on sale, full particulars of which may be had on application as above.

From the 'The Exeter Flying Post'....

Here they describe the climate in NZ for the purpose of health and production ...

"probably about the finest in the world. It is milder and more sunshiny than England, but not so hot as Italy or Australia. Whatever we grow in England will grow there" ... etc etc...

SCALE OF EMIGRANTS' OUTFIT

[illegible] may be obtained by payment of the under-mentioned Prices, at the Company's Office (Emigratio[illegible]), or of Messrs. Dixon and Co., No. 12 Fenchurch Street, London.

N.B. No other mattrasses, or bedding, will be allowed to be shipped, except such as have been approved by the Company as understated.

For each Adult Male	s.	d.
2 Fustian Jackets, lined, at	5	6 each
2 Pair do. Trowsers, at 4s.3d. Lined, at	5	3 each
2 Do. Duck do., at	2	3 each
2 Round Frocks, at	2	5 each
12 Cotton Shirts, at	2	0 each
6 Pair Worsted Stockings, at	1	6 per pair
2 Scottish Caps, at	0	11 each
6 Handkerchiefs, at	0	8 each
6 Coarse Towels, at	0	7 each
1 pair Boots, with Hobnails, &c., at	7	6 per pair
1 Pair Shoes, at	5	3 per pair
4 lbs. Soap, at	0	8 per lb.
1 Pair Blankets, at	12	0 per pair
2 Pair Sheets, at	5	6 per pair
1 Coverlet, at	3	0 each

For each Adult Female	s.	d.
2 Gowns, or 18 yards Printed Cotton, at	0	5½ per yard
2 Petticoats, or 6 yards Coloured Calico, at	0	5½ per yard
2 Do. Flannel, or 6 yards Flannel, at	1	2 per yard
12 Shifts, or 30 yards Long Cloth, at	0	6 per yard
6 caps, or 3 yards Muslin, at	1	0 per yard
6 Handkerchiefs, at	0	8 each
6 Aprons, or 6 yards Check, at	0	8 per yard
6 Neckerchiefs, at	0	8 each
6 Towels, at	0	7 each
1 pair Stays, at	3	6 each
6 Pair black Worsted Stockings, at	1	2 each
2 Pair Shoes, at	3	6 each
1 Bonnet, at	2	0 each
Needles, Pins, Buttons, Thread, Tape, &c., an assortment of	2	0
4 lbs. Marine Soap, at	0	8 per lb.
2 lbs. Starch, at	0	8 per lb.

	s.	d.
One Mattrass and Bolster for each couple, of coloured Wool	11	0
Knife and Fork, Plate, Spoon, Drinking Mug &c., say	3	0

Children must be provided with a proportionate Outfit, including Mattrass, &c., which may be had upon payment of the undermentioned Sum for each Child, viz:-

	£	s.	d.
One year of Age, and under Nine	1	0	0
Nine years of Age, and under Fourteen	1	10	0

What prompted Ann and Griffith Lowe to leave Wales and England, for an unknown place called New Zealand, where at that time very few white men lived, where there were no roads, no shops and no homes waiting on them to move into?

In 1830 there were no more than 330 Europeans living in NZ. By 1840 this number was about 2000, then the colonisation of NZ started with ships bringing settlers to Port Nicholson, Wellington, NZ. (SNZ)

> Life in the UK during the early 1800's at best can be described as difficult, however, there are many books detailing those conditions and problems, so we will just look at the decision made by our family.

1832, or about then, Ann and Griffith Lowe with two children moved near to the Wales / England boarder to live at the Hamlet of Sarn, near the English town of Threapwood, where Griffith found employment as a farm labourer. During the next 6 years three more children were born, with Mary arriving soon after the move. Here they were introduced to religion by the Church of England, Rector of Threapwood, Rev J F Churton, and he baptised Mary soon after her birth, and Joseph and William some years after they were born.

1839. Early in 1839, soon after the NZ Land Co was formed, one of the members will have offered John F Churton the position of Colonial Chaplain of a new town to be created in New Zealand. This must have appealed to JFC as he accepted and promised to emigrate with his wife and 7 children. He was also encouraged to select families from his present parish flock and 'sell' them the idea of *'a better future in a distant land.'* There were leaflets and posters detailing this chance of a better life in New Zealand. We can imagine lots of discussion between JFC, Ann and Griffith, as both Ann and Griffith were illiterate. JFC would have helped them with all the emigration qualification details and form filling.

The ship's records show our family *"... were engaged for emigration by Rev John Frederick Churton,"* aged 41 who also travelled on this ship but as a cabin passenger with his wife, 2 sons and 5 daughters. The Reverend was the second clergyman and first Church of England man to go to Wellington. The Rev John Butler and family, C of E, was the third clergyman and also joined the *Bolton* voyage to live in New Zealand.

In the book "Early Wellington" we found a copy of one of the advertisements and it is a long wordy document. We have selected some of the details most relevant to Ann and Griffith. Basically, the NZ Land Co purchased all the land they could in New Zealand, then sold it sight unseen by auction to wealthy UK residents and some of the emigrants, who would in turn sell it at a later date to NZ residents, who were probably then occupying or leasing their land.

The money the NZ Land Co raised paid for the purchase or lease of suitable ships, for the free passage of sponsored people and included provisions and medical attendance during the voyage. There is a long list of occupations deemed suitable but our Griffith Lowe qualified amongst the most desired as an Agricultural Labourer. (Farm hand or Farmer.)

Ann and Griffith had to supply a *"testimonial as to their qualification, character and health"* and this must have been supplied by their sponsor, Rev J F Churton. As an emigrant farm labourer, Griffith had to agree *"to go to NZ to work for*

wages, had to be of sound mind and body, and be aged not less than 13 and not more than 30 years and must be married."
(A later advertisement changes this to 'up to 40 for married agricultural men and up to 30 for single men'.)
"The rule as to age will be occasionally departed from in favour of persons having large families whose qualifications are in other respects satisfactory. The wives of labourers are also offered free passage with their husbands and children of parents emigrating receive free passage if under the age of 15, otherwise a fee of 3 pounds applied."

With some adjustment our family qualified to emigrate. Griffith was a farm labourer and was married and apparently in sound body and mind but he was born c1798 and therefore aged about 41. Ann was 35 with 5 children, so qualified under the age exemption. Someone bent the rules a bit and Griffith must have had a youthful face, as he joined the ship with his age recorded as 36. Marriage certificates had to be produced but no one asked for birth certificates. Five children and Ann, still of child bearing age, would also have helped them.

"All emigrant adults and children must have been vaccinated or have had the small pox."
"Embarkation is from London and emigrants have to pay their own way there."
"Every adult emigrant can take half a ton weight or twenty cubic feet of baggage."
"Emigrants must provide bedding for themselves and their children and the necessary tools of their trades. They should take strong plain clothing or materials for making clothes up on the passage which averages about four months."

Such was the rush of people to immigrate to New Zealand

that they could not be accommodated in the ships already chartered by the company and an additional ship was arranged, to take those who had been shut out of the previous ships. This was *the Bolton* *(White Wings)*

"The BOLTON"

Model of The BOLTON at The Bolton Hotel Wellington, NZ

> This photo is not the best as the model is backed by a mirror and a quick glance says there were 5 masts, but the mirror duplicates the first two masts and gives the impression the ship had two hulls… which it did not. (T)

The *Bolton,* a three masted Barque of 540 tons, left Gravesend London at half-past ten am on 19 November 1839 with 232 people on board. She was skippered by Captain John Percival Robinson and the Surgeon Superintendent was Richard Godfrey Lowe. aged 29, single and not thought to be a relation of our Lowe family.

The Bolton was the sixth ship to sail with a reasonable volume of emigrants for Port Nicholson, Wellington, the first area of major settlement in New Zealand.

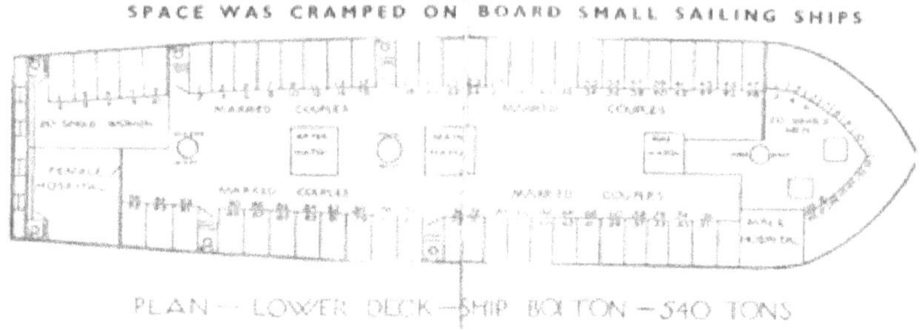

We are very lucky to have found this plan of the lower deck of the *Bolton* in the book *The Story Of New Zealand* (SNZ) which was home for all the non-cabin passengers including our 7 Lowe family. You will note the single men and single ladies were separated and married couples were housed in double bed sized boxes with another bed above them. No privacy.

There were 6 toilets on this deck but no sign of a bath or shower-room. The three masts are easily located and we are advised seating benches and long tables ran down the centre of

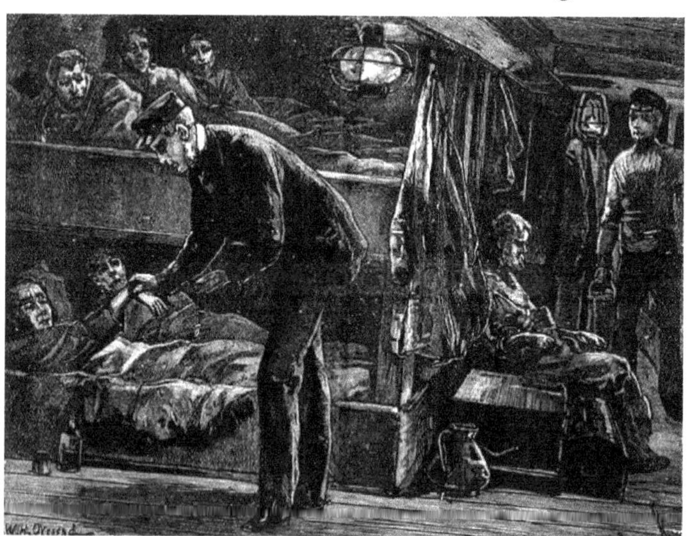

the 'lower deck' for relaxation and eating at. (PM,CW)

This picture of the 1840 Irish emigrants going to America, best shows the cramped sleeping arrangement on board.

Another vessel for New Zealand, the Company's ship Bolton, reached Gravesend last night, and will sail this afternoon. She carries labouring emigrants exclusively of the agricultural class, and several cabin passengers. Among the latter are the Rev. J. F. Churton, a minister of the Church of England, and family; Henry Shafto Harrison, Esq., of Yorkshire, and family; Joseph Minet, Esq., &c. &c. Mr. Churton goes out with an endowment from the Society for the Propagation of the Gospel, and carries with him a liberal grant of books from the Society for Promoting Christian Knowledge. The emigrants are supplied by the New Zealand Company with books for their amusement and for the instruction of their children during the voyage.—*Spectator.*

This **NEWSPAPER CUTTING** from *The Standard* 18 Nov 1839, gives more detail about the *Bolton,* especially the last sentence which we interpret as saying the children did not just run wild all over the ship during their 5 months at sea ... they received some education, maybe reading, writing and maths was included. (CW)

Steerage passengers were organised into COOKING groups. Each one was issued with food according to a set scale. The ration for one adult was ....

¾ lb biscuit a day ... 1 lb Indian beef Tuesday & Saturday only.
½ lb pork 3 times a week ... ½ lb preserved meat twice a week.
½ lb flour & ½ pint peas per day, ¼ lb rice and ¾ lb potatoes four times a week. Plus butter, sugar, tea, coffee, raisins, suet, pickled cabbage, salt, mustard and water.

The children on board received part of an adults ration but those under twelve months were not entitled to rations.

Proper medicines and medical comforts were carried on board and these included 12 bottles of port wine, 12 bottles sherry, 300 gallons of stout and 40 gallons of brandy per 100 passengers. Oatmeal, arrowroot and lemon juice was also available. Women who were breast feeding were issued with a pint of stout a day. (SNZ)

A CROSS SECTION of the ship *'Bolton'*

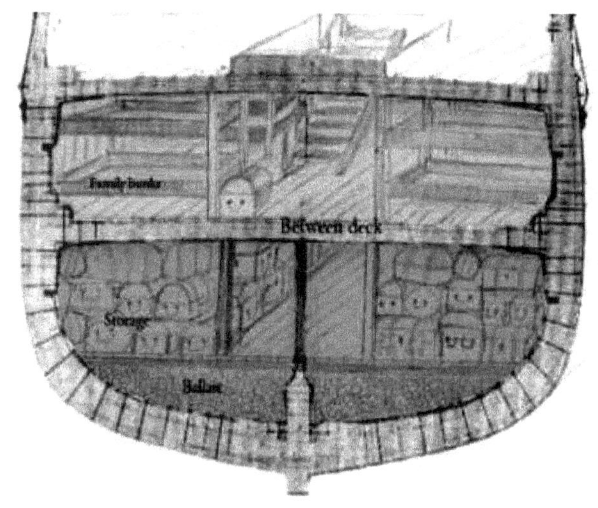

showing Ballast at the bottom, then the Cargo Deck, then the passenger's Lower Deck showing the double double-beds and stairway through the hatch to the Upper Deck. Every inch of space in the ship was in use.

The *Bolton's* ***'Register of Emigrant Labourers who received a free passage to NZ'***, lists 156 steerage passengers and 33 cabin passengers. A total of 189 people made up of 56 males, 47 females and 86 children.

(The book 'Early Wellington' records passengers as 66 married couples, 23 single men, 13 single women, 23 children 9 to 14, 60 children 1 - 9 and 8 under 1 years.)

The Steerage passenger lists included ....

101	Griffith Lowe	36 Married Man
102	Ann Lowe	35 his wife
103	Edward Lowe	12 years boy
104	Joseph Lowe	9 years boy
105	Mary Lowe	7 years girl
106	John Lowe	4 years boy
107	William Lowe	1½ years boy

(The children's and Ann's ages seem to be accurate but Griffith's age has been reduced by about 5 years.)

In another New Zealand book we found our family name misinterpreted and Griffith Lowe was noted as Louie Griffiths. Bit confusing but the above photo is the true entry.

--oo0oo—

The *'BOLTON'* sailed from Gravesend 19 Nov 1839, arriving at Wellington 21 April 1840.

THE VOYAGE:

It was a slow craft and its voyage took five months.
The Surgeon's records show that three days after leaving Gravesend the *Bolton* was off the Isle of Wight and took just under a month to reach Santa Cruz, Tenerife. It berthed here on the 12 December 1839 *"...to procure stock, severe losses by death amongst them, having taken place during bad weather."* The *Bolton* re-sailed on 15 December 1839.

The surgeon records 178 dinners were served to passengers at the Captain's table mainly of fresh meat or poultry and the cost of each dinner is recorded as two shillings. Mr Lowe further certifies that *'the following medical comforts were supplied and properly expended to the sick since Nov 14, 1839 and to May 7, 1840... oatmeal 1.5 hundred weight, arrowroot 75 pounds, preserved beef 75 lbs, lemon juice 69 gallons, sugar 558 lbs, 1.5 dozen each port wine and sherry wine, stout 13 dozen bottles and 240 gallons of draught, rum 52 gallons, and brandy 8 gallons.*
During the five month voyage three children were born and seven passengers died.

2 VOYAGE DIARIES: *Miss Eliza Hargreaves and Miss Sarah Falwasser were Wrexham residents before embarking on the Bolton. They provide us with a wonderful in depth picture of conditions of their voyage to this country and when they landed in New Zealand, through their diaries. (Our Griffith and Ann LOWE family must also have endured, observed and experienced these topics, even if they were not of the same 'upper class' with servants etc.* (T)

A letter attributed from Miss Eliza Hargreaves (1822-1845) to a Miss Calender. *Alexander Turnbull Library MS papers 3809.*

Miss Eliza was aged 17 on the voyage.

The letter has no date and the start seems to be missing........

I can assist you considering the distance we have come. We have seen very little and I have found out that the sea voyage is not such a terrific thing as I imagined and as to the wonders of the sea, I did not see many.

We met with very heavy seas in the Bay of Biscay and off Madeira the consequence was we lost many of our fowls, pigs and sheep here. The town of Santa Cruz has nothing particularly worth seeing in it but I was very well pleased with it. Everything and everybody looked foreign. The only buildings of any consequence are the churches, the interior of some are very magnificent but too gaudy. The ornaments are poor and showy, every niche in the wall has an image of some saint.

I should think they would worship a fresh one every day in the year. The altar piece they say is made of solid silver. The streets are clean and very quiet. You don't see a carriage or cart. The gentlemen ride on mules, the ladies on camels. These poor animals look very thin. They have very heavy loads of every description to carry and have very poor food. You never see a Spanish lady out of doors until after 12 o'clock. They have a great many fruits. The oranges are very sweet. I bought 200 for 1 Spanish dollar. The country is very barren and mountainous. There is no depth of soil consequently their trees are very much twisted in their growth and look very poor. I was very anxious to have seen the convents but we were told they did not allow English to go in.

On leaving Tenerife we were becalmed a week, the only thing we had to look at was the Peak, covered with snow. It reminded me very much of Snowdon in its shape. We saw the tip of it peeping above the clouds at the distance of about 40 miles. We soon fell in with the trade winds and we went gliding along without the least motion at 10 knots per hour. This was the most agreeable part of the voyage, however the winds forsook us about 7 degrees from the line (equator) and in one month we went a distance of 16 miles. At this time we had nothing but white squalls which never lasted more than 10-15 minutes. You can have no idea how beautiful the lightning of an evening was, the flashes were so vivid and came so quickly that you would see the surrounding seas distinctly and it was my delight of an evening to sit and look at the sea. The phosphorous in this latitude is very beautiful as far as you can see. It appears as one sheet of fire, during these calms.

We saw plenty of sharks and other fish. Five sharks were caught in one day, the largest measuring 14 feet. When the first was bought on deck there was such a tremendous whack to the side of the ship that two young men fell overboard. Fortunately the boat was soon lowered and they were both saved. A little boy five years old fell over another day. He was in the water a full ten minutes. He had very thick clothing on and was longest in the water. Although he may have perished, the next day he was running about as merry as ever. We lost six children on the voyage, all were under two years of age and the cook died just as we entered Port Hardy. (Nelson) Three infants were born on board and are the finest, fattest little things I ever saw.

We all dreaded the thoughts of rounding the Cape. Everything was made fast, stanchions were placed around the cuddy table, our royal masts were taken down and all made up their minds to something very dreadful, but our fears came too soon. We went around this formidable piece of land beautifully and were becalmed off it a day but we soon met with rough weather and during these storms we had some very ridiculous diners. Many of the falls some had were of rather a serious nature. At dinner some of the ladies tied themselves to the stanchions for it was no unusual thing for chair and self to go to the other end of the cuddy. The breakage of crockery and glass was dreadful. We were sadly reduced toward the end of the voyage. One day I was taken completely off my legs and sent with tremendous force against the bulwarks of the ship which gave me two black eyes. I wonder I did not go through. On another day Miss F was going through into her cabin, the ship gave a roll and she was forced through her doors and broke off the hinges. Wonderful to say she escaped without a bruise. Charlotte and baby often used to take a slide. She was a very poor sailor. Little Charles very much admired the rolling. Even in calm weather he could not sit still. I did not suffer from sea sickness after leaving the Channel, though many of the passengers were so whenever it was rough. I never enjoyed better health in my life.

After passing the Cape we saw great quantities of birds, the most beautiful certainly was the Albatross. They are generally perfectly white and very much resemble a swan. Their skins are very valuable for tippets or boas, but owing to the great quantity of oil in them, they are very difficult to prepare. Many of the passengers tried to dry them but did not succeed. It was famous fun trying to catch them. They run along the water the instant they see the bait, and if you are going anything like fast it is as much as you can do to pull them in. They make a noise like a goose. The largest that was caught measured twelve feet from tip of each wing. The Captain had some pies made and very good they were. The emigrants considered them a great luxury.

We only met with one ship that came near enough for the Captain to speak to her. The telegraphing between ships was really wonderful though we were so many miles apart they could ask any questions and understand each other perfectly. We were in company with her one week and should not have left her so soon but she put in at the Cape.

On the 2nd April we sighted Van Diemen Land and in ten days entered Cook Strait and had four or five severe gales here. I was rather frightened being so close to land and the Captain not knowing much of the coast. However, we reached D'Urville Islands in 11 days and had to put in to know how and where to proceed. The scenery is very bold high rocks stretch along, thickly covered with brushwood to the water's edge. In the harbour we soon spied a canoe coming along full of black curly headed natives squatting down just like monkeys. I think they are a species between baboon and a man for they are not quite human looking. As they came paddling along their appearance in the distance was very fierce having so much hair and being so long it blows in the wind and gives them a very wild look. Many of the ladies were very much alarmed when they saw them, but how could a little canoe with five natives in it harm us with 200 aboard. They had more reason to be afraid of us. The fish in the harbour was delightful eating and all had so much that we were quite tired of it. One fish the steward bought for an old knife. The weight of which was 83lbs. The name of it was Hapuku. *(Grouper)*

The decks for a week were covered with potatoes, pigs and natives. You could not stir without tumbling over them. Mr Harrison, one of the passengers bought 40 baskets of potatoes for five pence and five gun flints. Large pigs sold for eight or nine shillings but things can't be had at that price here in Port Nicholson. The Maoris are grown too wise, nothing will do for them but money or gold as they also prefer now.

We reached Port Nicholson in 154 days. We anchored at the mouth of the river that night and fired a gun for the pilot to take us in. The entrance is rather dangerous on account of a reef of rocks stretching nearly across the harbour, but when once in, it is very nice and sheltered and has excellent anchorage ground. It was a miserable rainy day when we came in and upon looking through our glass at the shore the prospect certainly was not very cheering. There were a few huts (as I call them) on the beach and a tent here and there, but the improvement and progress since our ship arrived is astonishing. Unfortunately it is the winter season now and therefore we feel every inconvenience much more than we should have done had it been summer. The natives build their own houses and do not at all consider doors and windows necessary to their comfort. They cut little holes through and their earthen floors are worse than anything for it causes so much dust. One thing speaks well for the climate, although we have been so much exposed to the weather, not one of us have taken cold and we are all enjoying excellent health.

The shock of earthquake frightened me very much at the time, but the natives think so little about them and they have never been known to do the slightest harm, that if another was to come I don't think I should be so alarmed. The idea of one is certainly not pleasant.

The country I can't tell you much about at present, but there are some delightful walks in the woods close to our house. I can sit for hours and listen to the birds singing most sweetly. There are great varieties, many very curious and many very pretty, we have not yet seen many flowers but in the summer we expect a great quantity. (Eliza Hargreaves)

---oo00oo---

ANOTHER VOYAGE DIARY:

The Rev Butler's daughter Hannah (22) kept a Diary of her voyage and the arrival of her ship, the *'Bolton'* to NZ. The selected extracts follow, including some interesting insights, but it generally agrees with the above letter.

Jan 1840. Drifting backwards. Saw a turtle... lowered a boat and went after it, but was disappointed, it being only a Squid Fish. Caught a dolphin. A man and boy fell overboard... not hurt, except for a good ducking, which they seemed to relish.

5th. Devine service held on deck by Mr Churton. An internal complaint attacking nearly everyone on board.

11th A little disturbance in the single women's cabin.

25th Spoke to an American Whaling ship, lat 18.15, long 35.40, the 'Rochester' by name.

29th Another child died, named Nankeville, making 5 boys and 2 girls.

Feb 1st. Disturbance with a young family... put in irons for being impudent to Doctor. The emigrants came up to the Captain and said ... if the person was not released immediately, they would release him themselves, and throw the Doctor overboard.

2nd Great confusion below during Divine Service, dogs barking and howling, pigs squealing and men cursing and swearing in a most shameful manner.

6th Caught a 10 foot shark. *(On this day, while the Bolton was still at sea, The signing of the Treaty at Waitangi in the Bay of Island took place. It was signed by the crown and 40 Maori Chiefs.)*

18th Caught an Albatross, 10 feet, tip to tip, on a fish hook.

26th Terrible night, the vessel rolling in a most fearful manner; no one had any rest.

March 21. Main topsail sheet broke in two; same time sea struck us and came through the windows.

April 1st. Passed Van Dieman's land about fifty miles off... weather foggy,

9th 60 miles from Cape Farwell at 12 o'clock; ship's cook died and cat Robinson's cow died.

12th Entered the heads of the harbour of D'Urville Island about 10 am. Another canoe came with a man and child; the man was tattooed all over his face.

14th A man and his wife came on board; we fired a gun at his request, to let the natives know they might bring pigs and potatoes; a few came. Our gentlemen went on shore with the native to his place for water. We saw a large canoe full of natives going towards our people, very much afraid they were going to do us some mischief, but they went up and shook hands and seemed very pleased; they sang and prayed before they retired.

15th Purchasing pigs and potatoes; the decks are strewed with potatoes. Two large canoes full went away, the owners were very much displeased.

16th Just going to breakfast when Mr Douglas came to fetch my father, a dispute having arisen among the natives about the water. My father went to make peace. We succeeded, the ship's crew getting as much water as they possibly could. The great chief Mako and his wife came off with the gentlemen who had been ashore, and remained with us until 9pm. Two natives will travel with us to Port Nicholson.

20th Arrived Port Nicholson; wind strong out of the harbour; endeavoured to beat in; only a little way into the heads but had to let go the anchor; fired two guns for a pilot, who came accompanied by a person named Northwood, a colonist. Mr Collett went on shore with the gentleman above named and stayed the night. About half past two Colonel Wakefield came on board but only stayed a short time.

21st. Anchored in harbour about 1pm. Went on shore with others. Had our dinner on shore, quite in gypsy style. The houses are not worth calling houses; such miserable place that we were quite astonished. Came back on board about 6pm.

Hannah Butler's comments from her diary continue later referring to … Life in NZ.

---oo0Ooo---

From Captain Robinson's report, the *'BOLTON'* saw 4 men die on the voyage and 8 men deserted in New Zealand … including our Samuel Morris.

--oo0Ooo--

NEW ZEALAND.

1840. WELLINGTON.

In the days prior to 1839 most Pakeha visitors to Wellington Harbour were whalers, sealers or missionaries. The 30th September 1839 was a decisive day in determining British settlement of the harbour which became known as Port Nicholson. On that date the *'Tory'* arrived in the harbour in the charge of Colonel William Wakefield, who had orders from the New Zealand Land Company to find a suitable settlement site in the Cook Strait area. (PP)

He liked two areas for settlement in the harbour ... at Petone beside the River, and Thorndon. The first five ships to arrive with any great volume of immigrants, were The *'Aurora'* on 22 January 1840, the *'Oriental'* 31 January, the *'Duke of Roxburgh'* 7 February, the *'Bengal Merchant'* 21 February and the *'Adelaide'* on 7 March. All disembarked their human cargo of 847 willing new New Zealanders onto the shore at Petone. Soon after their arrival the 176 passengers of the *Adelaide* made themselves acquainted with the respective merits of the two sites for their new town and gave their voices almost unanimously in favour of Thorndon. It was therefore decided by the 'Committee' to commence the survey of that district laying out roads and sections. (BC)

The first meeting of the Port Nicholson Council was held 4th April and they met weekly. Measures were put in readiness for all sorts of public works at the site of the new settlement around Lambton Harbour, the appointment of officers, the regulation of finances, and the selection of sites for a powder magazine, infirmary and other public institutions.

It was not until 28 November 1840 that the name Wellington was agreed upon for this town. (BC)

> **21 April 1840**. When the ***'Bolton'*** arrived, there had been five earlier immigrant ships, plus three survey and stores ships from England and 8 food and stores ships from Australian ports, in to this harbour.
> On reaching New Zealand the *'Bolton'* first stopped at Port Hardy (Nelson) on Sunday 12 April 1840 at 11.30 am, then, sailed for Port Nicholson (Wellington) 2pm on 18 April where she arrived at 2pm on 21 April 1840. A five month long trip, totalling 154 days since leaving the Thames.

BOLTON AT ANCHOR: According to the terms of the charter each ship after reaching Port Nicholson was required to remain at anchor for four weeks, so that their passengers would have somewhere to live while assembling their temporary accommodation. Every morning the people used to leave the ship in a flat-bottomed punt, work on their future homes and return to the ship at night to sleep. (WW)
Living on the boat awhile after arrival is confirmed by the *'Bolton'* ship's surgeon who wrote *"all passengers were victualled for 176 days"* and that our seven travellers, *"...disembarked on 7 May 1840,"* and *"...at 3pm Wednesday 20 May 1840 the last of the cargo was landed."*

FOOD: The heads of the New Zealand Company were not stingy, for their ships were always well provisioned, and ample stores of food were kept at Port Nicholson. For fresh provisions there were the Maori to depend upon for pigs, fish and potatoes, with cattle and sheep soon arriving from across the Tasman Sea. (WW)

Amongst those to set foot on Thorndon beach on 21 April 1840 were our Lowe family of 7.

Thorndon and Te Aro flats were the first areas to be settled after the settlement of Brittania (Petone) failed with the flooding of the Hutt River. (Te Aro by E Menzies)

LAND: Nobody named Lowe, Morris or Woods (except Robert Henry Wood – no relation) were amongst the original purchasers of the 100 by 1 acre sections in the new town of Wellington, held in London 29 July 1839, and issued in July 1840. (EW, UE)

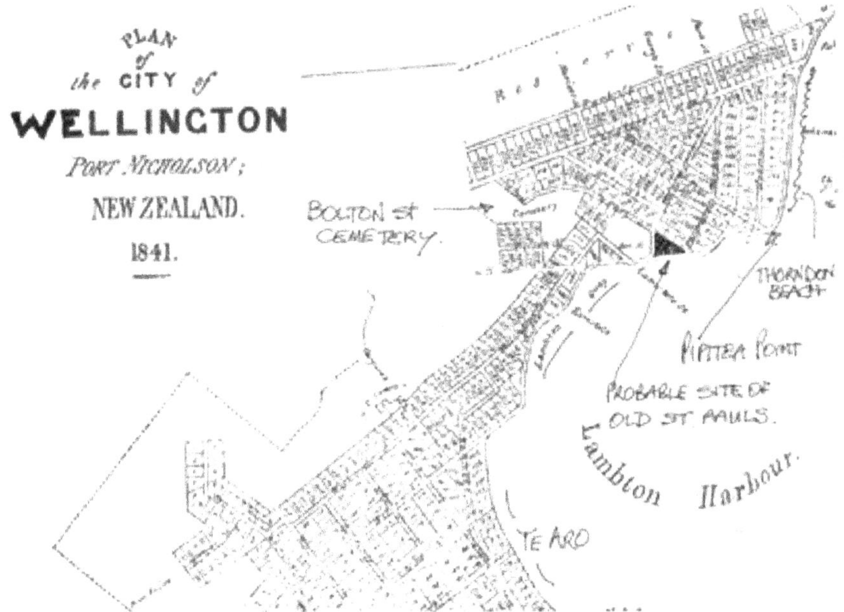

Hannah Butlers Diary part 2;

23 April 1840. Mr Wakefield came on board with the immigration agent, Mr Riddiford. The immigrants all went on shore to build their houses. The people were taken to a spot near to the native village, but the native chief would not let

them. He said it was his ground, and had not been purchased by the company off him, and they should not have it. A meeting with Mr Williams to be held tomorrow respecting it.
25th Mr Churton went on shore to preach. The sailors went on shore; came back at night very drunk. Also some men from the 'Adelaide' were on board, and caused a disturbance which was put to an end without much trouble.
May 7 Bought a house off Captain Gomm. (Mr Butler's house was situated next to Col Wakefield's home) Colonel Wakefield ordered Captain Robertson to take the luggage to Britannia. (Britannia was the name given to the Hutt Valley settlement where the first ships settled... that got flooded and they moved inland a bit and it became known as Petone.)
12th Mr Butler and Col Wakefield set out a churchyard.
17th After service, Major Baker called Mr Butler to go to the west end of the beach to settle a quarrel between a European and the natives about a son of Epuni being thrust through the doors against his will, and by means of force. After an inquest the body of H R Eaton (who had been speared by a native) was buried by Mr Butler.
25th A hurricane all night. Fire broke out in Cornish Row, and destroyed 15 dwellings, and nearly all the people's goods.
26th A dreadful earthquake took place at 5.30 am; all our houses rocked in a most fearful manner. We all ran out quite terrified, but then returned to bed. After three quarters of an hour we heard an explosion and a small shake. Upon enquiry we found there had been two earthquakes prior to this and since the arrival of the Europeans, but nothing so bad as this.
27th Another earthquake shock.
29th Two vessels arrived. The 'Bee' from Sydney and the 'Sally Ann' from Bay of Islands. They reported loss of three vessels off the coast.

30th A disturbance arose between some of the Scotch settlers and the natives about a knife. They came to Mr Butler to settle the affair. One of the Scotsmen had hit one of the natives with a piece of wood on the side of his head and made it bleed. They went into his house and took a blanket for payment.

June 4th Went to Thorndon with Mr Butler etc in Atoru's canoe. The Queen's proclamation was read by Mr Shortland, secretary to Governor Hobson, taking possession of NZ.

11th While at dinner a person of the name Todd came and wanted Mr butler to go to his house and pacify some natives who were pulling down his fence.

21st Epuni, a chief, dined with us, by special invitation and behaved remarkably well.

29th Mr Duppa's boat drifted away. Mr Butler agreed three natives could go with Mr Duppa... they returned and had supper with us. Buried Mr James Wilson, 37, seaman from the Bolton who drowned attempting to cross the River Hutt.

July 1 A large meeting held to petition Captain Hobson to make this place the seat of government. Col Wakefield was publicly solicited to convey the petition to the Bay of Islands.

4th A native lad stole two tomahawks from Mr Telford, who put him in irons, and came to Mr Butler requiring his assistance is this affair.

7 JULY. *"The Bolton"* **sailed from Wellington for England**.

The ship Bolton, which left England in November last, having on board the Rev. John F. Churton, the episcopal church minister, and family, with 160 settlers, arrived safe in New Zealand on the 20th of April.

(This notice appeared in The London Times, 15 September 1840 belatedly advising its readers of *The Bolton's* successful visit to New Zealand.) (CW)

27th Mr Butler went to Thorndon to attend a meeting about the division of the town land, to see that the natives were not imposed upon. Attended the funeral of a native from Pipitea.
22nd Paid the natives for building the house.... 2 pair blankets, 3 gowns, 4 shirts, 3 axes, 4 plane irons, 4 pound money. A total value of 17 pounds 5 shillings.
August 25. Mr Fowler's boat capsized opposite our house... 9 drowned.
30th Two earthquake shocks during the night.
Sep 28. Severe earthquake.
Dec 16. Severe earthquake.
Jan 22. Walked over to Wellington to attend the ball in commemoration of the foundation of the colony; had a splendid attendance, and were much amused. The ball broke up at five thirty Saturday morning.
30th January 1841 this **Dairy of Hannah Butler** ended.
(In between the selected items above, the Rev Butler was busy with baptisms, burials and sorting out continuous complaints throughout Wellington district and helping with the arrival of numerous ships from all over NZ and dealing with more new immigrants from Petone.)

--oo0Ooo--

ARRIVAL IN NEW ZEALAND:

A letter attributed from Miss Sarah Falwasser (1799-1868) to a Mrs Calender.

Alexander Turnbull Library MS papers 3809.
Sarah was aged 40 on arrival to New Zealand.

Port Nicholson (Wellington) 29 June 1840

We were disappointed to find the colony in a much less forward state than we had reason to hope, yet everyone seems to think that the capabilities have not been overrated. The climate is very delightful. It is now the depth of winter yet our fine days are equal to those in June in England with a clearness of atmosphere which is seldom experienced. Owing to the land not being surveyed we are obliged to supply temporary huts or as they are called here by the natives 'whares' and although they have neither doors or windows or flooring yet, we have not experienced any colds, although we feel the cold at times severely and we have had two or three rather severe white frosts. We occupy one of the better of these buildings and are making it comfortable according to our English notions as fast as we can.

The natives I think more than answer our ideas of savages in appearance, their only covering is a mat or English blanket and their faces are tattooed all over in different patterns according to their tribe. They receive us most gladly and favour us with their company from morning to night and come without hesitation even into your sleeping room. Until your home is quite completed or fenced or doors made, which, as they are the builders is a work of time, and they seem to feel a sort of contempt for the Pakeha (or Englishman) working in the wet or cold. "Not work!" say Maori "Not work to minehee" *(probably 'tomere'..= chimney)* but will do you the favour to squat around the fire, six or eight at a time. The Chiefs have a great idea of their own consequences. They are very capricious and require as much humouring as children but are as easily pacified. One day our servant was cleaning some knives and in joke held them up to a number of them who were around the fire. They were very much offended and one began with his tomahawk to chop away the chimney they are building. Others proposed to make the cry when they set up a dismal howling but what was most extraordinary they really shed an abundance of tears which they seem to do at pleasure. Mary, who was the only one of us at home tried to appease them but they said "Ka pai" *(good)*, getta ka pai Charlotte, ka pai the peramana *(?)* but ka kino *(bad)* Mary", and were a long time before they would be reconciled.

We have had a funeral of one of the Chiefs, the brother of the one who is building our house. We could not at first imagine what was the cause of a constant firing with which we were disturbed in the middle of the night, together with a most dismal howling. We were at that time lodging at the house of a native missionary that explained to us what it was and the following day we went to see the body lying in state. It was wrapped in their blankets and in a sitting posture with the face visible and he was surrounded with the whole of his wardrobe and muskets. Out in the open air all his friends seated around him making the most dismal noises and such as had not become missionaries, that has been converted to Christianity, were cutting themselves with mussel shells and bits of glass until the blood streamed down. The widow was in the midst of them, her head covered with evergreen matter mixed with a quantity of gold flowers. It was two days before he was buried. A few days after Mrs Churton was remonstrating with Powte through our interpreter Dr Ermis to whom we apply in every case of difficulty, when his reply was "How can the Pakeha expect me to work when the body of my brother is scarcely cold in the ground and the soul scarcely ascended to the great spirit." We are however very good friends and on Sunday he attended our service. He fixed his eyes very attentively on Mrs Churton and on having held out his hand called out "Ka pai" to the missionary. They seem most anxious to be instructed and nothing pleases them better than talking to them on religious subjects.

Every tree is an evergreen. The mountains and the soil is the richest you can imagine down to the edge of the sea. The survey of the town will be completed on the 13th July when I hope the construction of the house will continue and we will see what it is capable of producing. It is hoped that the Governor will make this his residence.

Everything sent out must be packed in lead cases lined with tin and soldered down and I thank you to direct it to the Rev J F Churton, care of Mr Manning, Colonist house builder, Holburn and insure to the amount of all you send out. Anything sent more than required may here be put into an auction and sold to advantage. Therefore anything you may meet with cheap will be acceptable provided it is pretty good of its kind. There are frequent losses on board ship. We experienced a very great one having lost the whole of our ironmongery which could not be replaced here for less than £ 60. We are informed we shall be entitled to the whole value. Several things we expect to replace here and for the remainder we shall be much inconvenienced.

The place we are now in is so dark that it is with the greatest difficulty we can see to do anything but we do hope in the course of next week we shall get windows put in which will make us much more comfortable.

The Queen was proclaimed here about a month since so that we are now under the protection of the Government. I have no doubt society will be very good when we are enabled to be as in a society but at present visiting is out of the question. We have seen the Governor's secretary who found us on a mud floor with a fire in the middle of the room and cooking going on as we had at that time no division from the servants. Wages are very high. A labourer 6/- per day and mechanics 8/-. Provisions are dear but not as much as they generally are in a new colony. The poor people all seem perfectly satisfied. (Sarah Falwasser)

--oo0oo—

PIPITEA PA.

The New Zealand Company draughtsman Charles Heaphy described the Thorndon area in 1839 as *'a flat land covered in fern, with about 50 Maori living at Pipitea.'*

The book 'Early Wellington' shows the Pipitea Pa situated about where we in 2010, find the junction of Mulgrave and Pipitea Streets, close to the Pipitea shore line, but up-hill a bit. An 1841 Wellington surveyor's map clearly shows Pipitea Street running fully down to Pipitea Point, and we also found Thorndon Quay and Lambton Quay used to hug the coast and beach line, but earthquakes and reclamation have moved the shoreline further away.

We learnt from Ann's granddaughter Mildred Fraser, that for her father George's birth on 5 February 1841 Ann was living near the Pipitea Maori settlement in what today is the Thorndon district in Wellington. (PM)

This is approximately where they disembarked from the *'Bolton'* and we believe the family lived here for their first few years in New Zealand. There were no maternity hospitals available at this time so George was probably born at his parent's home at Pipitea Point. Ann and Samuel and the children were still living at Pipitea in 1845.

MAP OF WELLINGTON HARBOUR:

This map shows early reclamation and the position of Pipitea Point where Ann and her children lived in their early years in New Zealand and shows the location of Thorndon Beach.

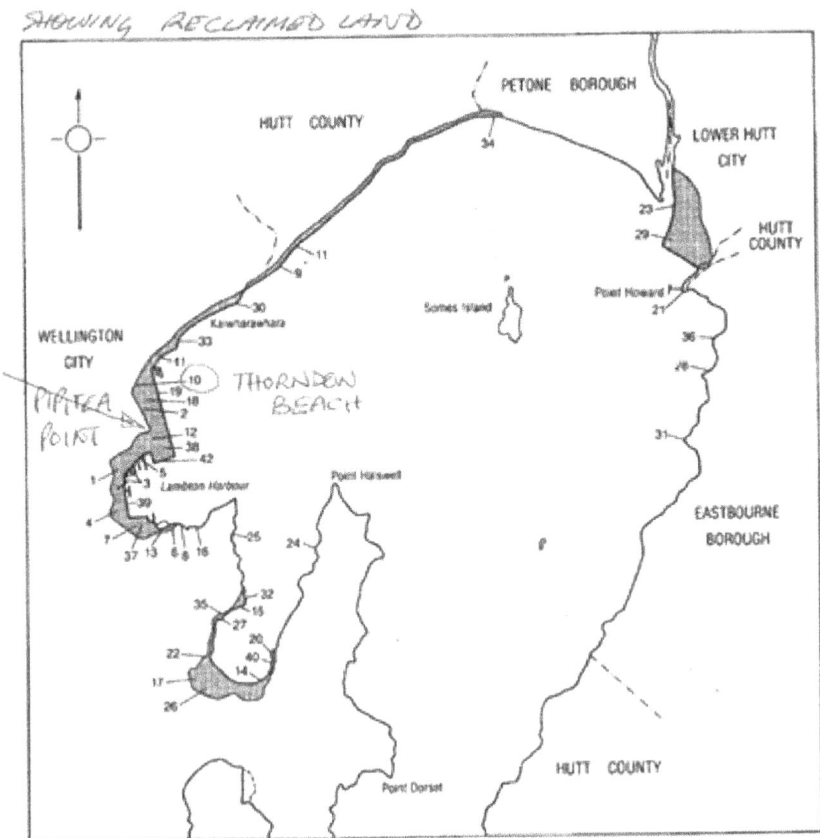

It is probable Ann's children Jane, Sarah and Henry Morris were also born at Pipitea. We have come to the conclusion they lived near to Pipitea Pa until the 1848 earthquake as son George advised grandson Gordon Fraser ....
"the earthquake left him homeless." A good time to consider a new home. They found a residence near to Plimmers Steps on Lambton Quay which was then the beach line. (MF)

George wrote... *"The beach at that time came up to Courtney Place and the tide at Lambton Quay used to go a long way out... a fact known to Maori women who congregated to gather pipis. There was only one house at Oriental Bay and the whole of Wellington's hills were clothed in bush, much of it very large trees."* (GF)

Mildred Fraser recalled stories of the family partaking in rat hunts on Lambton Quay beach. (PM) This area today is well inland, as in latter years the Wellington Council spent large sums on land reclamation work in the Lambton and Thorndon Bay areas. Gordon Fraser recalled stories of those early Wellington days, told to him by his grandfather (Ann's son George) and written down by him about 1925. George remembered his fear when aged about four (1845) there was a large native war dance of some 2000 Maori very near his home. On another occasion a tangi was held at the Pa for a Maori who had shot himself. (GF)

> Pipitea Pa must have been a continuous source of activity and entertainment and a worry for Ann and her family. The Pa had its own Maori Chief. Mr G. F. Angas wrote in 1845 that when he visited the Pa he found several canoes drawn up along the beach. Some of them were decorated with kokowai and red ochre. He said he met Ngatata, the chief of the Pipitea and Kumutoto Maori people, who lived just south of Pipitea Pa. (EW)

WELLINGTON'S FIRST HOSPITAL.

The first hospital in Wellington was the Colonial Hospital, erected in Pipitea St, Thorndon, on the site later occupied by Wellington Girls' College. It was the first of four such hospitals commissioned by Governor George Grey, the others situated in Auckland, New Plymouth and Wanganui.

Governor Grey insisted that each hospital be made available to both Maori and Pakeha.

The land for the Wellington Hospital was gifted by local Maori. The Colonial Hospital opened 15 September 1847.

It had 16 beds. The Colonial Administration appointed Dr John Patrick Fitzgerald as the hospital's physician and his administration included Maori members. (ccdhb, NZ)

ANGLICAN CHURCH. Wellington's Anglican Church meetings were held from the day they arrived, on their boats, then in a building that also acted as police court and post office. When this burnt down they used a humble wooden structure (known as St Pauls) erected in 1844 on part of the Government Reserve close to the Bolton St cemetery. (Church photo p101 EW)

This served the Thorndon community until 1866. About 1854 a larger St Pauls was built further away on Mulgrave St (known today as 'Old St Pauls') and a separate Chapel erected at the Cemetery. (EW)

In 1840 the Church Missionary Society was granted two acres of land, adjoining Pipitea Pa with a frontage to the beach and we believe that on this land the Old St Paul's Church was erected. The Rev J F Churton was appointed Colonial Chaplain to the settlement and established himself at Thorndon and the passengers from the *'Bolton'* and *'Adelaide'* served to form a fairly large congregation. (EW) Rev Churton's first entry in the Church of England registers was a burial on 14 May, then a baptism on 24 May 1840.

> Near the end of 1841 Rev Churton left Wellington to take up his appointment to serve in Auckland as the first minister of St Paul's Anglican Church then sited at Point Britomart. (A) The foundation stone for the first church built in Auckland was for St Paul's and was laid by Captain Hobson on 28 July 1841 in Emily Place. (CA) The site is easily located today in 1999 as a monument has been erected to Rev Churton where this church stood. The plaque describes him as.... John Frederick Churton L.L.B. the Colonial and Garrison Chaplain and 12 years minister of St Paul's Church, Auckland. Rev Churton died 26 January 1853 aged 54 at Auckland.

Bishop Selwyn arrived in New Zealand 12 Aug 1842 bringing with him Rev Robert Cole who replaced Mr Churton in Wellington. (EW)

> At least 3 of Ann's Morris children were baptised by Robert Cole at Old St Paul's Church.

1844 RELIGION: The Wellington districts now had a considerable number of settlers and most were well settled in. The Rev Butler who had knowledge of Maori customs and language, soon became Commissioner of the Peace. McFarlane (Presbyterian minister) had returned to Scotland and the Rev Churton who was appointed Chaplain by the Anglican Church, had taken up his duties in Auckland. The Rev James Duncan was attending to 433 Presbyterians, Rev Robert Cole 1240 Anglicans, Priests J P O'Reilly and M le Compte to 177 Roman Catholics, Rev Jones Woodward 64 Independents and Rev J Watkin and S Ironside administered to 300 Wesleyans. (book Earliest NZ)

EARTHQUAKES.

1840... On 25 May, only one month after our Lowe family stepped onto New Zealand soil they felt the effects of an earthquake. (EW) Hannah Butler's Dairy mentions earthquakes on these following dates and some of them 'severe'. 26 and 27 May and 2 on July 30, September 28 and December 16. We have found no records covering 1841.

1842... In August an earthquake caused damage to monumental work at the Bolton St Cemetery. (UE)

1848... For at least a week in October the Wellington district experienced a number a severe earthquakes.... buildings were damaged and people died. (UE) At 1.30 am during a severe gale and heavy rain on 16th October, the 7.5 earthquake struck and lasted a good 2 minutes and was followed by strong vibrations for 10 minutes, with after-shocks (est 100) continuing for 6 hours and seemed to cease when daylight broke. Although centred in the Awatere Valley in the Marlborough district in the South Island, it caused considerable damage in the Wellington area and was felt from Hawke's Bay to Canterbury. At the time 4,500 European settlers were living in the Wellington area while Marlborough was more sparsely inhabited. Maori settlements were scattered along the coast. More shocks were felt on 16th, 17th, 19th and 24th Oct, in Wellington where shaking damaged all brick and stone buildings, including many homes, commercial buildings, barracks, the jail and the Colonial Hospital.

Drawing of the HOSPITAL after 1848 quake.

Colonial Hospital

The Wesleyan large sod brick Chapel was shaken to the ground and the Congregational brick building was rendered too dangerous to use and was later collapsed. Both these churches were rebuilt using timber. Wooden buildings survived, but most lost their brick chimneys. Major shocks on 17 and 19 Oct bought down a number of buildings damaged in the first earthquake. Most buildings were damaged and repairs cost the community £ 15,000.00. (EW) As aftershocks continued, some people sought safety at night aboard ships in the harbour. Others decided to leave permanently… on 26 October the barque *Subraon* set sail for Sydney with over 60 settlers. It struck rocks near Wellington harbour entrance and although wrecked no lives were lost. Surprisingly only three people died in the 1848 tremors. Damage claims show no Lowe or Morris claims were made in the Thorndon Flat area but over the other side of the bay at Te Aro, a one storey, clay, thick walled residence owned and occupied by Mr Lowe had both gable ends destroyed. (We do not think this was our Griffith Lowe's home but we cannot be sure. T) (EW & teara.govt.nz)

Uplifted storm beaches, Turakirae Head

This photo shows a series of Storm beach ridges resulting from the uplifting of land at the eastern entrance to Wellington Harbour and the southern end of the Rimutaka Range. The four marked areas show the present storm beach level, the 1855 beach which is 6.4 metres above the present level, the 2,330 year old beach and about the 5,000 year old beach level all many metres above the present level.

George WD Morris (then 8) not only mentioned these 1848 quakes left him homeless but that the ground was unstable for two or three weeks. He wrote *"It was an awful time... most of the people were praying and many of them took to drink."*

Years later he warned of similar shocks returning some day and advised against erecting high buildings. (GF)

(Wellington has experienced many strong tremors over the years, however, NZ's strongest earthquake (magnitude 8.2) on 23 January 1855 occurred in southern Wairarapa just north of Wellington. It ruptured approximately 150m along the Wairarapa fault, had a horizontal displacement of up to 18m and uplifted the Rimutaka Range by about 6m. It created NZ's largest locally generated tsunami, with a maximum run-up of 10-11m. For Wellington the earthquake changed the landscape by lifting the land surrounding the harbour and all the way up to Otaki by 1 to 2 m. In Wellington Harbour ships were lying on their sides in shallow water and the wharves were left high and dry and a lot more land was visible.

(teara.govt.nz)

It was soon after the 1848 experience that Ann Lowe took her six children to live in Auckland and must have been very pleased she was not in Wellington in 1855.

INFLUENZA. Just before the earthquakes struck the town of Wellington in 1848, an influenza epidemic hit the town on 1 July 1848. Three quarters of the population were affected and scarcely a family escaped. (EW) Fortunately the town's hospital had been erected in Pipitea St the year before. This building however only lasted until the earthquakes shook it beyond repair. (sketch page 60)

Another hospital was erected on the same site in 1852. (EW)

UNREST. <u>The **1840 Treaty of Waitangi**</u> provided a legalised opportunity to repudiate any sales of lands and

immediately the Pipitea and Te Aro Maori complained of settler encroachment. The Maori had never intended selling any of their pa, cultivations or burial grounds. (PP)
Racial tensions must have been very high at this time. There was general unrest during those early years between Maori and Maori, and between Maori and Pakeha over land sales, over their different customs, over interpretations of general laws and ownership. (EW)

Life for all the early settlers including Ann, Griffith, Samuel and children, could not have been too comfortable or easy. We imagine the numerous and often near and frightening incidents, the strong winds and frequent rain and the relative safety of the younger but peaceful Auckland settlement, could all have influenced our family travelling to the northern town. Within the family today, we believe that the 1848 earthquake played a major role in giving Ann the strength to find a way to move herself and her children north.

Captain William Hobson had arrived in the Waitemata to select the site of this new town on 21 February 1840 and the first two organised immigrant ships to arrive at Auckland were the *'Jane Gifford'* and the *'Duchess of Argyle'* bringing 600 settlers in October 1842. (WW)

--oo0Ooo—

SAMUEL MORRIS.

1811 Samuel was born in England about 1811.

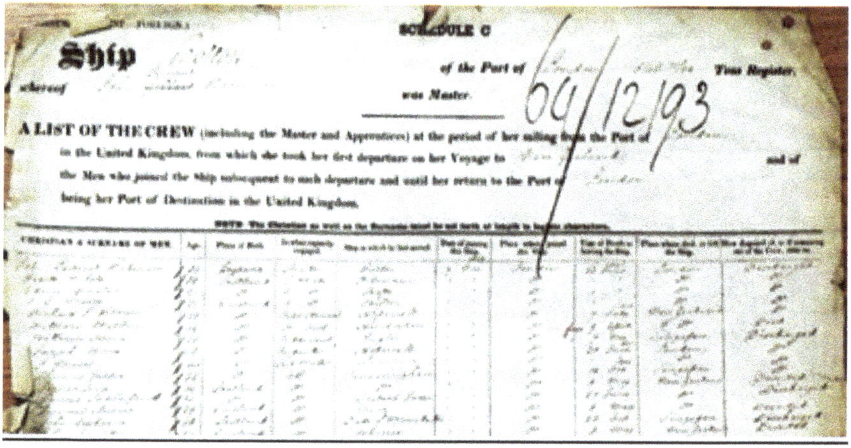
Ship

SCHEDULE C

of the Port of

was Master

A LIST OF THE CREW

64/12/93

<u>PHOTO of the "BOLTON" ship's CREW LIST</u> (CW)

Schedule C is a necessary form completed by the Captain, showing details of all crew on board for the coming voyage and those that returned to London with him or did not.

First on the list is Captain John Percival Robinson and listed in 13th place above, is **SAMUEL MORRIS, aged 29, born England, a Sail Maker, who had last served on the *'Elena'*, and joined *The Bolton* in London on 7 November 1839.**

This report also advises **Samuel left the ship on the 8 May 1840, while berthed in New Zealand and that he 'deserted' the ship at Wellington**. (CW)

So, **Samuel Morris** was born in England about 1811 and was working on *The Bolton* at the same time as Ann Lowe, her husband and 5 children were.

SEPARATION: It would appear that although the seven members of our Lowe family survived the voyage from England, the marriage of Ann and Griffith Lowe did not. This thought is confirmed by the birth of Ann's child George

(6 Feb 1841) about nine months after their arrival in New Zealand. As well as George he received the names of Walter Drake given to him by his father Samuel Morris who said he was a descendant of a younger brother of Sir Francis Drake. Sometime after the break-up of the marriage Griffith and the two eldest sons Edward and Joseph stayed in Wellington. Ann took charge of the three youngest Lowe children ... Mary Ann, John and William and together with three of her 'Morris' children, left Wellington by ship c1849 to make their home in Auckland.

--oo0oo—

1840 After arrival Ann seems to have immediately started living with Samuel Morris at Pipitea Point, Wellington.

1841 Ann Lowe gave birth to son George in Wellington, NZ. He took his father's name of Morris. At some time Ann and the three younger Lowe children started using the name Morris, even though Ann and Griffith had not divorced, leaving Ann and Samuel unable to marry.
Ann and Samuel Morris had four children ... **George 1841, Jane 1843, Sarah 1845 and Henry in 1847** while they lived in the Wellington area. Sarah died in 1846 aged 10 months.

The Rev Churton was well practised in baptisms and record keeping in Wales and we do not know why George WD Morris (or Lowe) was not one of the earliest entries in his NZ baptismal register. The St Paul's old-church records do show Jane, Sarah and Henry were baptised 'Lowe' at the first Church of England, erected in Wellington. (CW)

1844. In the Nov 22 issue of the 'NZ Spectator & Cooks Strait Guardian' newspaper, a 'Samuel Morris' is one of many who had 'unclaimed mail' at Post Office, Wellington.

1845 26 July. Samuel again listed with unclaimed mail. (T)

1845 ***Samuel Morris...Boatman of Pipitea,*** was listed in the Wellington Electoral Rolls. (This is the only official record, other than children's births, that we have found referring to Samuel Morris.) (CW)

Did SAMUEL die before 1849 on an Australian goldfield?
A GWDM family-records George (aged 6 or 7) saying to his mother while living in Wellington *"Dad's coming, he just passed the window". Ann was mystified when he didn't walk in and later discovered this 'vision' coincided with the time and date of Samuel's death.* (No proof found in Australia or NZ. T)

1848-9 Ann, with the help of her 16 year old daughter Mary Ann, left Wellington by boat, with her 6 youngest children. We have found no further recorded detail of Samuel in Wellington or in Auckland, so maybe he was dead by then.

1852 Gold was discovered on the Coromandel by Charles Ring. We researchers do not know if any of the Lowe/Morris older children rushed off to seek their fortune. We believe Samuel did go to a gold field and the separation broke up the 'marriage' as Ann remarried in 1858 to Moses Crocker. Did Samuel sail a boat over to the Coromandel, to Otago or maybe to the West Coast gold fields in NZ? We know he DID do some mining because (a) family descendants believe he had a ship and he and his crew left in it to search for gold in Australia and he died in a gold mine tunnel collapse. (No document support has been found, no newspaper article or death certificate.) And (b) when his daughter Jane (Polly) Thomas died in 1911, the informant gave her father Samuel's occupation as 'MINER'. But where ... Australia or NZ?

Photo: **Ann Griffiths Lowe** with **Samuel Morris**

Although the photo is named Mrs E Morris this lady appears in other photos named Ann Lowe. Ann married Moses Crocker in 1858 and this must have been taken before then. Moses was a tailor and this gent is extremely roughly attired and, in our opinion, it is not the way a tailor would dress himself. We have found no proof Samuel was ever a Captain of a sea-going vessel but he was listed as ......

Capt. Sam Morris; Mrs E. Morris

a *Boatman of Pipitea* in 1845 in Wellington. This implies he was a Captain or a Skipper of a vessel with one or two seamen helpers, who probably transported goods from visiting ships to shore, or transported goods from his base to other nearby villages and businesses such as coastal saw mills. We have regrettably found no proof other than the above statement.

–oo0Ooo–

The LOWE FAMILY:

GRIFFITH LOWE and SONS ....
EDWARD and JOSEPH LOWE.

It is thought Griffith 48 and his two eldest sons, Edward 20, and Joseph 18, stayed in the Wellington area when mother Ann left with the other children about 1849 for Auckland. Within the family in 2018 not much is known of them.

GRIFFITH LOWE born c1798 in Wales or England.

The book "Early Wellington" by Louis E Ward has a very good record of early happenings in Wellington, but they got our family listing wrong. On pages 37/38 they list the passengers for *The Bolton* and list the Lowe family as *"Griffiths, Louis and Ann with 5 children."* They have misread LOWE for Louis and decided Griffith was a surname and not a given name. (T)

1840... Griffith arrived in New Zealand on the ship *'Bolton'* aged about 42.

1845... Port Nicholson Jury List.

Griffith Lowe... Thorndon Flat ... Labourer. (CW)

1847... The Militia Roll lists,

Griffith Lowe... address Tinakori Road, Lambton Quay.

1848... The Colonial Hospital, Wellington, Admission Register, lists Griffith Lowe aged 49.

On the 16th October the Wellington area experienced a large 7.5 earthquake. The 'New Zealand Spectator' reported in issue 25 October, a letter from J Fitzgerald M.D. to the Lt Governor. In part it says ..... *"We the undersigned Patients, lately inmates in the Colonial Hospital which has been suddenly rendered uninhabitable by the severe shock of earthquake, express our sincere feelings of gratitude to you in coming to our assistance in our distress, and affording us shelter and accommodation in Government House.* These 15 patients signed the letter... *Charles Hobbs, Thomas Fitzgerald, John Atkinson, Thomas W Wellma, Thomas Northwood,* ***Griffith Lowe,*** *Ngakuaha, William Jones, James McNeil, Thomas Double, Richard Tomlin, Mary Wyburn, Mary Ann Peck, Hone A Ihake. Mateni."* (CW)

1849... The Colonial Hospital, Wellington, Admission Register, lists Griffith Lowe aged 50.

1850... Jury List ... Griffith Lowe, Porirua Road, Labourer.

1852... Griffith Lowe died 15 October 1852 at Wellington, aged 54 (his estimated birth 1798/9). He died of consumption (TB Tuberculosis). His certified-death-certificate provides no other facts. We believe he may have been interred at Bolton Street Cemetery, Wellington, but no headstone was raised and no burial record has been found. (PM)

The 'Wellington Anglican Burial's List' for the entire Wellington and Hutt areas, shows Griffith Lowe died on the date above, in the Colonial Hospital, Wellington, and gave his occupation as 'labourer'. (CW)

--oo0Ooo—

EDWARD LOWE born in 1829 in Wales:

1840... Arrived in New Zealand on the ship *'Bolton'* aged 11yrs 4 months.

1842... An advertisement in 'The NZ Colonist and Port Nicholson Advertiser' dated August 9, asks for a Public Meeting to be held for the arrival of the Right Rev. the Lord Bishop of New Zealand and that all religious denominations be invited. Twenty two people signed and Edward Lowe was one of them. (CW)

1843... On 17 June 1843, the first serious clash between Maori and British settlers occurred. A party tried to clear Maori off Wairau Valley land and arrest two Chiefs. Fighting broke out and 22 settlers were killed. A letter written 11 July 1843 from Wellington Residents to the population at Nelson expressing *assurances of deep and heartfelt sympathy in the severe calamity which has befallen the Colony, by the horrible massacre at Wairau.'*

About 130 people signed the letter including Edward Lowe.

(book Early Wellington by L E Ward) (T)

1845... The NZ Gazette, page 7, 1845, lists ***'Edward Lowe, Bookkeeper'***, under Wellington "Rate Returns". (T)

1847&1848 Jury List. Edward Lowe, Te Aro Flat, Clerk. (CW)

1848... A Wellington court case between 'Scott V Grimshaw & Another' was reported in The NZ Spectator & Cook's Strait Guardian on March 25. Edward Lowe was a witness and as a clerk he served the notice upon Mr Grimshaw on 7 January 1846 and also stated he knew both Mr Grace and Mr Grimshaw. (T)

1847... Jury List (NZ Spectator 10 Feb) Edward Lowe, Te Aro Flat, clerk, and his father Griffith Lowe, Tinakori Road, labourer were listed. (T)

1849... Jury List. Edward Lowe, Wellington, Clerk.

1849... 7 July NZ Spectator. The Nicholson Mechanics Institute was raising funds to erect a new Hall to serve as a Library, Reading and Lecture Room and Museum. The newspaper listed many donations and Edward Lowe donated one pound and 1 shilling to them. (T)

1850... A notice appeared in the 'Wellington Independent' seven times during June and July advising the partnership between 4 men, Printers and Newspaper Proprietors, was dissolved by mutual consent. Witness to the signatures was Robert Hart, Solicitor, Wellington and Edward Lowe, Clerk & Bookkeeper, Wellington. (CW)

1850... Jury List .... Edward Lowe, Tinakori Road, Clerk.

1852... A 'Jurors List' in the NZ Gazette, shows Edward Lowe of Tinakori Road, Wellington.

1852... 'The Militia Roll' lists, Edward LOWE, address Tinakori Road, Wellington. (He was aged 23) (CW)

1852... The NZ Spectator & Cook's Strait Guardian of 3 April, 1852, details anger by the people at proposed changes to the Land Claims Ordinance & Pasture Regulation by the settlers of Wellington and neighbouring districts. A very long list of signatories with ... *Edward Lowe, Landholder* ... listed amongst them. (T)

1852... On August 18, the entire cargo of the ship 'PERSIA" made a very long list in the NZ Spectator and showed to whom each article was to be delivered ... (E Lowe, 1 tierce.) My Collins English Dictionary states a tierce as an absolute measure of capacity equal to 42 gallons of wine.

1852... When his father Griffith Lowe died in October 1852, Edward was 24.

1852 ... E Lowe was a passenger on the ship 'GRECIAN' reported in the 3 November issue NZ Spectator. (T)

DEPARTURES.

October 31—Government Brig *Victoria*, 200 tons, Deck, for Port Victoria.

November 1—Schooner *Return*, 70 tons, Griffiths, for Port Victoria.

Same day—Schooner *Wellington*, 70 tons, Ferguson, for Ahuriri.

November 2—Brig *Grecian*, 212 tons, Gwatkin, for Melbourne. Passengers—Mrs. Craney, Mr. and Mrs. Halbert, Halbert, jun., E. Lowe, Ellingham, W. Galpin, Seed, Morris, Sleath, Smith, White, J. Herbert, W. Cocking, J. Hawk, J. Fisher, H. Phillips, P. Kelly, T. Benton, Benton, jun.

From this point there are no more mentions of Edward Lowe in NZ, except ....

1854... NZ Spectator (etc) advertised on 3 May 1854, that the Partnership between D Isaacs and L Levy was duly dissolved by mutual consent. Mr Lipman Levy would carry on the business on his own account. Witnesses to the agreement date 24 March 1854 were Edward Lowe, Melbourne and David Robertson, Melbourne. (CW)

1854... NZ Post advertisement of people who had not uplifted letters in their name up to the 30 September 1854, was published 14 October 1854 in the 'Wellington Independent' newspaper and Edward Lowe's name appears there amongst a long list of names. (T)

1856... Port Nicholson Jury List .... No people named LOWE were listed. (CW)

After his father's death in 1852, Edward Lowe seems to move to Melbourne, Australia.

--oo0Ooo—

JOSEPH LOWE Ann's second child was born in Wales and baptised in March 1831 at the Overton Parish Church, Flintshire, Wales. (refer page 17 for baptism photo)

The *'Bolton's'* papers state he was aged 9 in November 1839 when he boarded the ship. Joseph is thought to have lived his New Zealand life in the Wellington area. He would have been 18 when his mother and younger siblings travelled to Auckland and aged 21 when his father died. Our research has found numerous Joseph Lowes in New Zealand, (best in Auckland and Dunedin) during that era but no proof that any of them were 'our' Joseph. We have found no record of him past his arrival at Wellington in 1840. Did Joseph leave the area? Travel to some other part of NZ, maybe the South

Island? Travel to Australia? Did he move up to Auckland to be near his mother? Did he die early in NZ? No record of his death in the Wellington district, no Joseph Lowe death in the Anglican Church records and no Joseph Lowe buried at the Bolton St, Cemetery, Wellington. Quite a mystery! (T)

1849. AUCKLAND

We believe about 1849, Ann, and her six youngest children travelled from Wellington to live in Auckland. Ann's great-grandson Ronald Woods remembers being told *they travelled by ship to Auckland and set up home in Elliott Street.* Ann's children at this date would have been aged... Edward 22, Joseph 19 (these two may have stayed in Wellington) Mary Ann 17, John 15 and William 13, (these three Lowe children definitely came north with their mother) and George 9, Jane 6, and Henry 3 (these three Morris children came to Auckland also). Young Henry died in 1852 aged 5 in Auckland but unfortunately his death certificate does not give his parents street address.

We believe that from this time they all used the surname MORRIS, excepting son John who stayed with Lowe and with Ann and Mary Ann reverting to Lowe later when they married.

The population of Auckland reached about 1500 by the end of **1841** and in early **1850** there were 17 stone houses, 25 brick and 814 built of weather-board. (A)

In **1852** the total population of the Colony of New Zealand, including Maori was put at 130,000 people with 80,000 scattered throughout the Auckland Province (A)

Auckland town's population growth was quite rapid.

In **1858** when Ann married Moses Crocker there were 6,283 people and in **1868** when Ann died there were 11,510 people living there. To carry this a bit further we found that in **1899** when Mary Ann Woods left Chapel St for Canada St there were 33,109 people and in **1918** when Mary Ann died there was a population of 71,157 in Auckland City. (CA)

--oo0oo—

CHURCH in AUCKLAND.

At Overton in Wales and Threapwood in England, the Lowe children were baptised at the Church of England.

At Wellington they had arrived with their Church of England sponsor Rev J. F. Churton and remained part of his congregation in the district of Thorndon, where *'The Bolton'* families were housed and where the Rev Churton had been appointed. The Old St Paul's Church of England records, show the 'Morris' children, Jane, Sarah and Henry were baptised by the Rev Robert Cole at Old St Pauls.

1850. In Auckland we found Ann and family attending the Primitive Methodist Church. It was situated between 100 and 200 yards of their home and much closer than the Church of England. Here at the Edwards Street Chapel the families of **Lowe, Morris, Crocker, Woods, Gow and Thomas** all became members. They all knew each other and through marriages all later became related to each other.

Edwards Street was soon renamed Alexandra St and in 1993 it became Airedale Street.

In 1993 the Aotea Methodist Chapel was standing on the same site earlier occupied by the Primitive Methodist Church but now the larger Church faced onto Queen St.

'Register of Members of the Primitive Methodists.'

1850 – 1867 This register mentions members of our family.

Ann Morris was not registered as a member until 1853, although her daughter **Mary Ann (Lowe) Morris**, single, was registered each of the three years 1850, 51, 52.

Mary Ann married in this Church in 1853 and her entry in that year changed to **Mary Ann Woods**.

In a financial record book **Ann Morris** was mentioned as receiving 12 shilling and 6 pence ($1.25 in NZ dollars) for cleaning the Chapel in each of the years 1851, 1852 and 1853.

In 1853 **Ann Morris** first appears as a member.

In 1860 she was registered as **Ann Crocker** until 1867. At the age of 23 (1860) Ann's son **William Morris** was registered as a member of the Primitive Methodist Church at Edwards St.

Ann's son **George W D Morris** was a Trustee.

The **PRIMITIVE METHODIST CHURCH & SUNDAY SCHOOL HALL, AUCKLAND** seen immediately above car.

In the final year of the records, 1867-8 Ann's son George and wife Agnes were registered at both the Edwards St and the new Primitive group meeting at Sheridan St, Auckland.

AUCKLAND HOME.

We have not found where in Elliott Street in Auckland, Ann and her family's home was. Ann was not registered on Auckland Electoral Rolls for 1850 to 1858 when she married Moses Crocker.

> (Elliott St ran, and still does, from Victoria St to Wellesley St in Auckland's CBD.) Maybe her street was partially formed in 1849 and her home was built just 'off' Victoria St on the new road.

We have Ann's grandson Ronald Woods' memory of them *'setting up home in Elliott St, Auckland'* and in 1858 Ann married *'at her home off Victoria St'* and Moses Crocker, is first listed in Elliott St in 1862.

1852. Gold was discovered on the Coromandel by Charles Ring in 1852. We researchers do not know if any of the Lowe or Morris men went to the gold fields.

1852. Ann's son Henry Lowe/Morris died aged 5 on 4 July in Auckland.

--oo0Ooo—

<u>1886 MAP of AUCKLAND</u>

This map of Auckland in 1886 shows the wharves starting at Customs Street; the position of Elliott St where Ann lived; John and Mary Ann Woods home on Chapel St, (later known as Lower Vincent St) and the Primitive Methodist Chapel on Edwards St, today known as Airedale Street.

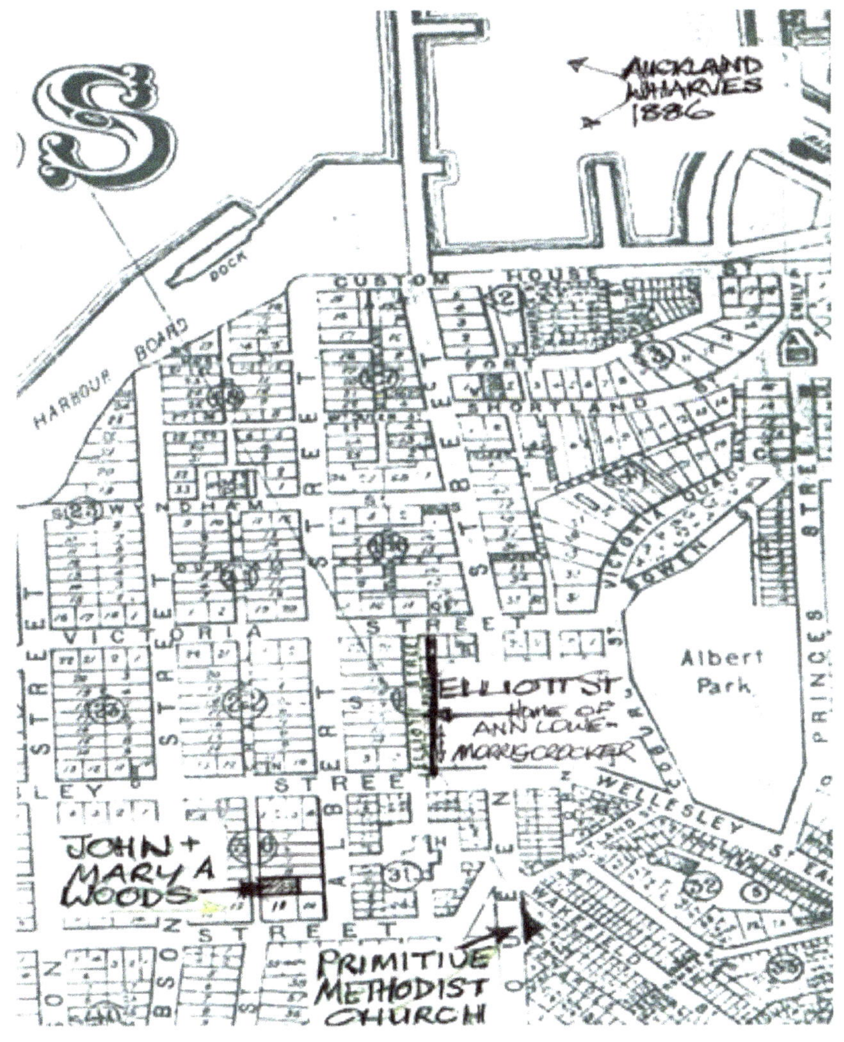

1852. Griffith Lowe died 5th October in Wellington at 54.

1853. In February, Ann's daughter **Mary Ann** married **John Woods** at the Primitive Methodist Chapel, Auckland.

1853: Ann's FIRST GRANDCHILD...... The Primitive Methodist Church records show that Ann's daughter Mary

Ann's first child **MARTHA ANN WOODS**, was baptised on 13 December 1853 by Rev R Ward.

1858. ANN REMARRIED.

Eighteen years after arriving in New Zealand, Ann Lowe (Morris) remarried in Auckland, on 28 October 1858 to **MOSES CROCKER** who stated he was a bachelor aged 43.

(Of her living 'Auckland' children, Mary Ann 25 now married with 3 children, son John was aged 23, William 21, George 17 and Jane 15.
(If still alive, Edward was 29 and Joseph 27)

Ann stated on her *'Intent to Marry Form'* (dated 26 October 1858) that she was aged 43. (she was actually 53) and had lived in Auckland 8 years. (therefore she arrived in Auckland late 1849 or early 1850)

NB.... Eldest son Edward was aged 29 but not in Auckland, so we think Ann reduced her aged considerably. Maybe she didn't want anyone to know she was about 11 years older than her new husband.

Ann aged 35 onto ship = born 1805. Her baptism in
Flintshire, Wales proves this date correct.
Ann 43 marries Crocker = born 1815.
Ann, death certificate = born 1814/5. (ex Moses)
Ann, headstone = born 1814. (ex Moses)

Moses advised that he was a tailor, a bachelor aged 43 and been in Auckland seven months. (Maybe he arrived from overseas, maybe Sydney, Australia about March 1858)

Ann originally told the BDM authorities she was Ann Morris but the next day on 27 October she returned and altered her name to *'Ann Lowe, widow'*

The wedding ceremony was held at *'Ann's house 'off' Victoria Street in Auckland'.*

Ann and Moses did not have any children.

(This 'Intent' statement seems to confirm that before Griffith Lowe died Ann had not gained a divorce and was in fact never married to Samuel Morris. Maybe Griffith had never agreed to give her a divorce.

1860 This Jury List shows Moses lived at Helleord (misinterpreted 'Elliott') St, Auckland and was a Tailor.

1862 'Moses Crocker, Elliott Street'. This entry in the Auckland West Electoral Roll. (T)

1863 NZ WARS: The New Zealand Wars between settlers and Maori started over a dispute of the Waitara Block in Taranaki in March 1860 and moved to the Waikato in July 1863. Finally the wars were concluded at Tauranga in October 1864. At no time did the scene of hostilities reach the town of Auckland but during 1863 and 1864 the entire adult male population was enlisted for compulsory service, either in the militia, volunteers or fire brigade and had to undergo military training. Some did duty at the various blockhouses placed at points of vantage overlooking the district. The blockhouses were situated where Auckland hospital now stands and at Domain Hill, Parnell, Newmarket, Karangahape Road, Great North Road and Freemans Bay. July 22, 1863 saw the First Class Militia and Volunteers join the field forces at Wairoa River, and in February 1864 the Second Class Militia comprising business and tradespeople were ordered into active service.

(ex 'THE CITY OF AUCKLAND' book by John Barr.)

1863: During these **NZ War years**, Ann's son Edward was possibly living in Melbourne, son Joseph was 33 and may have been in Auckland or Dunedin. Son John was single, 28, in Auckland, and son William 26 had 'removed' from Auckland. Son George WD was living in Dunedin area. Ann's husband Moses Crocker was then aged 48.
We wonder if some of these males had military experience we have not found in the Auckland City records. (T)

ANN Griffiths, Lowe, Morris, Crocker in later years.

The CROCKER family:

1776. JOHN CROCKER & **WILMET** of North Tawton, Devon, England, baptised son Thomas.
1806. THOMAS CROCKER married **JANE BODY** at the Church of England in Devon.
1813. THOMAS CROCKER (b 1776) Ag Lab and **JANE BODY** had five children .... Elizabeth b1813, Samuel b1814, **Moses b1816**, Jemima b1818, Matthew b1820.
1841. This English Census shows Thomas 64, Jane 55, Moses a tailor 25 and siblings Matthew 20 (born 25 June & bapt 13 Aug 1820), Jemima 25 and Elizabeth 27. Son Samuel had left home but had been baptised 27 Dec 1814. The family were living at Lanteglos by Camelford, in Cornwall, England.
1844 Pigot's Directory, under Shopkeepers and Traders... "Moses Crocker, tailor."
1850. Aged 35 Moses married **CATHERINE MERRIFIELD** (daughter of William and Elizabeth Merrifield) on 26 Dec 1850 at *'Newlyn near St Columb-Major'*, Cornwall.
1851 Census. Moses, married, aged 35, tailor, (No wife listed with him) living with father Thomas 74, and sister Elizabeth Crocker aged 37 at Lanteglos, Camelford. Wife Catherine was with her mother Elizabeth 51, widow, at Mitchell, Cornwall. She was recorded as '25, wife of a tailor'. Three siblings were also at home ... James 19, Peter 16 and Richard Merrifield 10. (Camelford to Mitchell = 27 miles via A9)
1852 to 1857. During these years Moses travelled from England, maybe direct to Sydney, Australia, then crossed the Tasman Sea by boat to Auckland in March 1858.
1858. In October 1858 Moses married **ANN LOWE** at her home in Auckland.
1862 & 63 & 66 & 67 In these Electoral Rolls *'Moses Crocker living in Elliott St, Auckland.'*

1865. Moses Crocker was found in the *Electoral Roll for West Auckland.* (Auckland City had two parliamentary districts … 'East' and 'West' off Queen St.)

1868. In the Electoral Rolls he stated he owned Freehold Lots 40 and 41 in Elliott St plus lot 6 Glengarry.

1869. Moses wife Ann nee Lowe died in November. We believe Moses had the headstone erected on her grave and saw that her other relatives were mentioned on it. He joined Ann in the Grafton Cemetery grave later in 1895.

1871/2/3 Electoral Rolls, Moses still living at Elliott St, but not listed 1874 to 1880.

1876. Moses Crocker married **MARTHA SMITH** …
ref 1876/2844 in New Zealand.

1881. Electoral Roll. Moses, a tailor, lived in England Street, Auckland. Owned 2 houses.

1882. In the *"1882 Freeholders of NZ"*, Moses Crocker recorded property in Auckland valued at 330 pounds. Also, Moses on Electoral Rolls … *'tailor, of Scotland St, Auckland.'*

1883. Electoral Rolls. *Moses Crocker of Scotland St, Auckland.*

1893. Electoral Roll. Martha Smith Crocker listed at Scotland St, Auckland.

1895. Moses died 27 August 1895, aged 80 (=b 1815/16) at Scotland Street, Auckland. He was buried by Wesleyan Rev E Best, at the Grafton Cemetery, Auckland. Moses left a WILL dated 31 May 1890, leaving an estate valued at £300, to his wife Martha Smith Crocker for her use, but when she died the house at Scotland St, Auckland was to go to his nephew William Henry Moore, a tailor living in Sydney, Australia. Nothing was willed to our Ann Lowe's family.

1904. Martha S Croker died 16 August. Her Will is held at Archives NZ, Auckland.

--oo0Ooo—

1869. On 18 November 1869, **Ann Crocker died** (Apoplexy) aged 54, (we think she was actually aged 63) and was buried at Grafton Cemetery, Karangahape Road, Auckland.

In the same grave are her son Henry Morris, her grandson S.R.H.Morris, her son-in-law John Woods and her last husband Moses Crocker.

The tall headstone at this grave reads ......

SACRED
TO THE MEMORY OF
ANN the beloved wife of
MOSES CROCKER
who departed this life
18 November 1868
aged 55.
also
HENRY MORRIS
son of the above
who died 11th May 1852
aged 5 years.
also
S. R. H. Morris
grandson of the above
who died 27 February 1868
aged 1 year 9 months.
also
JOHN WOODS
who was drowned in
Auckland Harbour
13 September 1882
aged 52.
Blessed are the dead
who die in the Lord.
also
MOSES CROCKER
who died 27 August 1895
aged 80.

Details of ANN's 9 children follows .....

ANN LOWE had 9 children as follows .....

Five to husband **GRIFFITH LOWE**

EDWARD LOWE	page 69 & 85
JOSEPH LOWE	page 72
MARY ANN LOWE	page 86 & 180
JOHN LOWE	page 88
WILLIAM LOWE	page 95

(William used the surname MORRIS)

and

Four to partner **SAMUEL MORRIS**

GEORGE WALTER DRAKE MORRIS	page 100
Children of George and Agnes	page 106
JANE (POLLY) MORRIS	page 123
SARAH MORRIS	page 127
HENRY MORRIS	page 127

--oo0oo--

ANN LOWE'S <u>5 children to Griffith Lowe</u>.

1 ...EDWARD LOWE was Ann's first child and born and baptised in 1829 at Overton Parish Church in Flintshire, Wales. (refer page 14 for baptism photo)
What we have managed to learn about Edward we have typed on pages 69 to 72.
Edward was last found living with his sick father, from 1850 at Tinakori Road, Wellington, and when his father died in October 1852, Edward was aged 23, a clerk & bookkeeper. We think he may have left Wellington for the larger towns in Australia. We found an Edward Lowe in Melbourne and in Adelaide but found no proof they were 'our' Edward.

--oo0Ooo—

2 ...JOSEPH LOWE

What happened to him is a complete mystery to his family.
What we know and speculate is on page 72.

--oo0Ooo—

3 ...MARY LOWE Ann's third child was probably born in the Sarn district of Flintshire in Wales in 1833 but was baptised MARY, at the nearest Church of England, over the boarder at Threapwood in England in February 1833.

(refer page 22 for photo of baptism record)

At some early part of her life, and before she was seven and recorded in the Bolton ship's passenger list, the middle name of ANN (after her mother) was added. (MARY ANN LOWE)
Mary lived until 1918 (85 years). She married John Woods and they had 10 children. Because of the volume of detail we have gathered, we will record Mary separately starting page 180.

--oo0Ooo—

4 ...JOHN LOWE Ann's fourth child was born in the Sarn district of Flintshire, Wales in **1835,** and somehow he was never baptised in Wales or England. This is explained on pages 22 and 23. His descendants thought he was born in Bolton, Liverpool or Lancaster in England... but that is not so.

1839 to NZ. John was aged 5 in November 1839 when added to *"The Bolton"* ship's passenger list for the trip to New Zealand. Here he first lived with his mother Ann and her new partner Samuel Morris, at Pipitea Point, Wellington.

1849. John aged 15, was with his mother Ann and the other children when she travelled to live in Auckland around 1849. What happened to John over the next 23 years in Auckland? No records have been found within the family, but he did remain single until aged 38 when he married Rebecca.

1873 MARRIAGE: On December 2, at the dwelling house of Mrs Taylor in Cook St, Auckland, **JOHN LOWE** (38) married **REBECCA TAYLOR (Beccy)** (20). The certificate shows John was employed as a 'Storekeeper'. Rev Charles Waters officiated, with Francis Collingwood Taylor (Rebecca's brother) and Martha Ann Woods (John's niece) as witnesses. Both bride and groom signed their names. (CW cert)

SURNAME: His mother Ann, his brothers and sisters started using the Morris surname soon after they arrived in Auckland... but all records of marriage, children's birth registrations etc, show John kept the LOWE surname.

CHILDREN: John and Rebecca had three daughters.
1884 **ALICE** born at Karaka St, Auckland.

1886 **MARTHA** born at Karaka St, Auckland.
1892 **EVELINE** born at Fernleigh St, Ponsonby, Auckland.
Details of the 3 children's lives follow on page 90 ......

1894 DEATH of JOHN LOWE. After he married he was a Gum-sorter and Storeman by occupation. John died aged 58 at Cook Street, Auckland (mother-in-law's house?) on June 2, 1894. The Rev W.S. Potter of the Primitive Methodist Church buried John Lowe at the St Jude's Avondale Cemetery, plot 197e, (the name changed to George Maxwell Memorial Cemetery in the late 1980s) beside his brother William Morris.

John and William's grave is immediately beside that of Jane & George Thomas. Jane being Jane (Polly) Morris ... John and William's half-sister.

No headstone was erected. His certificate advises he was born in Bolton, Lancashire (wrong) and he had been in NZ 55 years. His daughters were aged 10, 8 and 2. (PM)

WEDDINGS: Unfortunately daughter Alice died aged 22. Martha married in October 1911 in Rotorua and Eveline married in 1910 in Rotorua, NZ.

GRANDCHILD: John and Rebecca's first grandchild was born in March 1912 to Martha (William Fitzroy Melton) and the second in Dec 1912 to Eveline. (Trevor Allan Carnachan)

1907 John Lowe's widow, Rebecca 44, married WILLIAM GIBBONS HARP 45, widower, at Alexander St Primitive Methodist Church, Auckland, on 10 March 1907. Francis Collingwood Taylor and Mary Ellen Taylor (both Rebecca's siblings) were witnesses. (CW)

1934 Rebecca (81) died at Waikato Hospital, Hamilton, NZ, on November 30. Her certificate notes her father was William Morrow Taylor a 'shipwright' and her mother Ann nee Collingwood. Rebecca was born in Sunderland, Durham, England, and had been in NZ 70 years. (CW)
Rebecca's daughters Martha (48) & Eveline (42) survived her.

1939 Rebecca's second husband W G Harp (builder) died aged 87, on 21 December 1939 at Pahiatua, but had been living in Hamilton. William had been married before to Jennie Walker of Cambridge, NZ, and a male 63 and two females 51 & 47 survived him. Another daughter had died. Rebecca and William were buried at Hamilton East Cemetery. (CW)

Rebecca's **TAYLOR FAMILY details** .... see page 94.

--oo0Ooo--

Rebecca and John Lowe had 3 daughters..........
Alice, Martha and Eveline

1884 ALICE MAUD GRIFFITH LOWE was born 21 July, while the family was living at Karaka Street, Auckland. John was aged 46 and a 'gumsorter'. Rebecca was 21 and born in Sunderland, England. (near Newcastle) (CW)
1906 Aged 22 on November 29 at Devonport, Auckland, Alice died and was buried at O'Neil's Point Cemetery in the Presbyterian section. (CW)

--oo0Ooo—

1886 MARTHA ANNE COLLINGWOOD LOWE was born at Karaka Street, Newton, Auckland, on August 15. John was aged 48 and a 'gumsorter'. Again he nominated Liverpool as his birthplace and got his marriage date wrong recording February 1872 and gave Rebecca's age as 32… also wrong.

1911 Martha married **WILLIAM GEORGE MELTON** at the Bainbridge Memorial Church in Rotorua on 7th October 1911. She was 25 employed as a domestic servant and William was a Hotel servant aged 35 (1875/6) and a son of William Henry Melton a 'Housekeeper to a Company' and Elizabeth Anne Scates and was born at Bury Saint Edmunds, Suffolk, England. William George Melton may have been a crew on the ship 'Zelandia' which plied between NZ, Fiji and Sydney ports. There are 15 entries between 19 January 1904 and 9 April 1905 where WGM mostly worked as a Bedroom Steward. His job at a Rotorua Hotel in 1911 matches this activity. When Martha married, her father had died and her mother had remarried.

1951 Death. Aged 75 William G Melton died at Greenlane Public Hospital, Epsom on Dec 2 and was buried at Waikaraka Cemetery by Rev M A Moore an Anglican. William was a retired Hotel employee and had last lived at Kain St, Mt Roskill, Auckland. (CW)

1958 Death. At 72 Martha died at Cornwall Public Hospital, Epsom, Auckland on July 30, a widow living at 31 Hargest Rd, Mt Albert, Auckland and was cremated at Waikumete Cemetery. The certificate shows she had a son aged 46 alive on this date… (William Fitzroy, born 1912) (CW)

1973 Death. The son of William and Martha Melton … **WILLIAM FITZROY MELTON** born March 15, 1912, an electrician by trade, died aged 61 on June 21, 1973, at North Shore Hospital, Auckland. William (30) married **EDITH MABEL EUNICE BALCHIN** (22) in 1942 but there were no children noted alive on his death certificate. Edith was born 10 October 1920 and died in 1976. William F M (and probably Edith) was buried at North Shore Memorial Park, Schnapper Rock Road, Albany, Auckland. (CW,TP)

--oo0Ooo—

1892 EVELINE ELIZA JANE LOWE was born June 24, 1892 when the family was living at Fernleigh St, Ponsonby. Father John was 54 and Rebecca 39.

1910 MARRIAGE. In Rotorua, Eveline E J Lowe married **ALLAN BARR TAWAKEHEIMOA CARNACHAN,** b 1887, Maketu, Te Waiariki, who became a Grocery Assistant.

3 CHILDREN ...

TREVOR ALLAN CARNACHAN born Dec 15, 1912.
VALERIE EVELYN CARNACHAN born March 26, 1920.
JOY VERONICA CARNACHAN born Aug 3, 1925.

1918 WW1. Allan served in The Great War as a Quartermaster Sergeant #31946, NZ Rifle Brigade, 28th Reinforcements, H Company. During this time his family lived in King St, Rotorua. On July 28 Allan then a corporal, was number 910/1 on the Wounded – Casualty list. (He recovered)

1931 UNION St. Before this date the family moved to 20 Union St, Rotorua where they remained. The electoral rolls show Allan & Eveline there in 1931, 1943 and Allan 1949/51, 1954, 1963. Their children... Trevor was at 20 Union St, a teacher, 1935, he married 1936, he and wife there in 1949/51, they moved to 19 Malfroy Road for 1954. Daughter Joy was at Union St 1949, and 1954 after she married. Daughter Valerie was at Union St 1949/51, 1954, then she married and soon became a widow, living at 20 Union St in 1957 and 1963.

1944 Death. Eveline died at her residence, 20 Union St, Rotorua on Sept 9, 1944 aged 52. She was buried at Rotorua Cemetery Block 2, Section 62, Plot 17. She died 'intestate' (no Will) and the courts awarded her estate to husband Allan. (T)

1971 Death. Allan B T Carnachan 84, died at Rotorua Hospital May 27, and was buried at Rotorua Cemetery RSA plot 396.

--oo0Ooo--

8 GRANDCHILDREN of Allan and Eveline Carnachan.

TREVOR married 1936 **VERONICA GLADYS (Vera) EVERSFIELD ......** and they had three children .... **JUDITH, BRUCE & GILLIAN Carnachan.**

VALERIE married **GEORGE HENRY LAWRENCE** and named a child **EVELYN Lawrence.**

JOY married **CLIVE SELWYN SHARP** and named four children **ALLAN BRIAN, RODNEY SELWYN, MURRAY and KEVIN Sharp.** (BC/CW)

4 GREATGRANDCHILDREN of Allan and Eveline include... Anne-Marie, Gerard, Bernadette & Scott. (Allan's Obit 1871)

--oo0Ooo—

Allan's CARNACHAN family of Scotland

Four generation brief tree

1 **Robert** Carnachan married Agnes McKinlay in Scotland. They had a son **David** in 1820.

2 **David** Carnachan married Elizabeth Friars in Scotland They had 11 children ... Martha 1856, **Fox Maule** 1857, Elizabeth SS 1859, Lauderdale 1861, Catherine 1863, William

1866, David 1867, Jeanie 1869, Blanche E 1871, James 1874 and Robert 1877.

3 **Fox Maule** Carnachan came to New Zealand and married in Te Puke 1881 Sarah Hera Mokaiwhakanui Piercy and they had 9 children ...

Robert 1882 & 1884, Ellinor Steton Stuart 1883, **Allan Barr 1887**, Elizabeth K 1889, Edward Piercy 1892, Angus Te Poroa 1894, Kate Te N 1896, and Fox Maule jnr 1899.

4 **Allan Barr Carnachan married Eveline Eliza Jane Lowe** in 1910 at Rotorua, New Zealand.

(These Carnachan details were gathered from official records and Family Trees on Ancestry... CW & T)

--oo0oo—

Rebecca's **TAYLOR family details** ....

JOHN TAYLOR 1763- died 1794 aged 31, had married **THOMASINE KIRKUP 1765-1827** and they had 4 children ...
Robert 1791, Ann 1793, Thomasine 1793-1793, John 1795-1796.

ROBERT TAYLOR 1791-1871 bapt 20 March 1791 at Bishopwearmouth, Sunderland, County Durham, England. He married **REBECCA BRECKENRAGE** on 23 February 1812 at St Michaels, Bishopwaermouth and they had 10 children ...

Robert 1813, George 1815-1816, Susannah 1817-1877, Rebecca 1817, Dorothy 1819-1879, **William Morrow 1824,** George 1826, Jonathon Storey 1827-1827, Huddleston 1829-1880, and Rebecca 1832. In the 1841 Census the family were living at Whitburn St, Monkwearmouth. Mother Rebecca died Jan 1863 at 4 Waterloo Place, Monkwearmouth.

WILLIAM MORROW TAYLOR born 14 August 1824 at Monkwearmouth - died 10 May 1867, (became a shipwright).

William married **ANN COLLINGWOOD** on 15 August 1846 at Gainsborough, Lincolnshire. Ann was born in March 1823 in Lincolnshire, England. They had 7 children ...
William born 1845, Francis Collingwood 1848-1933, Sarah Ann 1851-1921, **Rebecca born 19 July 1853** at Hardwick St, Monkwearmouth Shore, Durham, England, and baptised 7 August, Joseph 1855, Susannah 1857-1936, and Mary Ellen born 1862 in New Zealand, died 1934. In the 1851 census this family was living at Back Rendlesham, Monkwearmouth.
1859 This Taylor family emigrated to New Zealand on 6 June, leaving from Gravesend, on board the *"Spray of the Ocean", (Capt. Slaughter)* arriving at Auckland 1 September 1859.

Rebecca Taylor 1853 married John Lowe

(We are grateful to Arthur Owen Ryan for the research he has done and shared two of his Ancestry Family Trees. T)

--oo0Ooo—

5 WILLIAM MORRIS was Ann's fifth child born and was baptised LOWE in Wales / England on June 16, 1838. He was entered in the Bolton passenger list as aged 1½ in Nov 1839 which confirms he was born about May/June 1838.

For his baptism record see page p22.

BIRTH William's death certificate suggests he was born at Bolton in Lancashire. However we found he was Welsh born and baptised at the Threapwood Church in England by the Rev J F Churton. (The ship's name & Town being confused)
He boarded the ship *'Bolton'* with his parents aged one and a half years. William remained unmarried for all his 72 years and used his stepfather's surname of Morris.

1849 William, (11) travelled with his mother to Auckland.

1869/66 The *'Register of Members of the Primitive Methodist Church'* in Auckland. William Morris' first entry was in 1860 when he was *single and 23.* In 1861 and 1862 he was recorded as a member. In 1863 the comment *Removed* is written. (removed from Auckland ... not the Church) In 1864 William was... *At Port Waikato* and in 1865 he has... *Left the province.* In 1866 William Morris was recorded as... *Gone to Sydney.* (T)

1866-1891 He remained a bachelor and became a Methodist Lay Preacher and Sunday School Superintendent in Sydney.

AUSTRALIA. In 1866 William left Auckland for Sydney, Australia and we think he went into a Methodist Training School where he graduated on December 9, 1870. He was presented with a certificate on that date from the members of his 'class'. It reads..... *"Presented to WILLIAM MORRIS by the members of his class, previous to his departure to visit his friends in New Zealand, as a slight expression of their High Esteem for and Christian Love towards him,* unsigned but from, *Crown St, Sydney."*

William must have returned to Sydney quickly as he spent 25 years in total there, being a useful Methodist.

1868 WILLIAM MORRIS

On the rear of this photo is the photographers name Robert Stewart, successful in Sydney, and in Melbourne. It was taken at 348 George St where Robert moved to in July 1868 and then he moved to Melbourne in 1870.

So, this photo was probably taken around William's 30th birthday.

1891 A bible was presented to William when he finally left Australia to return to New Zealand, and the fly leaf dated 15 February 1891 reads..........

Presented by the Teachers and Scholars of the Primitive Methodist Sunday School, Albion St, Surry Hills, (Sydney) *to Mr William Morris in recognition of his diligent and faithful service as the 1st Superintendent of the School, and of his thoughtful and courteous bearing towards the Teachers and Scholars.*

(Signed)
J. W. Holden. Minister.

1891 William returned to Auckland and he joined his sister Mary Ann Woods and her son Harry (just turned 16) at Lower Vincent Street.
(Was called Chapel St until 1884)

1898 Early this year John Haslett (Mary Ann's daughter Janes' husband) purchased 7 sections in Canada Road, Mt Eden. (Canada Rd was later renamed Kawaka St.)
On 30 March 1899 he sold lot 6 and part of lot 5 to William Morris. (approximately 21 perches.) Here William built a house and soon Mary Ann and son Harry (then aged 24) moved to live with him. Title CT92/12 shows W M owned this house and land, known as 8 Canada Road until he died.

1907 William's Will (signed 5 August 1907) gave this property to nephew Henry Joseph Woods (Harry)... tailor, who officially received it on 18 March 1911. Harry was by now supporting his mother Mary Ann. William also left 100 pound to his mother Mary Ann Woods and 50 pounds to his sister Jane Thomas, widow. He appointed John Woods, shoemaker and John Haslett, settler, as his Trustees and Executors.
After Harry married and had one child, his mother Mary Ann then aged about 80 (who Ronald Woods called "Grandma") moved to live awhile with daughter Jessie Gow (about 1914) in Prospect Terrace. (RW) At some future date Mary was living with daughter Jane and John Haslett in their Pah Rd, Epsom house, where she died in November 1918.

1910 WILLIAM DIED aged 72, on 4 July 1910 at his residence ... 8 Canada Road, Mt Eden, Auckland.

The Rev H White of the Primitive Methodist Church buried William Morris with his brother John Lowe in plot 197e at St Judes Avondale cemetery. The undertaker for John and William was Thomas J Mclvor of Auckland. No headstone was raised.

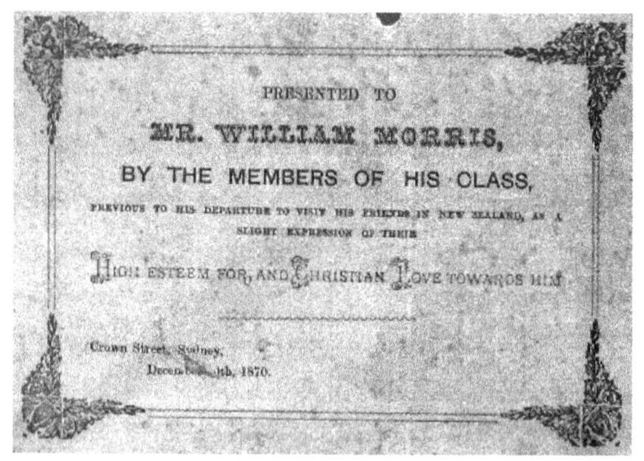
PRESENTED TO
MR. WILLIAM MORRIS,
BY THE MEMBERS OF HIS CLASS,
PREVIOUS TO HIS DEPARTURE TO VISIT HIS FRIENDS IN NEW ZEALAND, AS A SLIGHT EXPRESSION OF THEIR
HIGH ESTEEM FOR, AND CHRISTIAN LOVE TOWARDS HIM
Crown Street, Sydney,
December [illegible]th, 1870.

1870 certificate

1891 certificate
Inside bible cover

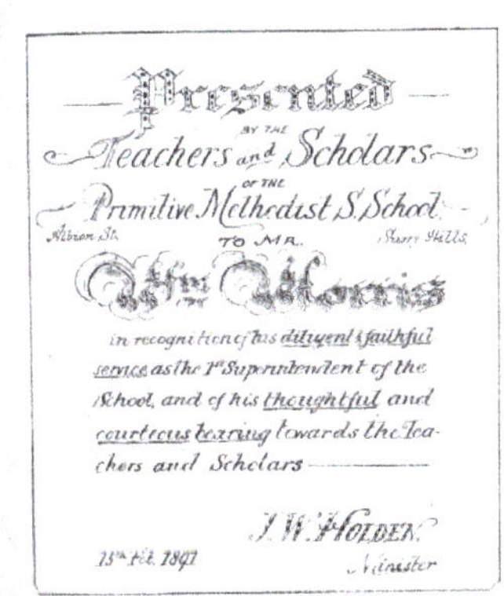
Presented
by the
Teachers and Scholars
of the
Primitive Methodist S. School.
Albion St. TO MR. Surry Hills.
Wm Morris
in recognition of his diligent & faithful service as the 1st Superintendent of the School, and of his thoughtful and courteous bearing towards the Teachers and Scholars

J. W. HOLDEN.
15th Feb. 1891 Minister

WILLIAM MORRIS

8 CANADA Road, Auckland.

ANN LOWE's <u>4 children to Samuel Morris.</u>

(numbers 6 to 9) George, Jane, Sarah and Henry,
We have found the following ....

6 GEORGE WALTER DRAKE MORRIS. senior

1841. George was born February 6 at Pipitea Pa, Wellington and became a master builder. (MF/PM)

George was named by his father Samuel Morris, and after Samuel's predecessor ... the younger brother of Sir Francis Drake ... Walter Drake. (GF)

George's family believed for a time George was the first white child born in Wellington Feb 6, 1841. He may in fact have been the first European born in the Pipitea/Thorndon district. However, on February 29, 1840 Thomas Rogers was born in a small manuka bach on the Petone Beach. His parents had landed at Petone about 4 weeks prior to the birth. (GF/PM)

1846. About this year George started his education at a Dame School near Hobson St in Wellington. (MLF/PM)

1848 Earthquake.

We covered this Wellington earthquake earlier on page 59 but George, then 7, recalled *"it knocked him over and made him homeless. The ground was unstable for 2 to 3 weeks. The beach at that time came up to Courtney Place and the tide at Lampton Quay used to go a long way out ... a fact known to the native women who congregated to gather pipis. There was only one house on Oriental Bay and the whole of Wellington hills were clothed in bush, much of it very large trees."* (GWDM,GF)

1849 Travel. Soon after that large earthquake George (about 8) travelled by boat with his mother and siblings to live in Auckland and continued his education and learnt the trades of carpenter and builder. (PM)

Auckland. George's memories of his arrival in Auckland include *'it being a city of mud and encountering a woman digging a child out of the mud in Queen St opposite what is now (1973) the Post Office. Kauri gum was plentiful ... it could be dug up in the yards and streets and people used it for lighting the fire.'* (GWDM/GF)

George learnt his trade from James Gilbert of Auckland, who was the founder of the Sash and Door Company and he completed his term in 1861. (JH/BE)

1861/2. George was registered as a member of the Primitive Methodist Church, in Auckland in this year when aged 20. Added beside his name is the note... *Gone to Otago.* (T)

Grandson Gordon Fraser writes ... *"Grandfather Morris (GWDM) was smitten with gold-fever with the news of finds in the Dunedin area (*Gabriel's Gully gold found 23 May 1861) *and sailed there in the schooner 'Surprise' calling in on the way at Napier where at that time there were no more than 20 houses." "When he arrived in Dunedin he noted it was a beautiful place, with bush covered hills, the streets of mud, the beautiful women and the fine lassies, most of whom wore top boots."*

But he found the people very much opposed to new arrivals unless you belonged to the clan. He went to church several Sunday mornings but no one took any notice of him or offered him the Psalms. So he went to buy one, but the old man at the shop wouldn't sell him one because he was not a Scot. He supposed he took him for a larrikin.' (GWDM/GF)

"One day in a Dunedin St he saw a young woman to whom he was very attracted. Six weeks later he met her at a party and soon after he and Agnes were married." *(MLF/PM)*

1863 NELSON *George spent a week in Nelson which he viewed at that time as a town of gardens. A big hop garden was quite close to the Trafalgar Hotel, and nearly every house had a fruit garden.* *(GWDM/GF)*

1865 CHRISTCHURCH George recalls arriving at Christchurch and having to walk over the hill from the port, then go by coach to the scattered settlement. (GWDM/GF)

1865 MARRIAGE.

GEORGE (24) married **AGNES ANN TURNER** (20) on May 4, 1865 at Sumner Valley, in Christchurch, NZ. (GF)

ROBERT TURNER born 1819 in Leeds, England, (died 1899 Hotham, Victoria, Australia) and married **AGNES ANN CORLESS** on 10 January 1839. (Agnes born 1816 in Leeds, England and died 26 Feb 1868 in Victoria, Australia) Robert and Agnes had three children ....
Mary Ann T 1839, William Robert T 1842 and
Agnes Ann T born 17 January 1845 at Akaroa, NZ.

Note : Agnes' brother William Robert Turner married Martha Ann Woods, daughter of George W D Morris' half sister Mary Ann (Lowe) Woods. (GF)

CHILDREN. George and Agnes had 10 children .... Henry Robert Samuel 1866, Agnes Ann jnr 1868, Ada 1870, these three born in Auckland, George Walter Drake jnr 1873 born in Wellington, and William Charles 1875, Arthur Corless 1876, Edith Elfreda 1879, twins Joseph Lewis and Edgar Wilfred 1882, Mildred Lefemia 1884, these six all born in Christchurch. (more children's individual details follow later) (T)

1867/8 George and Agnes were both registered as members of Primitive Methodist Church at Edwards St and at the same time were members of a new group meeting at Sheridan St, Auckland. There are no church records later than this. George was also listed as a Church Trustee. (T)
In an article written by George's grandson Gordon Fraser he noted that *"George was very religious and they always had a bible reading and prayers after breakfast."* *(GWDM,GF)*

They soon attended the Franklin Road Chapel of Primitive Methodists and here their first three children were baptised **HENRY R.S.** 11 May 1866 by Rev W Colley. George listed as carpenter of Elliott St. **AGNES A** 21 May 1868 by Rev W J Dean. George a storeman of Queen St. **ADA** 28 August 1870 by Rev W J Dean. George was a carpenter living at Sheridan St, Auckland. (Methodist Records/ T)

1868. Their first born, **HENRY R0BERT SAMUEL MORRIS** born in Auckland April 14, 1866, died one year and nine months later on February 16, 1868. When Henry died they lived in Queen St, Auckland.

WELLINGTON: George and Agnes left Auckland and travelled to Wellington where George found work as a joiner. George WDM senior was born in Pipitea St where his parents lived near the Pipitea Pa. George WDM junior, was also born in Pipitea St but probably at the Hospital there.

1873. Son **GEORGE WALTER DRAKE MORRIS** (junior) was born 19 March, at Pipitea St, Wellington to George and Agnes.
Between 1973 and 1875 the family shifted to Christchurch where George was in business for seventeen years. (JH/BE)

1875 Electoral Roll. George and family were living at Phillipstown, Christchurch East.
1880 Electoral Roll. Same as 1875 with George a carpenter.
1885 Electoral Roll. George living in Phillip St, Stanmore, Canterbury.

1887 HUNTERVILLE. During this year Jane Haslett records George moved his family to Hunterville. (JH/BE)

1893 NZ Women gained the right to vote and *Agnes A Morris … Domestic Duties,* was listed #4554 Rangitikei Electorate, living in Hunterville, NZ.
1896 Electoral Roll. George and family living in Hunterville.

1897. From 'Vol 1 NZ Cyclopedia' produced in 1897, we learn G W D Morris was a Cabinetmaker, Upholsterer and Undertaker and owned the Hunterville Furnishing Warehouse in Bruce Street. His private residence was on Onga Road. Although a native of Wellington he learned his business with Mr James Gilbert of Auckland finishing in 1861. For 17 years he was a builder in Christchurch and for 2 years after this was in Wellington. He settled in Hunterville in 1887 where he established his Furnishing Warehouse. The building he designed and erected himself… 2 stories of wood and iron on leasehold land. His business extended all over the Pareakaretu district. He made everything required for his furnishing business. He was an ex-member of the school committee and a member of the Oddfellows Court. (PM)

1900 Electoral Roll. George & Agnes, GWDM junior a butcher, Arthur Corless a carpenter and Ada Mabel were all living at Hunterville.

ODD FELLOWS. George was one of the oldest members of the Order of Odd-fellows in the Dominion and in Hunterville he was a member of the local School Committee. (JH/PM)

1902. An October 1902 article in the "NZ Methodist Times" magazine advises ......

> *"George (WD) Morris, many years a loyal worker in our Alexander St Church, now resides in Hunterville."*

George was a master builder and he once built a clinker dinghy and I rowed with him to Porirua Heads to get fire-wood. We gathered a big load and nearly swamped the dinghy and had to land on a beach and wait for the sea to moderate before we could get closer to home. (Gordon Fraser)

1905 Electoral Roll. George and Agnes living at Hunterville.
1911 Electoral Roll. Living in the Wellington Suburb of Plimmerton were George (builder) & Agnes, and daughter Edith a spinster.
1914 Electoral Roll. Agnes, Edith and George (builder) were living in Durham St, Levin.

1915. GOLDEN WEDDING. George and Agnes celebrated their 50th at Plimmerton on May 4th and family who attended were son GWD Morris of Marton, AC Morris of Wanganui, Mesdames W Wilson, Hunterville, HJ Fletcher of Normanby, JA Fraser of Nelson, and Miss Morris of Plimmerton. (PM)

1919. AGNES DIED February 15th, aged 74 and was buried at Karori Cemetery, Wellington.

In her **WILL** Agnes nominated her husband George as sole executor and trustee. She gave George all her plate, linen, china, glass, books, pictures, prints, furniture and other household effects. George received all her money as trustee, to invest with income from this to go equally to her unmarried daughters, and upon George's death her capital was to be divided equally between all her children.

1919 Electoral Roll. George WD Morris and daughter Edith of Plimmerton, appear on the Roll for Wellington Suburbs, Supplementary Roll.
(No mention of Agnes of course)

PHOTO OF GEORGE taken c1924

1926. GEORGE DIED July 1, 1926 aged 85 at Plimmerton, Wellington.
He was buried at Karori Cemetery, Wellington, with Agnes, Area 02, Block B, Row 11, Plot 015. (PM)

George's **WILL** was filed at Wellington on 11 August 1926.
It notes George was a retired builder of Plimmerton, Wellington.
He made son George and William Wilson a Hunterville farmer, his trustees.

All of his estate was to be equally divided between his children, and if one of them predeceased him, then their share was to be divided equally amongst that child's children upon their reaching 21 years. (T)

1928 Electoral Roll. Although he had died by this date George was still listed, with daughter Edith, living at Karehana Bay, Plimmerton.

KARORI CEMETERY. Their headstone reads....

In Loving Memory of **AGNES ANN**
beloved wife of G. W. D. MORRIS
went home 15 February 1919 aged 74.
"Asleep in Jesus"
also **GEORGE WALTER DRAKE MORRIS**
who departed this life 1 July 1926 aged 85 years.

"Forever with the Lord"

--oo00oo--

Details of the 10 children of
GWD and Agnes Morris follow ....

The 10 CHILDREN of GEORGE & AGNES ……

1 **HENRY ROBERT SAMUEL MORRIS** born 14 April 1866 he was baptised HENRY R.S. 11 May 1866 by Rev W Colley of the Franklin Road Primitive Methodist Church.
HENRY died one year and ten months later on February 16, 1868, of inflammation of the brain, while living in Queen St, Auckland. Father George was at this time a Clerk. (CW cert)

--oo0Ooo—

2 **AGNES ANN MORRIS** (junior) was born in 1868, baptised on 21 May 1868 by Rev W J Dean of the Franklin Road Primitive Methodist Church, Auckland.
1892 Agnes (24) married **WILLIAM WILSON**
They had two children ……… sons Vivian and Graham
1893 Agnes was listed in the first Women's NZ Electoral Roll.
1915 The Golden Anniversary of Agnes' parents was held at their home in Plimmerton on May 4th and Agnes was there.
1937 William was born in 1859 and died 3 April 1937 aged 78 at Wanganui & buried at Rangatira Cemetery, Hunterville.
His Will is available at NZ Archives, Wellington.
1973 Agnes, aged 105 died at Plimmerton on 24 June and joined William at the Hunterville Cemetery.

A 1893 **VIVIAN STANLEY MORRIS WILSON** married **RACHEL MARY MEADS** in 1920 and they had 1 child, **BARBARA WILSON** born 24 March 1922 at Hunterville. (Barbara married **WALTER ANDREW CHESSWAS**, a farm manager, on her 23rd birthday 24 March 1945 and they had three children. Barbara died 21 December 1988 at Stratford, NZ. Walter was born 16 April 1923 and died 13 November 1999 at Hamilton)

Vivian died 27 January 1964 at Tauranga and his Will probated 7 Feb 1964 & available at Auckland Archives. Rachel died 23 November 1983 at Stratford, NZ.

--oo0Ooo—

B 1899 **GRAHAM HOWIE TURNER WILSON** was born 19 April. He started school at Hunterville, then his mother enrolled him at Plimmerton School on 3 July 1905. Graham married **HILDA MURIEL LOURIE** in **1924** and they had 2 children ...

BRYAN LOURIE W born 26 Dec 1926 & died 2007.

NOEL MURRAY W born 1 Nov 1930, died 1 May 2010.

1945 Hilda, born 1903, died at Wanganui on 8 August aged 42, and was buried at Rangatira Cemetery, Hunterville. Her parents were Samuel Duncan Lourie 1873-1969 and Elizabeth Ann Green 1876-1911.

1977 Graham, a retired farmer, died 30 July 1977 aged 78, and rests at Rangatira Cemetery, Hunterville. His Will probated 29 Aug is available Archives Wellington.

--oo0Ooo—

3 ADA MABEL MORRIS born in 1870 was baptised 28 August at the Franklin Road Primitive Methodist Church.

1893 NZ women were allowed to vote and Ada was listed as #4556 in the Rangitikei Electoral District, Hunterville town, employed on Domestic Duties. Her mother was #4554.

1895 Ada (25) married Rev **HENRY JAMES FLETCHER** (27) on 21 January 1895. Ada and Henry had 9 children ....

A **GLADYS IRENE** born 1895 at Hunterville, married 1916 **JOHN THOMAS McCRANE.** John, a Civil servant, died Dec 1939. His Will was probated 18 Dec and available at Archives Auckland. Gladys died, a widow, in Oct 1964 at Stanley Bay, Auckland. Gladys was cremated at Purewa Cemetery. Her Will was probated 23 Dec 1964 and available Archives Auckland.

B **JOHN** born 1898 at Hunterville, was enrolled at Taupo School in 1903.

C **CYRIL MORRIS,** born 2 Aug 1900 at Hunterville, married **JANE VICTORIA O'KEEFFE,** who was born in 1908 and they had 2 children.......... Cyril died 16 March 1963 at Taupo aged 63, and was buried Presbyterian block C plot 10 near his parents.

D **AGNES ALFREDA** 1901. NZ Gazette p641 records Agnes as a Teacher.

E **HENRY JAMES** jnr 1903. Died at Taupo and his Will was probated 1991, available at Wellington.

F **HINA MAIRA** 1907. NZ Gazette 1933 p641 plus 1940 p582 & p515, advise Hina was a Teacher. Remained single, her Will 1984 at Taupo, available at Wellington.

G **ANNIE RONA** 1909. Admitted to Taupo School 1915.

H **HARRIET VERA MADGE** 1911,

I unnamed still-born child in 1913.

--oo00oo—

Henry J Fletcher was a descendant of Sir Philip Fletcher of Kent, England, who married French Countess Claire De Valecourt during the French Revolution. (PM)

1868 Henry was born 29 February 1868, at Denton, Kent.

1871 Census England. Living in Clapham Cottage, Northfleet, Kent, were ... William Fletcher born 1839 (carpenter) and his wife Jane Ann Fawcett (laundress) born 1839, and their children... Harriet 9, William H 8, Thomas 5, Henry James 3, and Mary Ann aged 1.

Father William died in 1914 and mother Jane in 1926.

1874 Henry James Fletcher, 5, arrived in NZ with his parents on the *'La Hogue'* on 26 June 1874. He was fourth of six children. He was educated at Rangitikei and left school aged 13 and apprenticed to a wheel-wright. He soon changed his life and became a student Missionary at Turakina Pa. His first year salary as Maori Missionary was 65 pounds at Te Reureu Pa at Onepuhi Bridge. He learnt Maori from the Chief and was there six months teaching children in 1894.

1890 Electoral Roll. Turakino, Wanganui. Henry a Missionary.

1895 Henry was in charge of the Taupo District from January 1895. He served the Presbyterian Maori Mission for 30 years. It was a very large district, including 16 native settlements, some sixty miles from headquarters.

1896 to 1911 Electoral Roll. At Taupo. Henry … a Missionary.

1897 Henry joined the Polynesian Society in 1897 and during this time he published two books and numerous papers that appeared in the *'Journal'*. Henry and father-in-law George Walter Drake Morris built a small four roomed cottage in Heuheu St that stood for 70 years.

1898 Henry was licensed and ordained in September 1898.

1898 The KAIMANAWA MANSE In 1898 a large manse was built in Kaimanawa St, Taupo which became the Fletcher's home until 1925 … when they moved to Opanake.

It was here in Opanake, that Henry became ill and died in the New Plymouth Hospital.

(You will find much more detail in two articles "Henry's Obituary by the Polynesian Society" and in "Ketetaupo")

1913 The first church in Taupo opened in 1913. This was called First Church, later renamed St Paul's. Henry's daughter Madge Fletcher was the first baby christened at First Church on opening day 14 December 1913.

First Church, Taupo

1915 The Golden Anniversary of Ada's parents was held at their home in Plimmerton on May 4th and Ada was there.

Henry was a keen astronomer making his own instruments.

1919 Electoral Roll. Ada and Henry were listed at Taupo. Henry as Presbyterian Minister.

1928 Electoral Roll. Ada, and Henry listed as Presbyterian Minister at The Manse, Normanby, near Opunake.

<u>1933 Henry died</u> 22 January 1933 aged 65.

A Land transmission was dated 11 April 1933, Land Info SA/Z32522 Opunake/Taupo.

WILL. Henry, Presbyterian minister, Opunake, NZ. His Will was very simple … everything was left to his wife Ada.

<u>1966 Ada,</u> widow, died 20 Feb 1966, aged 95 years, at Mairangi Bay, Auckland. Ada and Henry are buried at Taupo Cemetery block C, plots 6 & 7. (5 empty plots beside them)

Ada's Will probated 23 March 1966 and available at Auckland Archives.

--oo0oo—

4 **GEORGE WALTER DRAKE MORRIS** (junior), was born March 19, 1873 Pipitea St, Wellington. His father George was a Joiner and mother Agnes Ann nee Turner. (T cert)

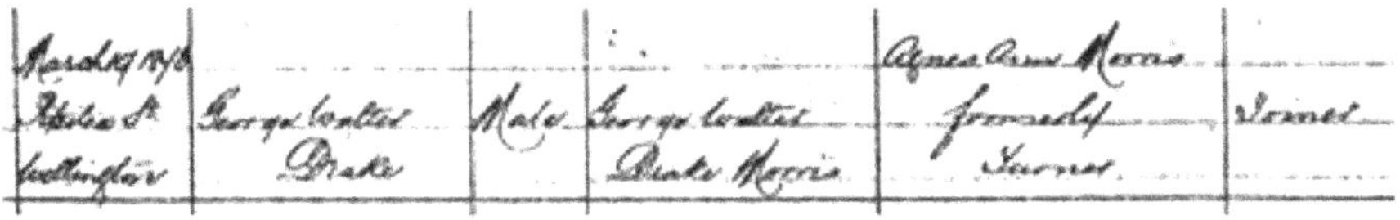

March 19 1873 Pipitea St Wellington	George Walter Drake	Male	George Walter Drake Morris	Agnes Ann Morris formerly Turner	Joiner

1896 Electoral Roll. George, a single man, lived in Hunterville and was a butcher. **Hunterville.** This town is situated 16 miles north of Marton and in 1906 the population was 645, of these 159 were ratepayers and GWDM was one of them.

1899 George married **MATILDA ALBERTINA KREGER.**
Matilda was born in 1876.
George and Matilda had 3 children ....Myrtle, Blanche, Rita.

1900 MYRTLE EDINA MORRIS Died 1920 (20 yrs)

1901 BLANCHE LEFEMEA MORRIS was born 8 Nov and remained single. 1837 & 1838 Blanche lived at 37 'Cuba' (actually Cubbabballa) Street, Marton.
1946 to 1957 aged 56 she lived at the Marton Hotel.
1963 Blanche with her mother, widow, at 17 Follett St.
1972 lived 18 Cuba St noted as a Law Clerk.
1981 lived 18 Cuba St noted as 'retired'.
Blanche died in 1984. (also refer mother's Will p114.)

1903 RITA IRENE MORRIS was born 5 Feb 1903, at Hunterville and married **KENNETH (Ken) ROBERT SCOON** in 1929. Ken was born in Oamaru, NZ, in January 1899, and was a Stock Agent. We have found 2 children ... Jill and Suzanne. (Also refer to mother Matilda's Will on page 116.)

1935 & 1938 Rita and Ken lived at 8 Ross St, Marton.

1942 Ken, (full name) aged 43, of Stewart St, Marton, an auctioneer, is on a Dec 1942 Ballot List for WW2, Military Area # 6, Wanganui.

1967 Ken died aged 68, on 20 July, retired Stock Buyer and was buried, Rose Garden B, Row 14A, Aramoho Cemetery, Wanganui.

1946 to 1981 Electoral Rolls advise Rita (widow) was living at 47 Stewart St, Marton.

1996 Rita died in 1996 and joined Ken at Wanganui.

NZ CYCLOPEDIA and the 1907 photo of GWDM jnr

Mr. G. W. D. Morris

The 'Wellington etc' section of the Cyclopedia details **George WDM junior** as .. *"A member of the Hunterville Town Board since its inception, and takes a keen interest in local public affairs. He was born in Wellington, NZ, in 1873 and educated at Mount Cook public school in (Wellington) and the West Christchurch School. For some years after this, he was engaged in general work including butchering in the Wellington province and in Australia. Later he established a butchery business in Hunterville, but three years afterwards the business was sold. In 1898 Mr Morris opened his present butchery business, which is conducted in a commodious shop in Bruce Street* *and gives constant employment to three persons. Mr Morris is also a general dealer in live-stock. He is a member of the Domain Board, The Gun Club, and the Presbyterian Church. Mr Morris is married with 3 daughters".*

1901 FIRE newspaper → George is listed as a grocer.

1911, 1914 & 1919 this family lived at Bowen St, Martin.

1915 George's parent's celebrated their Golden Wedding Anniversary on May 4th. This was held at their home in Plimmerton and George (of Marton) was present.

1919 George's Mother died at Plimmerton, 15 February.

1926 George's Father died at Plimmerton on 1st July.

Electoral Rolls ….
1928 George, a butcher, and Matilda, Blanche and Rita were all living at Cubbabballa St, Martin.

BIG FIRE AT HUNTERVILLE.

(PER PRESS ASSOCIATION.) 1901

MARTON, January 21.

Shortly after midnight a fire broke out in the front portion of Mr David Hallam's store, Hunterville, and quickly spread to the adjoining premises.

Fifteen shops and the Argyle Hotel were destroyed

The premises destroyed were as follows:—W. C. Hancock, saddler; C. Bray, hairdresser; J. McEldowney, draper; Argyle Hotel and stables; Ryan, tailor; A. E. Remington, chemist; Skerman and Co. (new premises); Mrs Currie, fruiterer; G. W. D. Morris, grocer; Temperance Hall; Library; Yuen Lee, fruiterer; J. W. Batt, dentist; and a portion of Harper's stables.

A Chinaman's cabinetmaking shop was also destroyed.

Only three shops at the extreme end of Bruce street are now standing. These would have been destroyed had the brigade not pulled Harper's stables down in the other street.

Large sheets of iron were placed against a portion of Argyle stables. This prevented the fire from attacking the Argyle Hall and the shops adjoining.

Messrs Ellis Bros. and Valder's store was damaged considerably, and it was only with the assistance of wet blankets that the building was saved.

The damage is estimated at £20,000.

(HAWERA + NORMANBY STAR)

1935 & 1838 George, Matilda and Blanche were living at 37 Cubbabballa St, Martin.

1946 & 1949 & 1954 George, butcher, (aged 73 to 81) and Mildred were living at Okanagon, Bulls.

1957 Electoral. Both George (retired) and Matilda were living at Scott's Ferry, near Bulls, NZ.

1959 George died aged 86 on 8 May at Scott's Ferry, near Bulls and was buried at Aramoho Cemetery, Wanganui, at cremation site ... Rose Garden 1175. In his Will, George was a retired butcher of Marton, and left all to his wife Matilda.

1963 Matilda, (87) widow, lived at 17 Follett St, Marton.

1965 Matilda died aged 89, April 30th while living at Scott's Ferry. She was cremated at Palmerston North and her ashes joined George at Wanganui. Matilda's Will appointed daughter Blanche, law clerk of Marton as executrix and she bequeathed 50 pounds each to her two granddaughters ... **JILL ELIZABETH SCOON** and **SUZANNE MARGARET SCOON**. To Blanche all jewellery, furniture, household and personal effects. The balance divided equally between her daughters, Blanche and Rita. (T)

(We are grateful to Ruth Turner, Brenda Cress and Joanna Fountain for sharing their family research on Ancestry. T)

--oo0oo—

<u>5 **WILLIAM CHARLES MORRIS**</u> was born in January 1875 but unfortunately died in March 1875 and was buried at Barbados Cemetery, Christchurch.

--oo0oo—

6 **ARTHUR CORLESS MORRIS** was born 17 February **1876** and became a carpenter.

1896 Arthur married **ADA MABEL BOURNE** who was born 29 April 1878 at Christchurch to John Moses Bourne born 1849 Pentham, Kent, England, died 1900 buried at Waimangaroa, Westcoast, NZ, and Frances Hyder 1845-1913.

(Waimangaroa is a small coal mining village on the coast below the Denniston coal mining area, north of Westport.)

1913 Electoral. Arthur Corless, a carpenter, was living at 186 Dixon St, Masterton.

1914 Electoral. Arthur & Ada living at 37 Albert St, Masterton.

1915 The Golden Anniversary of Arthur's parents was held at their home in Plimmerton on May 4th and Arthur was there.

1917 WW1 Army Reserve Roll for 2nd Division, NZEF, shows Arthur was a carpenter, of 37 Albert St, Masterton and detailed as a reservist with three children.

1928 Electoral. Arthur living at 116 Riddiford St, Wellington.

1938 Electoral. Arthur living at 23 May St, Wanganui.

1946 Arthur died, a retired builder aged 70, on 26 March at 22 Manuka St, Wanganui. He was buried at Aramoho Cemetery Wanganui, block R, row 4, plot 202. His Will (spelt Corlass) appointed son Percy as executor and left all to his wife Ada.

1948 Ada died, widow, at Otahuhu, Auckland on 28 March, aged 69 and was buried in the Presbyterian section at Wanganui Cemetery with Arthur. Her Will probated 19 May 1948 available Archives Wellington.

Arthur and Ada had 6 children ....

a **VICTOR BOURNE MORRIS** born July 1897 and died Jan 1898 at Hunterville, NZ.

b **ESTHER HYDER MORRIS** was born January 1899 at Hunterville, and married 1920 **HARRY REGINALD BATEMAN.** (nothing more found)

c **HAROLD ROY CORLESS MORRIS** born 1900 died 1902. He was buried at Waimangaroa, Westcoast, NZ.

d **PERCY BOURNE MORRIS** born 1902 at Waimangaroa married 1928 **CISSY WINIFRED TAYLOR**, daughter of ALFRED and ANNIE TAYLOR.

Percy died in 1970 and his headstone at Waikumete Cemetery, Auckland reads .... *"T 124 C.E.R.A P. B. Morris R.N.Z.N. 1939-45 War, died 17 Jan 1970 (69) also in loving memory of Cissy Winifred Morris passed away 12 Feb 1972 (68) ... item 28447 plot 76."*

e **LEONARD CORLESS MORRIS** born July 1905, married **NANCY ETHEL BREEN** in 1930. Nancy was born 21 Aug 1908 registered at Bulls, NZ and died a widow aged 80 on 1 April 1989 in Auckland and buried with her mother Mary M Breen in plot 147 at Waitara Cemetery, Waitara, NZ. Nancy's parents were TIMOTHY BREEN born 1854 Ireland and MARY MARTHA PAULINE BUFE. Leonard died in 1958 and was buried at Waimangaroa, Westcoast, NZ.

f **ARTHUR DUDLEY MORRIS** born 25 Feb 1922 at Wanganui, and died August 2010. Arthur married 30 Mar 1946 at Te Awamutu, to **ROSALIE MAY BLAKE** born 6 Feb 1927 to **ALFRED FRANCIS (Frank) BLAKE** born London, died 1978 Auckland, and **ELVIE RUTH FINER** born 1908 NZ, died 2001 NZ.

2010 Arthur died 14 August, a retired Ambulance Officer, aged 88.

2012 Rosalie died 4 Nov aged 85. They were buried together Te Awamutu, NZ, block 11, B Row, plot 518.

Arthur and Rosalie had 6 children ....

One of these, **JOHN ARTHUR MORRIS,** born 3 March 1947, a Sales Manager, lived at Mt Manganui, and died 22 July 2012 aged 65 at Tauranga. (RNZAF # 81662) John was buried at Te Awamutu, NZ.

John's wife and the other 5 children are thought to be still alive in 2016. --oo00oo—

7 **EDITH ELFRIDA MORRIS** born 1879

Edith went with her parents when they moved to Plimmerton.

1915 The Golden Anniversary of Edith's parents was held at their home in Plimmerton on May 4th. Edith was there.

1919 Edith E M was listed on the Wellington Electoral Rolls.

1930 Edith (51) married **ERNEST NELSON** (born 1876).

1950 Edith died aged 72, on 12 November 1950 and was buried at Aramoho Cemetery, Wanganui, in block H row 6, plot 327 by herself. Ernest died in 1954 aged 78.

--oo00oo—

8 **JOSEPH LEWIS MORRIS** and

9 **EDGAR WILFRED MORRIS** were twins, born in October 1882. Joseph died aged 1 month & Edgar at 8 months.

--oo00oo—

10 **MILDRED LEFEMEA MORRIS** born on 26 Dec 1884.

In **1907** Mildred married **JOHN ANDREW FRASER** (b1870)

The FRASER FAMILY.....

John A Fraser was son of ALEXANDER FRASER (1841-1912) who married 1862 MARGARET LIDDLE (1845 1912) They had 5 children born in Otago. ... Annie 1863, Sarah Grace 1865, Mary 1866, John Andrew 1869 and William Alexander 1872.

Mildred and John had 5 children ....

1 **GORDON MORRIS FRASER** born 20 March 1909, married **RUTH ANTHONY ALLARD** born 10 March 1913. They lived in Bronte Road East, Mahana, Nelson area, where Gordon was an orchardist. They had a son and a daughter. Gordon died 2 August 1980 (71) Whakapuaka cemetery, Nelson. Gordon was an executor of his father's Will. His own Will is at Archives, Wellington. Ruth aged 90, died 21 February 2004 and is with Gordon. (Block 22 plot 25)

2 **MARJORIE FRASER** born 1910 at Nelson, and **LAWRENCE VICTOR STRINGER** born 24 May 1901 at Nelson, married 1930 at Nelson. Marjorie and Lawrence had 7 children including Jean Margaret 1932–2015, Muriel Ena 1933-2016, the others are 2 girls and 3 boys. Marjorie died 4 Jan 1981 (70) bur Whakapuaka Cemetery, Nelson. Lawrence died 6 Sept 1988 (87) and is with Marjorie. In 1946 they lived at Mahana as farmers. Both their Wills are at Archives Wellington. Lawrence was a son of Arthur Stringer 1870-1951 and Emma Louisa Eban 1876-1945 who had 7 children including Lawrence. (BS)

3 **JOHN LIDDLE FRASER** born in 1913, died 27 January 1980 aged 66, an orchardist in Motueka and was buried at Marsden Valley Cemetery, Nelson, block 20A plot 063. John married **NORA WINN** in 1946 and had a son & 2 daughters. John's Will is at Archives Wellington.

4 **DONALD (Don) FRASER** born 24 April 1916, married **ELSMIE <u>FREDA</u> CHALLIS**. In 1946 they were both

single in the Nelson area. In 1954 they lived at Mahana, Nelson area, where Don was an orchardist.

Don and Freda had 4 daughters. In 1963 & 1972 & 1981 they lived at Appleby, where Donald was a sheep farmer. Donald died 24 June, 1997, aged 81 and buried at Block 22, plot 24 at Wakapuaka Cemetery, Nelson.

5 **LINDSAY GEORGE FRASER** born Feb 21, 1921, an orchardist and died 4 June 1983 at Mahana, Nelson.

1915 The Golden Anniversary of Mildred's parents was held at their home in Plimmerton on May 4th. Mildred was there.
1919 John & Mildred listed in the Wellington Electoral Rolls.

1948 JOHN A FRASER DIED on 14 September 1948 aged 79. He was an orchardist at Mahana, Nelson. In John's Will he appointed his son Gordon and wife Mildred as executors and left all his worldly goods to his wife Mildred.

1977 MILDRED DIED a widow, on 5 March 1977, aged 93 at Tahunanui, Nelson. Her Will was probated on 2 August 1977 and is available at Archives, Wellington.

We are advised that the Nelson Mail newspaper carried an 'Obituary' for Mildred on page 16, of issue 3 March, 1977.
Buried in the Anglican section of the Wakapuaka Cemetery, Nelson, in Block 22 plot 25, are husband John Andrew Fraser, Mildred Lefemea Fraser, their son Gordon and his wife Ruth Anthony Fraser. In the same Anglican block, next to these 3 and beside Donald in plot 24, is an unnamed baby who died at 0 age, in plot 23.
The grave plot 25 is now known as New General 22025-A:

PHOTO of MILDRED as a Bridesmaid 1907 aged 21.

Her son **GORDON FRASER** lived at Bronte Road East, Upper Moutere, Nelson region and wrote his memories of his grandfather George W D Morris, printed in a newspaper 18 August 1973, all of which we have quoted. Gordon is known in this record as (GF).

Mildred was known to her cousin Jane (Woods) Haslett, as 'Milly'.

Upper **PHOTO** supplied by Mildred in 1972 to researcher and relation Peggy Meikle who wrote to Mildred. She advised Peggy her name Mildred was chosen by her older sisters, because at that time they were reading a book called *Little Milly* and her father's choice was Lefemia, the name of a ship which once took his fancy. (MLF/PM)

This **PHOTO** supplied by Barry Lee Stringer a descendant of Mildred's daughter Marjorie.

--oo0Ooo—

Ann Lowe's children with Samuel Morris
continued ....

#7 ... JANE (POLLY) MORRIS, was the second child of Ann Lowe and Samuel Morris. Known as Polly she was born on 2 October 1842 at Pipitea Point, Thorndon, Wellington.

Polly was nearly aged 18 when she married 22 year old **GEORGE THOMAS** on 7 July 1860, at her mother's home *'the home of Moses Crocker, Elliott St, Auckland'* by the Rev Joseph Long of the Primitive Methodist Church. One of the wedding witnesses was *'John Woods, Boatman of Chapel St, Auckland.'* (T)

CHILDREN: Jane and George had 13 children ....
Selina Ann 1861, Eliza Jane 1862-1879 (aged 16), Elizabeth 1864, John Henry & Mary Ann 1866, John 1867, William 1869, George 1871, Richard Henry 1873-1875 (21 months), Esther 1875, Edward Ernest (Ted) 1877, Alfred Samuel 1880, and Hilda Jane 1883. (more details follow later)
George and Polly Thomas had their first 7 children baptised at the Primitive Methodist Church between 1861 and 1875.

> George Thomas' 2 nephews, William Thomas and wife Eliza nee McKay, and John Thomas and wife Phebe nee Woods, also had children baptised by the Primitive Methodist Church of Auckland before they both moved to the South Island in 1877.

1902 George Died. George Thomas, Polly's husband, died on 5 October at his Avondale home, Auckland.
"SUDDEN DEATH: A very sudden death occurred in Avondale last night. Mr George Thomas, storekeeper, was sitting near the fire between eight and nine o'clock, talking to his wife, when he suddenly fell back dead. Mr Thomas who was well known in the district, had reach the age of 65." (NZ Herald 6 Oct 1902)

George's death certificate states *"Verdict of Jury, Heart Failure"*

1911 Polly Died at her residence in Great North Road, Mt Albert Auckland on 28th August 1911, aged 68, of Paralytic Dementia.
A family member gave Thomas McIvor the Funeral Director Polly's details and noted she was the daughter of 'Mr Morris' who was a 'miner'. Polly was survived by 5 sons and 5 daughters aged 29 to 49. She was buried with husband George, by Rev Harris of the Primitive Methodist Church, at St Judes Avondale Cemetery. (in 2016 St Judes became known as George Maxwell Memorial Cemetery.)

PHOTO is of their headstone.

The GEORGE THOMAS' family ....

George was the 5th child of William Thomas and Elizabeth nee Lewis, born 21 August at Bradwell Mill, West Down, 7 miles south of Infracombe, in northern Devon, and baptised 10 Sept 1837 at the Church of England, at West Down.
George Thomas b1837, younger brother of 1829 John Thomas, who with wife Jane nee Coates and their two sons, emigrated to NZ from Devon in 1853 & 1855.
(Also refer ***"The THOMAS family"*** 1993 book, by TNPrice, for greater details in Devon, England and in NZ and their descendants family trees from 1700.) (More details p232)

--ooOOoo—

POLLY & GEORGE THOMAS'... 13 children

1 **SELINA ANN** born 1861, married 1884 to **ROWLAND HILL** and they had at least 3 children ... **Elsa, Ada and Ruby.** Selina died at Takapuna, Auckland, 39 April 1932, aged 71.

2 **ELIZA JANE** born 1862. Unfortunately Eliza died aged 16 in 1879.

3 **ELIZABETH** (Lizzie) was born 1864, married 1881 **GEORGE HENRY HARPER.** They had 4 children **Harold, Ivy, Albert and Hilda.**

4 **JOHN HENRY** birth registered 1866 (maybe twin Mary Ann) Have not found death registration.

5 **MARY ANN** was born 1866, married 1888 **THOMAS JOHN STEWART** and they had 7 children ... **Linda, Muriel, Myrtle, Olive, Algar, Doris and George.** We have found 53 descendants of Mary and Thomas as at Easter 1993.

6 **JOHN** known as Jack, was born 1867, married 1894 **ISABELLA MARY STEWART** and they had 4 children ... **Rita, Mabel, Leila and Norman.** We have 40 descendants.

7 **WILLIAM** was born 1869, and married 1898 **BERTHA WINNIFRED BICKNELL**, and they had Ernie and George. Bertha died and William married 1906 **LILLY DAVIES** and they had a son Stanley. 75 descendants to Easter 1993.

8 **GEORGE** was born 1871, and married 1895 **MARY ANN 'Minnie' MORGAN.** They had **Albert, Victor** and

Ernest. Minnie died giving birth to **Victoria** then Victoria died aged 3 weeks. George remarried 1906 to widow **MARY PARNELL PURCHON** with 1 child **Alice Mary Purchon**. We have 131 descendants to Easter 1993.

9 **RICHARD HENRY** born 1873, died 1875 at 21 months.

10 **ESTHER** born 1875, married 1901 **JOSEPH SEARLE KIMBER** and they had 4 children ... **Gordon, Dora, Frances and Norman.**

11 **EDWARD ERNEST** known as Ted was born 1877. In 1900 he married **CECILIA MARY STEWART**. They had 4 children ... **Dulcie, Muriel, Allan and Jean.**

12 **ALFRED SAMUEL** born 1880, married 1903 (MAGGIE) **MARGARITA BURKE,** then married 1919 **ISABELLA McMAHON.** No knowledge of children.

13 **HILDA JANE** born 1883, married 1912 **RODERICK FORRESTER LEWIS,** had 2 sons **Neville and Maurice**.

--oo00oo--

Anne Lowe's children with Samuel Morris continued ....

#8 ... SARAH MORRIS. Sarah was the third child of Ann Lowe and Samuel Morris, and born 17 Feb 1845 at Wellington. Sarah was baptised on 2 October 1845 at the Church of England... *Sarah Lowe, daughter of Ann Lowe.*
Sarah died 6 January 1846 aged 10 months 'of teething', as recorded by Rev Robert Cole in the Old St Paul's register.
She is thought to have been buried at the Bolton St Cemetery, Wellington. The author of 'Early Wellington' also recorded Sarah's death on page 460 as ....
"1846... Mrs Lowe's daughter, 1 year, teething."

--oo0oo—

#9 ... HENRY MORRIS was born 17 May 1847 son of Ann Lowe and Samuel Morris, at Wellington. He was baptised Henry Lowe on 11 June 1847 probably by Rev R Cole as he was still at St Pauls until mid 1849.
Henry died aged 5 at Auckland on 4 July 1852, his death certificate advises 'of decline' and he was buried at Auckland's Grafton Cemetery and his mother joined him there many years later.

--oo0oo—

The WOODS family

Early generations & page locations

1st Gen **JOHN WOODS 1720 & Elizabeth Bartram (Norfolk)**

6 children ... Rebecca, Mary, John, Robert, Samuel, and **ROBERT 1760**. (page 129)

2nd Gen **ROBERT WOODS 1760 & Hannah Cook**

(Norfolk) 7 children ...

Jane, Phoebe, William, **JOHN 1792**, Robert, Amy, and Samuel. (page 131)

3rd Gen **JOHN WOODS 1792 & Mary Ann Reynolds**

(Norfolk) 5 children ...

Phebe 1815, Emma 1818, Martha Ann 1824, **JOHN 1828**, George 1834. (page 144)

The **REYNOLDS** family (page 170)

4th Gen **JOHN WOODS 1828 & Mary Ann Lowe**

(New Zealand) 10 children ... Martha Ann 1853, Phebe 1855, Jesse 1856, George 1859, John 1861, Jane 1863, Agnes 1866, William 1868, Edward 1870, and Henry Joseph 1875. (page 174)

The **LOWE** family (page 6)

--oo0oo—

JOHN WOODS 1720 & his son ROBERT 1760

1720 JOHN WOODS was born in Norfolk, England.
1st generation of our Woods family

1744 JOHN WOODS (b1720) married by banns, **ELIZABETH BARTRAM** at St Catherine's Ludham Parish Church, on 16 Dec.

John Woods & Elizabeth Bartram both of Ludham — Dec: 16
Singlefolks married by Banns

St Catherine's Church LUDHAM PARISH, Norfolk, England.

Elizabeth Bartram was probably born 1720 – 1725 in Norfolk, and we found 6 baptised within the Trunch – Ludham area but none that offered proof. Her surname was spelt … Bartrum, Bortram, Bertrem, Bortrom, Bartram, and Barbram.

Ludham Parish is in the north east section of Norfolk County, England, an area known today (2010) as The Norfolk Broads.

Ludham's Church in the centre of the village, is a large Gothic structure built during the 14th and 15th century, replacing an older, smaller building. St Catherines' has an East Anglian-style 15th century font. (genuki)

Ludham village is surrounded on three sides by three rivers ... the Ant, Bure and the Thurne. The Parish population in 1845 was 924 people. (Ludham iSite)

JOHN and ELIZABETH's children baptised at Ludham Church.
REBECCA WOODS 19 Jan 1746
MARY WOODS 4 Oct 1747 but buried 20 Oct 1752 aged 5.
More children may have been born during the next eight years, 1747 -1755, while the family lived in another Parish nearby.
JOHN WOODS 9 Feb 1755
ROBERT WOODS 13 Feb 1757 but buried 1 May 1757, 3 mths.
SAMUEL WOODS 30 April 1758
ROBERT WOODS 23 March 1760 ... he is our 2nd generation

Father JOHN died 13 December 1759 at Ludham.

Then wife Elizabeth had 2 more children .....
A daughter, ELIZABETH was baptised 16 Jan 1763 at Ludham to Elizabeth Woods and Isaac Lamb.
Elizabeth (widow) and Isaac Lamb (single) married 16 July 1764 at Ludlam St Catherine's Church.
A daughter, ANN was baptised for Elizabeth and Isaac Lamb 25 Nov 1764 at Ludham. (T)

--oo0Ooo—

<u>ROBERT WOODS 1760</u> .... 2nd generation

ROBERT WOODS was baptised 23 March 1760, son of John and Elizabeth Woods of the Ludham Parish, Norfolk.
The registrar noted that father John was deceased by this date. Robert's 1836 death certificate states he was aged 76 when he died. After many weeks research we found only one Robert Woods baptism in Norfolk in 1760, so, if the death certificate is accurate then this must be our Robert Woods.

Robert, Son of John Woods deceased & Elizabeth his wife — 23

Baptismal entry at Ludham for Robert Woods 23 March 1760.

Inside St Catherine's church at Ludham

Banns and Licence Marriages.
The Church of England required 'Banns of Marriage' to be called once each week for the three weeks before the proposed marriage date. This enabled anyone to raise any impediment and prevent an invalid marriage ... say, a pre-existing marriage, or a couple being too closely related as detailed by law. However, if for any

reason you did not wish to wait the 3 weeks for bann-calling a Licence could be purchased.

A reason for a 'quick' Licence wedding would be if the lady was already pregnant or if both parties were leaving the home parish very soon, say, for employment in another parish.

(Wikipedia. C of E iSite)

<u>ROBERT WOODS</u> and LITTLE BARTON village.

We found 1760 Robert at the village of Little Barton in Suffolk, where aged 23, he married Hannah Cook 24 in 1783. They both stated they were *'of this Parish'* but, that just meant they had *'lived in that Parish for at least the past three weeks'* . (CW)

Both Robert and Hannah were born some miles away in Norfolk. At some point they must have been searching for employment, gone to their local 'market-town' and gained work at or near Little Barton Village, where they met.

1783 MARRIAGE: ROBERT WOODS and **HANNAH COOK** both single, married on 5 Oct 1783, at St Mary's Parish Church, at Little Barton in Suffolk County, England. (cert CW)

St Mary's, Little Barton Parish Church, Suffolk.

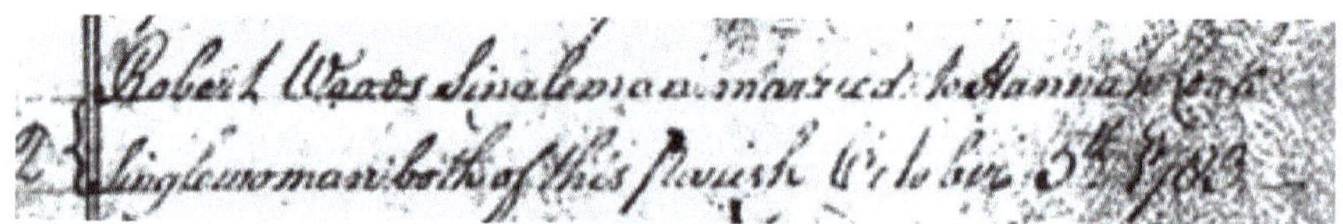

Robert Woods Singleman married to Hannah Cook
Singlewoman both of this Parish October 5th 1783

Little Barton is found about 12 miles NW of the town Bury St Edmonds. The village was originally called Barton Parva (Little Barton). The name changed in the eighteenth century to Barton Mills and is found on the banks of the River Lark. (Wikipedia)

Hannah was baptised at Bacton Parish Church, Norfolk 25 Feb 1759, daughter of William & Hannah Cook (cert T) She had a brother Robert, born 1758, died 1833.

Bacton is both a seaside Village and Parish, at 4 ¼ mile from the market town North Walsham. The village is well known for its very quiet sandy beaches and offering miles of walking along its beach and cliffs. (Wikipedia)

We feel **Robert and Hannah** almost immediately travelled from Little Barton, north east into Norfolk, to St Lawrence Parish, where their daughter JANE was born ten months later on 21 August. They then travelled north and settled in the Trunch Parish area where Robert must have found work. On the 27 Dec 1784 they baptised Jane at St Botolph Parish Church at Trunch. The settlement of Bacton where Hannah was born, was only 3.7 miles from Trunch, so she was now nearer to her family.

Three St LAWRENCE locations in Norfolk.

A 'St L' is an ancient Parish in the city of Norwich.

B 'Beeston St L' is a Parish 10 mile south of Trunch.

C 'South Walsham St L' is a Parish 19 mile south of Trunch.

We think A is out but the other 2 are possibles as in farming country and may be the area Robert referred to.

AG LAB : We wonder if Robert's occupation was Agricultural Labourer. No occupation is listed on all the certificates we have obtained, but the towns of, Little Barton, St Lawrence,

Gimingham and Trunch, where Robert was found living from 1784 to 1836, are all small villages within farming country.

CHILDREN. All born in Norfolk, England

ROBERT WOODS b1760 m 1783 **HANNAH COOK** b1754

They had 7 children ....

A	JANE	1784-1840	m James Martins, 13 children
B	PHOEBE	1787-1802	died aged 15 years ....
C	WILLIAM	1789- 1849	m Ellen Boulter
D	**JOHN**	**1792 .....**	**is our 3rd generation**
E	ROBERT	1795-1865	m Maria Sydle .... and m Charlotte Dyball, 8 children
F	AMY	1798-	?
G	SAMUEL	1802-1878	m Elizabeth Flowerdew, and m Sarah Newstead.

More details of these children start on page 135.
We will next be following the life of son John and his son John.

St BOTOLPH Parish Church, at TRUNCH.

TRUNCH. The final six of Robert and Hannah's children (B to G) were baptised at St Botolph Parish Church, at Trunch.

1836 Death. Robert died in 1836 aged 76 and was buried at Trunch Parish Church burial ground 27 March. (cert)

1839 Death. Hannah died in 1839 at Tuttington, Norfolk and was buried at the Trunch Parish Church burial ground 28 April.

It would seem that after her husband Robert died, Hannah moved to live with daughter Jane and husband James Martins and family in Tuttington, Norfolk. (cert CW)

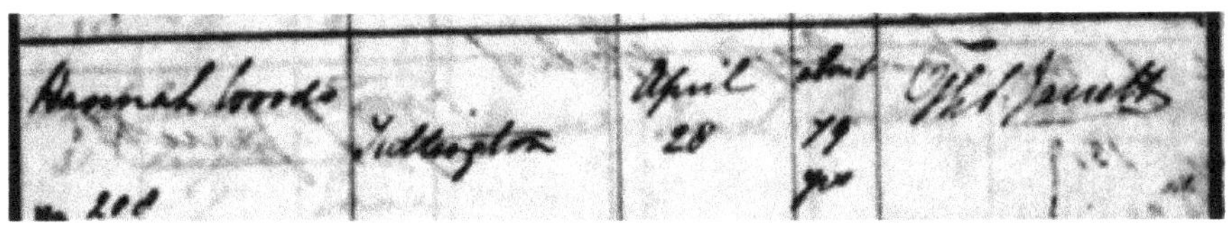

Hannah Woods No. [illegible]	Tuttington	April 28	abt 79 yrs	[illegible]

--oo0oo--

The 7 Children of ROBERT and HANNAH WOODS

A **JANE** was born 21 Aug 1784 in St Lawrence parish and was baptised on 27 Dec 1784 at Trunch. (cert)

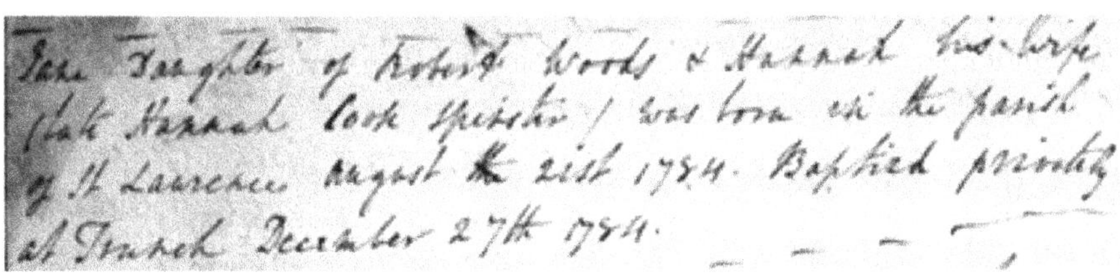

Jane Daughter of Robert Woods & Hannah his Wife (late Hannah Cook Spinster) was born in the parish of St Lawrence August the 21st 1784. Baptized privately at Trunch December 27th 1784.

JANE married **JAMES MARTINS** 17 Feb 1807 at North Walsham Church, Norfolk. Jane and James had 13 children .... And we have found 21 grandchildren.

1 **Elizabeth** born 23 Oct 1807* North Walsham and was baptised there Nov 15, 1807*:

2 **James** born 1811 and worked all his life as a black-smith. He married 20 Feb 1837* at Trunch, to **JANE GIBBONS** (1816-1891). They had 9 children ... **Mary** 1838, **Emily** 1840, **Robert** and **Martin** 1842, **George** 1843, **Jane** 1846, **Harriet** 1848, **Eliza** 1850, **Mary Ann** 1857. Living at Southrepps Road, Trunch 1841, Warren Lane, Trunch 1851. James died at Aylsham 1859*.

3 **Jane 19** born March 1812 at Tuttington, Norfolk.

4 **Elizabeth** 24 Oct 1813* at Tuttington.

5 **William** 5 June 1815* at Tuttington.

6 **Amy** 8 Sept 1817* at Tuttington.

7 **Robert** 23 Aug 1818 at Tuttington, married 3 March 1840 at St Augustine, Norwich, Norfolk, to **SOPHIA VINCK** (born 1821 Erpingham.) They had 6 children, **Jane** 1841, **Harriet** 1844, **Ann Elizabeth** 1845, **Alfred** 1847, **George** 1849, **Martin** 1851. Robert died Sept 1851 at North Walsham. Sophia died ?

8 **George** 3 Sept 1820* Tuttington, bur 22 Feb 1902 Suffield.

9 **Mary** 6 Jan 1822* at Tuttington and died 15 July 1847.

10 **Harriet** 17 Aug 1823* at Tuttington.

11 **John** 27 March 1825* at Tuttington, died March 1892, John (black-smith) married **MARY HALL** (1820-1895) with child **Walter John Martins** born 1851 at Aylsham, Norfolk. (1861C)

12 **Martin** 5 July 1829* at Tuttington, died 29 Aug 1830.

13 **Margaret** 21 Nov 1830* at Tuttington, married 2 Oct 1849 at Tuttington, **ROBERT BROWN**, shoemaker born 1828. They had 5 children ... **Robina Helen** 1851, **Robert** 1860, **Margaret A** 1863, **Jane Elizabeth** 1868, **Rosetta H** 1870. They were living at

Whitehart St, Aylsham in 1851 then moved to Pelton, Durham, England where they were living in 1861 and 1871 Censuses.

James Martins, the father was born 1785 at North Walsham and died 1870 at Tuttington, Norfolk. His parents were James Martins born 1743 Worsted, Norfolk and Elizabeth Burridge born 17 Aug 1755. They married 27 Dec 1781 at Felmingham, Norfolk and had 3 children **Margaret** 1783, **James** 1785 and **William Burridge** 1793.

Jane Martins, the mother died aged 56, at Aylsham and buried 5 Nov 1840 at Tuttington Parish Church, Norfolk.
(* star, notes our possession of Parish Church baptism record)

--oo00oo—

B **PHOEBE** (Phebe) was born and privately baptised on 16 Feb 1787 at Trunch.* (cert)

Phebe Daughter of Robt Woods & Hannah his Wife late H. Cook Spinster, was Born & Baptized Privately Feb 16th 1787.

She died and was buried at St Botolph Church yard, Trunch, on 8 August 1802, aged 15. (cert)

--oo00oo--.

C **WILLIAM**, born 5 Oct, 1789,* was baptised 7 Oct 1789 at St Botolph Church, Trunch. His father Robert noted as 'pauper'. (Of the 10 baptisms on William's page, 6 fathers were 'paupers.')

William son of Robert Woods & Hannah his Wife late H. Cook Spinster was Born October 5th 1789. Baptized privately Octr 7th 1789 - - Pauper.

William (Ag Lab). Banns were called January 6, 13, 20th and William married **ELLEN BOULTER** on 4 Feb 1811 at St George Parish Church, Hindolveston, Norfolk. The witnesses were Martha Boulter and Jeremiah Whitaker. (cert)
Ellen (Elen) was born 1781.

William and Ellen had 6 children ……

William bp 22 Aug 1813, **John** bp 16 Jun 1816, died 22 Mar 1846, **Sarah** bp 10 Jan 1819, **Robert** gamekeeper, bp 25 Feb 1821, married 9 Jan 1845 Jemima Codling, dressmaker. Jemima parents were Elijah Codling 1796-1868 and Martha Sarsby 1796-1881. **Charles** bp 6 Aug 1826, married DecQ 1845 at Aylsham to Maria Brett, had 2 children … Charles 1863-1865, Mary Ann 1860-1864. **Hannah** bp 25 Sep 1831, died 29 May 1849.

Father William died 22 Jun 1849 at Hindolveston.

Mother Ellen died 24 Oct 1868 at Hindolveston.

--oo0oo—

D **JOHN** was baptised 25 Dec, 1792 at Gimingham Parish Church, Norfolk. John is third in this family tree. He married **MARY ANN REYNOLDS** and we follow his life on page 142. Their son John Woods born 1828 came to New Zealand.

--oo0oo—

E **ROBERT** was baptised July 18, 1795 at Trunch. (cert)

Robert son of Robert Woods and Hannah his Wife
(late Cooke) was baptized July 18th

Robert married **MARIA SYDLE** on 14 March 1815 at St Mary's Parish Church at East Ruston, Norfolk. Maria born 17 May 1795 at Antingham, Norfolk and was the daughter of Thomas and Amy Sydle, but aged 24, died 27 June 1819 at Suffield, Norfolk. (cert) .. Robert, widower, married **CHARLOTTE DYBALL** single, on 25 Oct 1819 at St Margaret Parish Church, Suffield, Norfolk. The witnesses were Richard Dyball and Mary Burton. Charlotte was born 3 April 1796 and baptised 24 July at Suffield, the daughter of Philip Dyball and Sarah Money. (cert CW)

Robert and Charlotte had 8 children ....

George born 1821 at Colby, Suffield. 1841 & 1851 census George an Ag Lab working for John Kendle farmer of Suffield. George married in 1853 **SARAH GOTTS** (b 1829 at Aylmerton) They had 6 children ... **Charlotte Rebecca** b1853 Colby, d1924, **George** 1855-, **Emma** 1856-, **Robert** 1858-, **John** 1861-, **Mary E** 1873: 1861 census George 32 (40) Sarah 32 with the first 5 children. 1871 Emma, Robert & John still at home. 1881 Census George 60, Sarah 50 and Mary 8 at Colby, 1891 census George and Sarah living by themselves. 1901 census George 80, Sarah 72 with daughter Charlotte, single 42 as Cook / Domestic duties for Mum and Dad. Father George died 1902 at Suffield, Erpingham. 1911 census Sarah 82 widow and Charlotte 57 single.

William born 1824 at Colby, Suffield. William married **ANN LOUISE WOODS** (dau Robert and Susan Woods, so not thought to be related) on 4 Feb 1843 at St Giles Parish Church, Colby, and they had 6 children ... **Emily** 1843-1919, **Elizabeth** 1848, **John** 1850, **Ann** 1856, **Susan** 1858, **James** born 1866, married Caroline Bates and had 4 children ... **James E** 1887, **Ada Beatrice** 1889, **Arthur** 1890, **John William** 1896 at North Walsham Parish. (Probably all baptised at Colby).

1861 census William 37, Ag Lab, wife Ann aged 36, John 11, Ann 5, Susan 3, all living at West Beckham, Norfolk.

1871 census William 47, a yardman, Ann 46 with children Ann 17, Susan 13, James 5, granddaughter Anna 8, and son John 21 married to **Rebekah** 21 with child **Charlotte** 2 months, all living at Thurgarton, Norfolk, son **William John** bp 18 Dec Westwick.

1892 William (68) died at Smallburgh Parish, Norfolk.

1901 census. Son James married **Caroline** and had 4 children by the 1901 census ... **James E** 1887, **Ada** 1889, **Arthur** 1891, **Johnny** 1896. James' mother Ann lived with them in the 1901 census, aged 76, at White Horse Road, North Walsham.
1906 Wife Ann (born 1825 at Corby) died 1906 at Smallborough.

John 1825-

Margaret born 1826 Dec 9 and baptised at Colby 16 Dec (father Robert a Labourer). She died 16 April 1869 at Erpingham.

Philip Dyball baptised 11 April 1830 at Colby, died 30 May 1900 at Alby-with-Thwaite. Philip married 1854 **SARAH PUXLEY** (1831-1855) then married 26 Oct 1865 **SARAH MUER** born 1829 Suffield. No children found to date.

Richard born 29 Aug 1832 at Colby, died January 1909 at Erpingham. Richard married 1852 **ELIZABETH GRAY** (b1832 Wickmere, died ?) they had 7 children ... **Mahala** 1853-1929, **Elizabeth** 1856-, **James Robert** 1859-1953, **Mary Frances** 1862-, **Sarah J** 1864-, **Hannah** 1867-, **Rose Ann** 1871-.

James born 11 April 1835, bapt 10 May 1835, died 21 Feb 1868 aged 33 at Suffield. 1861 census James was 25 and a Tea Dealer. James married Oct 1862 at Aylsham, to **AMY HICKS.** Amy and James had 3 children ... **James** 1864-1930, **Eola** 1866-1922, **Jabez** 1868-1899. (Amy was born 11 Dec 1834 at Felmingham and died March 1924 at Dewsbury, Yorkshire. Amy's parents were Edmund Hicks 1804-1889 and Susan Slapp 1808-1890. When James died, Amy married April 1873 John Ellis 1832-1891 with a child William Charles Ellis 1874-1898.

Hannah born 15 Dec 1838. 1841 census aged 2 with parents at Colby. 1851 census aged 12 a scholar, with parents at Colby. 1861 census aged 22 no occupation given, living with parents. Hannah married 1862 Oct-Dec **JOHN GRAND** (born 1835) at Aylsham. Hannah died aged 24, 24 May 1863 at Colby, Suffolk.

Robert, the father died 18 Feb 1865 at Suffield, Norfolk.
Charlotte died 2 April 1865 at Colby, Suffield, Norfolk.

--oo0Ooo—

F **AMY** was baptised 10 March 1798 at Trunch. (cert)

Amy Doughter of Robert and Hannah Woods was baptized March 10th

Nothing more found... no death, no marriage, no censuses.

--oo0Ooo—

G **SAMUEL** was baptised Jan 17, 1802 at Trunch. (cert)

1802.
Samuel Son of Robert and Hannah Woods was baptized January 17th

1824 Samuel married **ELIZABETH FLOWERDEW** 12 Oct at St Nicholas Parish Church, North Walsham. Groom's Parish shown as Gimingham, Norfolk. Witnesses unknown? (cert)
1841 census Samuel and Elizabeth (Betsy) were living at Spa Common, North Walsham.
1851 census Samuel 48 Ag Lab, Elizabeth 51 (born Norwich) were living at Whitehorse Common, North Walsham
1861 census Samuel 58 Elizabeth 61 (now born Walpole, Suffolk) living at Whitehorse Common, Norfolk.
No children were shown on any of the censuses but may have left home before 1841. Elizabeth born 1800 died before 1862.
1862 Samuel (widower, Ag Lab) married **SARAH NEWSTEAD**

on 11 Aug (a spinster) at St Mary's Parish Church, Coslany, Norfolk. Grooms father Robert Woods, a witness was George Newstead. (Sarah's relation?) Both bride and groom's fathers were noted as deceased. Sarah born 1810, died 1891. (cert)
1871 census Samuel 69, Ag Lab, and SARAH 62 born Calthorpe, and living at Whitehorse Common.
1891 Sarah died SepQ, aged 81, registered at Erpingham. (BDM)
1878 Samuel died aged 76 and buried 22 Dec, North Walsham.

--oo0Ooo—

MAP: North East corner NORFOLK COUNTY, England.
The attached map shows the various parishes of Norfolk where over time, the John and Robert Woods descendant families mentioned above, lived …………

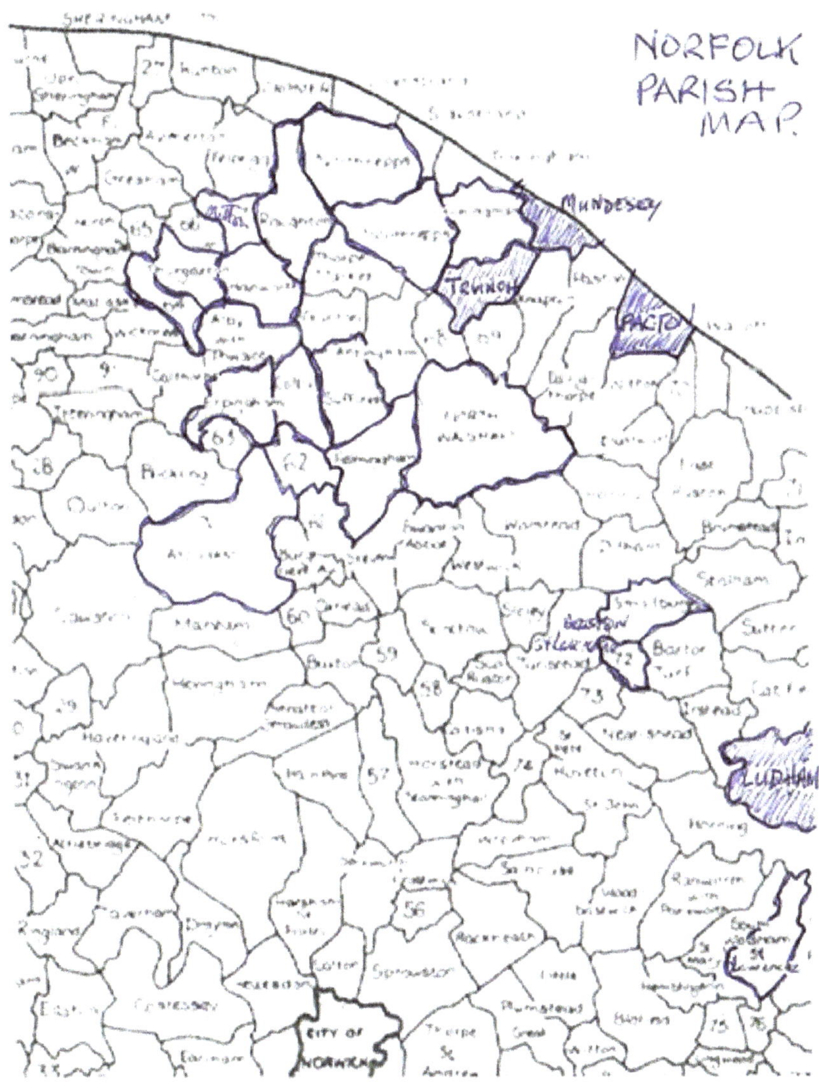

PARISHES showing ... Ludham (low right), 2 St Lawrences near Ludham, plus Mundesley, Trunch & Bacton (shaded upper) Suffield, Felmington, North Walsham, Erpingham, Gimingham, Colby, Alby, North & South Repps, Roughton, Thurgarten, Aylsham, Tuttingham, Metton, Smallburgh & Banningham.

3rd generation ... the JOHN WOODS family

There are two JOHN WOODS who married a Mary Ann
3rd generation... Mary Ann Reynolds and
4th generation... Mary Ann Lowe

3rd Generation BRIEF DETAIL ....
JOHN WOODS 1792-1858 m 1814 **MARY ANN REYNOLDS**
They had 5 children ....

PHOEBE	1815-1887	m George Emmerson.
EMMA	1818-1910	m Rueben Ashford ... 4 children
MARTHA ANN	1824-1903	m Richard Everard ... 9 children
JOHN	**1828-**	**came to New Zealand** ...... (page 174) **and married Mary Ann Lowe.**
GEORGE	1834-1874	died in Argentina.

The MARY ANN REYNOLDS family....
details follow on page 170.

JOHN WOODS 1792-1858

John 1792, is the **<u>3rd generation</u>** of this **WOODS FAMILY.**

John Son of Robert & Hannah Woods was baptized December 25th Pauper.

1792 John was born in 1792 and baptised 25 December at the **All Saints Gimingham Parish Church, Norfolk**, the fourth child of seven, of ROBERT WOODS and HANNAH nee COOK.

Of the twelve baptisms recorded on the same page as John's, there were nine fathers noted as 'pauper'. I think this excluded them from having to pay the baptism fee. (T)

'John 1792' is mentioned also on page 128.

John's six siblings were all baptised at the Trunch Parish Church.

GIMINGHAM. John's father Robert must have been employed as an agricultural labourer within Trunch's neighbouring parish, when son John was born. *The Gimingham All Saints Church is barely a mile from the North Sea and 4 miles from the market town of North Walsham. The village is small and strung out. Most cottages and farm houses are along a lane which runs from the coastal road towards Trunch township* (Wikipedia)

MARKET TOWN.

North Walsham was the market town for that part of Norfolk county. A town allowed to hold markets and fairs. These were first established in the 13th century with travellers and locals allowed to meet and trade their wares over a nominated week. In early 19th century times the majority of the population were living through agricultural and livestock farming and most lived where they worked. At the markets the unemployed made themselves available and farmers were able to vet and hire people to work on their farms. (Wikipedia)

AG LAB. This is an abbreviation of Agricultural Labourer, a description for all kinds of occupations needed in farming. First used in the censuses when writing the full terms was laborious.

1814 MARRIAGE

John Woods (21) married **MARY ANN REYNOLDS** (22) at St Botolph's Trunch Parish Church by Banns, on 18 November. The witnesses were Robert Woods (probably John's father) and Mary Reynolds. All four signed by their X mark.

MARRIAGES solemnized in the Parish of Trunch in the County of Norfolk in the Year one thousand, eight hundred, and fourteen

John Woods of this Parish
Single Man
and Mary Ann Reynolds of this Parish
Single Woman
were married in this Church by Banns with Consent of
this eighteenth Day of
November in the year one thousand, eight hundred, and fourteen
By me W. Rees Curate

This Marriage was solemnized between us { The mark of John Woods / The mark of Mary Ann Reynolds

In the Presence of { The mark of Robert Woods / The mark of Mary Reynolds

Photo of the TRUNCH FONT and the rare FONT CANOPY, with Harriett and descendant Murray Meikle. (2000 CW)

TRUNCH. *This is a village in the North East of the Norfolk County of England, situated about two miles from the North Sea, in the rolling country close to North Walsham. The church, St Botoloph, is an imposing structure with a fine tower. The octagonal font aged from about 1350 has a bowl with plain tracery and it's stem neatly inset with flint flashwork. The St Botoloph's Church was built in the 14th century and its finest feature is inside ... it's font canopy, one of the finest in the land. The font canopy (1500) is carved in oak depicting foliage, birds, fruit and animals and is one of only 4 left in the UK.* (Wikipedia & CW church leaflet)

TRUNCH CHURCH (CW)

1817 Between the birth of their first and second child, the family moved from Trunch, to live in Mundesley on the coast.

MUNDESLEY. *(pronounced Munsley) Is a coastal village near the exit of the Mun River and is 5 miles north of market town North Walsham and had a population of 333 in 1831. Mundesley grew rapidly when the Victorians brought visitors to the district by opening a railway station at North Walsham in 1889. The beach there is of fine white sand. The All Saints Mundesley Parish Church in Church Lane was founded before 1185.* The present church was erected in the 14th century, then reduced by a violent storm in 1779 and enlarged in 1844 when Mundesley population doubled after 1800. Between 1903 and 1954 refurbishment of the interior was completed. (Genuki, Wikipedia, & CW church leaflet)

MUNDESLEY ALL SAINT'S CHURCH
taken by descendant Christine Woods in 2000.

A MUNDESLY BEACH SCENE, Norfolk.

Inside MUNDESLEY ALL SAINT'S CHURCH (2000 CW)

John and Mary Ann Woods had 5 children ....

PHOEBE, EMMA, MARTHA, JOHN and GEORGE.

More details to follow, starting page 152 ...

1835 John's wife Mary Ann died 18 Sept 1835, aged 44 (maybe in childbirth) and was buried at Mundesley Church burial ground on 27 September. (cert CW)

1836 John Woods 44 widower, married on 30 May **ELIZABETH SHALES,** 43, single, at the All Saints Mundesley Parish Church by Banns called 15, 22, 29 May. John and Elizabeth signed with their X marks. Witnesses were Francis and Sarah Gray nee Nave. (Not thought to be related to us) (cert CW)

MARRIAGES solemnized in the Parish of Mundesley in the County of Norfolk in the Year 1836

John Woods of this Parish Widower
and Elizabeth Shales of this Parish Single woman
were married in this Church by Banns with Consent of
this 30th Day of May in the Year one Thousand eight Hundred and thirty six
By me Robert Beele Rector

This Marriage was solemnized between us { John Woods X his mark, Elizabeth Shales X her mark
In the Presence of { Francis Gray, Sarah Gray
No. 53

<u>**John Woods & Elizabeth Shales MARRIAGE certificate**</u> (CW)

1841 census. Living in Church Lane, Mundesley, Norfolk, were John Woods, fisherman, 40+ and children Martha 15, John 12, and George 6. Where was new wife Elizabeth? (CW)

1851 census. At New Road, Mundesley were John Woods, 58, Ag Lab, and his daughter Emma 32, single, washer woman and her daughter Sarah A aged 5, scholar, born at Mundesley. Where was John's wife Elizabeth? (CW)

1854 Elizabeth died aged 61, in Sept and was buried 21 Sept at Mundesley burial ground. (CW)

1858 John died aged 65 in Dec and was buried at Mundesley Church burial ground on the 21st (cert CW)
No Will for John Woods has been found.

--oo0Ooo—

The 5 Children of John and Mary Ann Woods.....
Phoebe, Emma, Martha, John, George

PHOEBE 1816-1887 married GEORGE EMERSON 1811-1885

1816 Phoebe (Phebe) was born 5 May at Swafield, (sometimes is Swaffield) Norfolk and baptised June 9 at Swafield Parish Church, to John and Mary (Mary Ann) Woods.

Born May 5 Bap'd June 9 No. 13	Phebe	John & Mary	Woods	Swafield	Labourer	[illegible] Curate

1841 census George 30+ was at Gimingham and occupied as a Millers J. (journeyman?)

1844 Phoebe married George Emerson at the All Saints Gimingham Parish Church on 19 April.

1851 census living in Church St, Gimingham, George 40 Ag Lab and Phoebe 34 a dressmaker.

1861 census at Heacham Beer House, George 45 a publican and Phoebe 44 and Sarah A V Woods, niece 15 Beer House assistant.

1871 census Snettisham at Southgate, George 54 Inn Keeper, and Phoebe 48.

1881 census Snettisham in a cottage, George 71 Ag Lab and Phoebe 63.

George was baptised 5 Oct 1810 at Gimingham Parish Church, son of George and Hannah Emerson.

1885 George died JunQ 1885 reg Smallborough, Norfolk.

1887 Phoebe died 3 Jan 1887 Lunatic Asylum, Thorpe, Norfolk, aged 71, of chronic brain disease, widow of George Emerson, Ag Lab of Snettisham. The Superintendent of the Asylum notified the authorities. (cert CW)

--oo0oo—

EMMA 1818-1910 married RUEBEN ASHFORD (4 children)

1818 Emma was born July 28, daughter of John and Mary Ann Woods and baptised at the Trunch Parish Church August 16. Father John noted as Ag Lab. (cert CW)

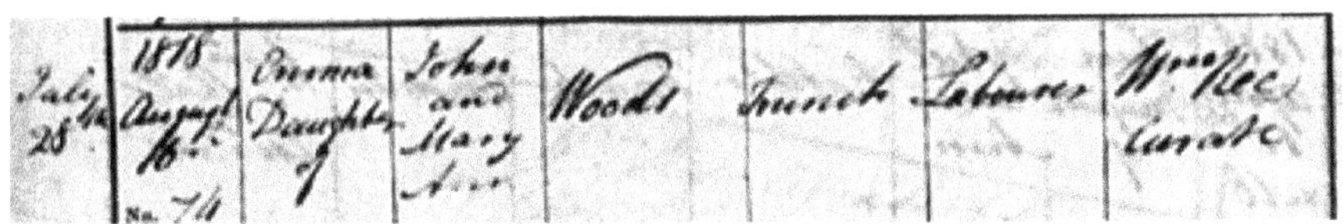

July 28th	1818 August 16th No. 74	Emma Daughter of	John and Mary Ann	Woods	Trunch	Labourer	Wm [illegible] Curate

1842 Emma gave birth to WILLIAM WOODS at Mundesley on Feb 15 and he was baptised 18th. Sadly William died and was buried at Mundesley Church Feb 24, 1842 about 1 week old. No father's name is mentioned on the Baptism record. (2 cert CW)

1845 Emma named her second child SARAH ANN VINCENT WOODS, who was born 8 July and baptised 21 July at All Saints Mundesley Church. (CW)

Sarah married by licence, on April 8, 1869 to JOHN AUGUSTUS MORGAN ROBERTSON (1847-1892) at Christchurch Parish Church in Surrey, England. John's father noted as John Robertson, a Tailor. Sarah died JunQ 1917 at Lambeth, Surrey, England. (cert CW)

1851 census. Emma 32, was living with her widowed father John, and daughter Sarah aged 5, at Mundesley. (CW)

1856 Emma (38) married RUEBEN ASHFORD (26) (born May 6, 1830) after Banns, on Oct 5 at Holy Trinity Church, at Mile End Old Town, Parish of Stepney, Middlesex, London. Rueben's parents were Thomas and Frances Ashford. Emma stated she was a widow, Reuben a Labourer and both had been living at 4 St Dunstan Rd, Middlesex. Emma's father noted as Fisherman, and Reuben's was a Labourer in a Distillery. (cert CW)

1859 Emma's third child was JANE FRANCES ASHFORD born at Bromley, Middlesex, London. (CW)

Emma's child **Jane** married EDWARD MOSS (1860-1939) in October 1882 at West Ham, Essex. 1910 Jane was present at her mother Emma's death.

Jane and Edward Moss had 9 children .....

Emma Ashford 1880, Rose 1883, Edward George 1885, Lily Miles 1887, William 1889, May 1893, Donald 1894, John (Jack) 1897 and Jane Dorothy 1900. (JP)

1938 MarQ Jane died at Deben, Suffolk.

1861 census Reuben 30 Distillery Labourer, Emma 35, Jane 2, Harriett 4. Reubens father Thomas 74 widower and brother George Ashford 25. All living at Bromley, Middlesex. (JP)

1861 In July at Bromley, Middlesex HARRIETT ASHFORD was born, the fourth child for Emma. (CW)

1879 **Harriett** married JAMES HARRISON (born 1841 & died MarQ 1917 at West Ham) on 23 Dec 1879 at Poplar, Middlesex. 1881 census. James 35 Manure Dealer born Norfolk, Harriett 21 born Bromley, and son James aged 1 born West Ham, Essex. All living at 34 High St, West Ham. 1901 census. James 60 General Dealer, Harriett 40 and children Charles 7, Rose 4 and Kate 2 living at 117 Livingston Ave, Stratford, Essex. (JP)

Harriett (61) died DecQ 1922 at Westham, Essex. (CW)

1871 census. Reuben Ashford 39, labourer born Bromley and Emma 45 with Jane 12, and Harriett 10, and Martha Everard, servant, visitor aged 26 (Emma's sister Martha's eldest child) living at Three Mill Lane, Bromley, St Leonards, Lower Hamlets.

1881 census. Reuben 53 labourer, Emma 60, Jane (dau) 22 single, servant unemployed and daughter's child Emma, born at Manchester, aged 6 months. All living at Bromley, St Leonards, Lower Hamlets. (JP)

1901 census Reuben patient at the District Metropolitan Asylum at Leavesdens. Aged 71 he was listed as a Whisky Distiller. (JP)

1903 Reuben died Jan 1903 at Watford, Hertfordshire, England.
1910 Emma died aged 94, on 5 July at London St, Swaffham, Norfolk. Informant was Jane Moss, daughter, present at death. (cert CW) Emma was buried at St Peter & St Pauls parish Church, Swaffham ... headstone reads *'In loving memory of Emma Ashford who died July 5, 1910 aged 94 years.'* (cert CW)

--oo00oo--

<u>MARTHA ANN 1824-1903 married RICHARD EVERARD</u>

1824 Martha was born 6 Sept and baptised 3 October at Mundesley Parish Church, daughter of John and Mary (Mary Ann) Woods. John was an Ag Lab. (cert CW)

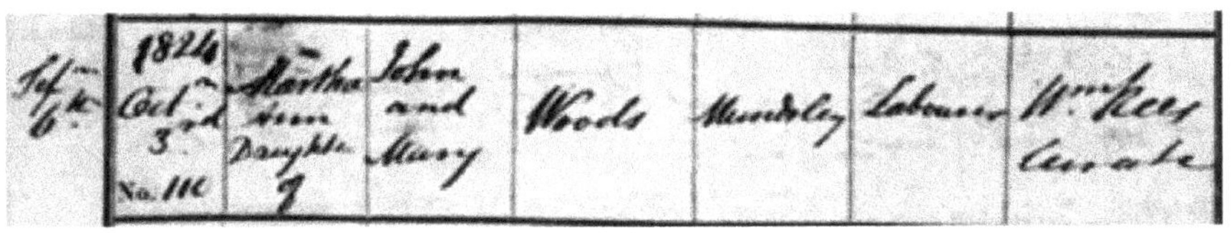

Sept 6th	1824 Oct 3rd No. 116	Martha Ann Daughter of	John and Mary	Woods	Mundesley	Labourer	W. [illegible] Curate

1841 census Martha was 15+ living with parents at Mundesley.
1844 Martha married RICHARD EVERARD on 1st July 1844 at St James with Pockthorpe, Norwich, Norfolk, England. Martha 20 years old and Richard 40 widower, a fish merchant. They both lived in Barrack St, Pockthorpe. Martha's father was an Ag Lab and Richard's father was also Richard Everard, a Farmer. Witnesses seem unrelated. (cert CW)

Martha and Richard Everard had 9 children ....
Martha Ann, Richard John, William, Elizabeth, George, Mary Ann (Annie), Phoebe, Charlotte Emma, and William Arthur Everard.

1851 census Martha 26, Richard 48 carrier born Gimington, and children Martha 6, Richard 3, Elizabeth 5 mth at Mundesley. (JP)

1861 census. Living at 12 Town's End, Mundesley were, Richard 51, a carrier, Martha 37, and children Martha 16, Richard 13, Elizabeth 10, George 6, Mary Ann 3 and Phoebe 5 months. (JP)
1871 census Richard 68 carrier, Martha 47 and children Elizabeth 20 servant-cook, George 16 carrier, Mary Ann 13, Phoebe 10, William A 3, Charlotte 5 months. They were living at Paston Road, Mundesley. (JP)
1881 census Richard carrier 79, Martha 57, daughter Martha single 36, William A 13, and grandson John L Everard 2. (JP)
1883 Richard died aged 81, DecQ reg at Erpingham. (CW)
1891 census Martha widow 66, living at third house near Royal Hotel, with her was Charlotte 25 single, house-maid. (JP)
1901 census Martha 75 mother-in-law to Albert Miles 41 a railway auditor, born Tillington Sussex, and Phoebe 40, living at 1 Florence Villas, Gaywood Village, Norfolk. (JP)
1903 Martha died aged 79, widow of Richard Everard, on 27 November at Aylsham Road, North Walsham, Norfolk. (CW)

The 9 children of Martha and Richard Everard.

1 Martha Ann, born 1845 and baptised 14 Jan. Father was a fisherman.(CW) John Larter Everard, born 20 Jan 1879 died 1966.
1881 census Mundesley. Martha was 36, single, with son John Larter Everard aged 2, living with her parents. (JP)
1882 Martha 37 married **ROBERT BATES** widower aged 40 born Lessingham, Norfolk, on 22 Oct after Banns, at North Walsham Parish Church. Martha and Robert baptised 2 children on 27 Sept 1888 ... Richard Everard Bates born 3 April 1884 – died 1912 and Benjamin Ernest Bates born 7 June 1886 (JP)
1891 census At Great Yarmouth, Norfolk were Robert 49 shoe-maker, Martha 46, John Larter 13 born Mundesley, Maude 12, Richard 7, and Benjamin 4 – these 3 born North Walsham. (JP)

1901 census Robert, shoemaker aged 57, Martha 56, Maude 28, Richard 16 and Benjamin 11 at Great Yarmouth. (JP)

1910 Martha died MarQ aged 65 at Gt Yarmouth, Norfolk.

1911 census Robert widower 72, shoemaker, Richard 25 single, photographer living at 5 Grosvenor Rd, Gt Yarmouth. (JP)

1924 Robert died aged 86 (Dec Q) Smallburgh, Norfolk. (CW)

------

2 Richard John, was born 5 Sept 1847 and baptised 3 Oct at Mundesley. His father was noted as a Carrier. (CW)

1851 census Richard aged 3 was with his parents in Mundesley.

1861 census Richard, 13, scholar at Mundesley, with parents.

1866 Richard married CHARLOTTE ANN SPICER (b1840-d1896) at Norwich City, Norfolk, in the DecQ 1866. (CW)

1871 census Richard 23 and Charlotte 33 lived at 204 Devonshire St, Mile End, Old Town, London, where Richard was a Brewer.

1871 Richard John died DecQ 1871 aged 24, at Mile End, Middlesex, London.

1877 Charlotte had a child John Kittle Everard born Gt Ormsby.

1881 census Charlotte widow 40, and John Kittle Everard 4. Charlotte was housekeeper for John Richard Conyers 33 Ag Lab and his daughter Sarah Conyers aged 9 at 32 Cobholm Terrace, Gt Yarmouth, Norfolk.

Charlotte then married James Richard Conyers 22 Sept 1881.

Charlotte's father was Richard Spicer of Great Yarmouth, NFK.7

------

3 William born 15 Aug 1849 was baptised 16 Sept but died and was buried on 26th Sept 1849 at Mundesley Parish Church. His father Richard was a carrier of Mundesley (2 cert CW)

------

4 Elizabeth born DecQ 1850 at Mundesley. In 1851 census. Elizabeth aged 5 months with parents at Towns End,

Mundesley. Father was a Carrier. 1861 census. Elizabeth aged 10 was a scholar at Towns End, Mundesley.
1871 census. Elizabeth 20, servant at Liberation, living Paston Rd, Mundesley, with her parents.
1874 Elizabeth (23) married GEORGE ALFRED BELL (1848-1918) on Oct 16, at Great Bircham, Norfolk. (CW)
1881 census. Aged 30, Elizabeth and husband George 34 were living with George's parents William 76 and Jane Bell 74, at Fring Road, Great Bircham, Norfolk. (JP)
1884 Son WALTER EVERARD BELL was born at Gt Bircham.
1891 census. At 6A Market Place, North Ormsby, Yorkshire George labourer and Elizabeth and son Walter 3. (CW)
1901 census. George 53 Labourer Blast Furnaces, Elizabeth 50, Walter 13 Errand Boy, at 6 Customs Road, Nth Ormsby. (JP)
1911 census. George 63 Mineral Water Dealer, Elizabeth 60, with three boarders. George and Elizabeth had been married 36 years and had 3 children with one alive at this date. (JP)
1918 George died aged 70 in Sept, at Middlesbrough. (JP)
George had been baptised May 27, 1849 at Gt Bircham.
1843 Elizabeth died MarQ at Middlesbrough, Yorkshire. (JP)

------

5 George was born at Mundesley in Oct 1854. 1861 census George (6) was with his parents and 1871 census aged 16 a carriers son. In Sept 1877, George married VIRTUE PITT (1852-1934) In the 1881 census George 26 coal carter born Mundesley, Virtue 26 born Trunch and son James George aged 7 months born Trunch, living at Gillings Yard, Norwich St Pauls. (JP)
1891 census. George 36 builder's labourer, Virtue 37, James 10 scholar, Rosen 9, Martha 6 (was born July 23, and bapt Dec 7, 1884 at Eaton, Norwich) and Lily Gertrude aged 2, all living at Lyons Yard, Norwich City. (JP)

1901 census. At Norwich, 19 Chapel St, were George 46 general labourer, Virtue 47, Rose 19 born Sth Repps and Martha 17 born Eaton, both Domestic Servants, Lilly 10 born Eaton, Richard John 9 born Eaton, St Andrews, Norwich and William 7. (JP)
1911 census. George 56 a carter, Virtue 58, William 18 a baker. They had 10 children but only 5 alive at this date. Family living at 13 Salford St, Norwich, Norfolk.
1933 George died aged 78 in JuneQ at Norwich, Norfolk.
1934 Virtue died aged 81 in JuneQ at Norwich, Norfolk.

------

6 Mary Anna was born in JuneQ 1858 at Mundesley, the 6th child for Martha and Richard Everard. Her baptism not yet found.
1861 census she was aged 3 with her parents.
1871 Aged 13 Mary was with her parents and a scholar.
1881 Mary, known as 'Annie' aged 24 was at 14 Northwick T'ce, Marylebone, London, a servant to William 33 and Mary C Wall 31 and their 3 children and 2 other servants. Did she marry?

------

7 Phoebe. Born in Oct 1860 to Martha and Richard Everard at Mundesley. Baptism not located.
1861 census. Phoebe was aged 1 with her parents at Mundesley.
1871 census. Phoebe aged 11 at Mundesley with parents.
1881 census. Living at Paddington, London, Phoebe (20) was servant to Edmund Holland, a clergyman and his family
1884 Phoebe (24) married ALBERT MILES (1859-1941) in the JunQ, registered in Erpingham district of Norfolk.
1885 Son Albert Everard Miles was born, but died 1891. (JP)
1890 Son Herbert Leopold born and died 1890 at Kings Lynn.(JP)
1891 census Phoebe 30, Albert 31, son Albert EM aged 6 living at Woodgreen, Middlesex, London.
1894 Daughter Mary Gwen was born - died in 1895 Kings Lynn.

1901 census. Phoebe 40, Albert 41 and Phoebe's mother, Martha aged 75 were living at ....
1903 Phoebe's mother Martha died aged 79 at North Aylsham.
1911 census Albert 51 was Chief Railway Audit Clerk, born at Petworth, Sussex. Phoebe 50, was now joined by her sister Charlotte 45 widow a servant. Albert and Phoebe by 1911 had been married 26 years and had 3 children but none of them had survived to this date. They were living at 'Waverley' Gaywood Rd, Kings Lynn. (JP)
1941 Albert died aged 82 at Kings Lynn, Norfolk.
1945 Phoebe died May 9, aged 85 at Gaywood, Kings Lynn.

------

8 Charlotte Emma born in Sept 1866, the 8th child of Martha and Richard Everard and baptised 24 Oct 1866 at Mundesley.
1871 census. Charlotte aged 5 with her parents in Mundesley.
1881 census. Charlotte 15 was a domestic servant for Mary A Gray, licensed victualler of the White Swan, North Aylsham.
1891 census She was 25 and domestic servant, living with her mother Martha 66 widow, three doors from the Royal Hotel.
1896 Charlotte 30, married EDMUND THOMAS FIRMAN 39, (Oct 1857 -1903) on 10 December at Mundesley. (JP)
1901 census. Charlotte 35, Edmund 42 Brewers Manager, living at Aylsham Road, North Walsham.
1903 **Edmund died** 10 July registered Smallburgh, Norfolk.
1909 Charlotte 43 married in DecQ 1909 to JAMES WILLIAM NASH 63 (born 1846) at Green Eggham, Surrey.
1910 **James died** aged 64, 21 May, 1910 at Windsor, Berkshire.
1911 census Charlotte was living with her sister Phoebe at 'Waverley' Gaywood Rd, Kings Lynn, Norfolk. (JP)
1942 **Charlotte died** in JunQ, aged 76, at Kings Lynn, Norfolk.

------

9 **William Arthur** was born 1868 at Mundesley, and with his parents aged 3 in 1871 census and aged 13 in 1881 census. (CW)
1901 census. On March 31, William aged 33, was mentioned as a crew member Royal Navy ship *"Terrible"*, a 1st class cruiser, Commander Percy M Scott and at Wei-hai-wen, China, (JP)
1911 census. William (41) born at Mundesley, was working as a butler at Bournemouth. (JP)
1941 **William A died** at Rugby, Warwickshire, England. (CW)

--oo0Ooo—

JOHN 1828 ...... John came to New Zealand.

1828 John was born in 1828 and baptised 17 August, son of John and Mary Ann Woods, at the Mundesley Parish Church.

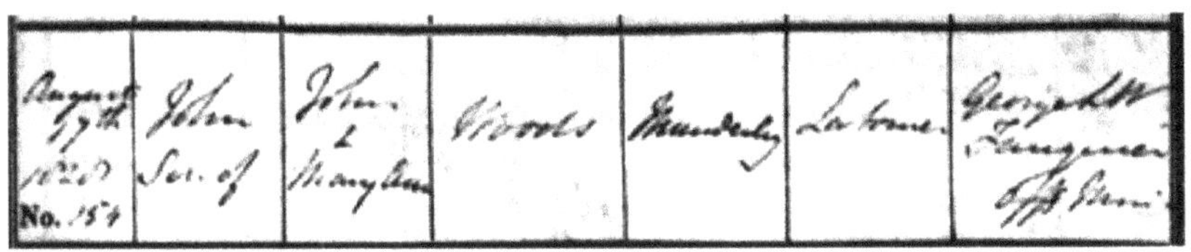

August 17th 1828 No. 154	John Son of	John & Mary Ann	Woods	Mundesley	Labourer	George H W Longmore Offg Minister

His father John was an Ag Lab. John is our 4th generation in the Woods Family Tree and his life is detailed starting on page 174.

--oo0Ooo—

GEORGE 1834-1874 born Norfolk, England ...died in Argentina.

1834 George was born 24 Dec, baptised 25 Dec at Mundesley.

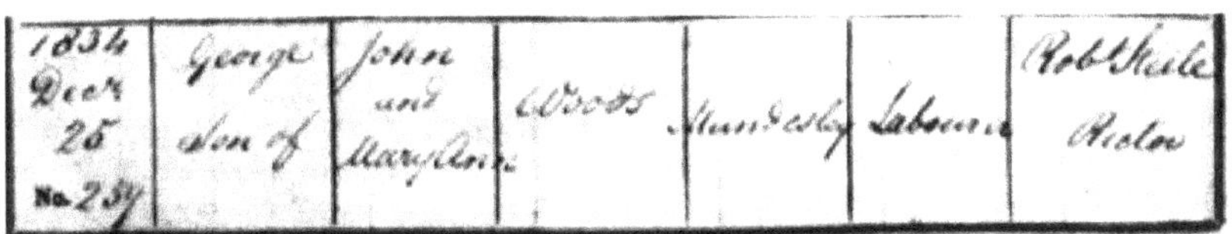

1834 Decr 25 No. 234	George Son of	John and Mary Ann	Woods	Mundesley	Labourer	Robt Steele Rector

1835 George's mother died 18 Sept. George was 9 months old.

1841 census George was aged 6 living with his father in Church Lane, Mundesley, Norfolk.

1851 MERCHANT NAVY: On April 2nd, George aged 16, called at Navy Offices in Stockton, (thought to be Stockton-on-Tees, Durham) and enrolled in the Merchant Navy as an apprentice. He gave his birth date as 24 Dec 1834, was from Mundesley, Norfolk and was given the Navy ticket number 518111.

> (It seems he arrived at Stockton with a Mundesley friend ... Robert Clarke from Mundesley, who also joined up that day and was issued number 518112.)

The records show George first went to sea in 1851, and served on the *"Victory & Albert"* during the period 14 Oct 1852 to 17 Oct 1854. When George left the Merchant Navy and joined the Royal Navy his new Commander completed a form stating George had served on the *"Beatitude"* and the *"Mary Ann"*. (?)

1855 ROYAL NAVY: George enlisted in the Royal Navy on 26 January 1855, aged 20. He was from Monsley, (Mundesley) Norfolk, born 25 Dec 1834, 5'6" (1.68m) tall, of fair complexion, with brown hair and hazel eyes, he had a tattoo on his right arm ... 'GW' and an 'Anchor'. George signed on for 10 years *"to serve honestly and faithfully in the Royal Navy"*. A Navy Commander and 2 others named Rutherford, Morris and Murphy certified George after examination, as *"of perfectly sound and healthy constitution, free from all physical malformation, active and intelligent and fit for Her Majesty's service."* George became Royal Navy member 18883 and was first sent to the ship ***"Powerful"*** as an AB.

> (AB = Able Seaman ...was the second lowest naval rank and he received this rank because of his more than two

years' experience as a Merchant Navy man. An AB was able to steer, (take the wheel for a two hour shift) use the lead, (sound or measure the waters depth) and work aloft on the sails. An AB received about 25% more wages than an Ordinary Seaman.)

The ship's records we studied were unfortunately short of detail or had confusing information but during his 10 years in the Royal Navy we believe George served on 6 different ships……

"Powerful" 1855 to 1856. The Powerful was built in 1826 and broken up in 1864. She was a 'second-rate, 84 gun ship'.

"Victory" Item 454 records George's report as V Good, at 1 October 1856 when George was aged 21.

"Shannon" George on board 18 October 1856 to 15 January 1859. The Shannon was a Liffey-class frigate built at Portsmouth, a fully rigged ship, also with steam power. The Shannon played an important role in the Indian Mutiny, landing a naval brigade which fought the Siege of Lucknow. The records show George was one of the 560 crew who boarded between launch and final fit-out which was complete 29 Dec 1856. (Wikipedia)

George was on this ship during the 'Relief and Capture of Lucknow 1857/8'.

The "Shannon"

The ***'Relief of Lucknow', India Medal*** presented to George on 28 June 1861 at Devonport Naval Base, England, where his ship was berthed.

"Victory" Between the 16 Jan 1859 and 24 Feb 1859 George was not away on a ship but on land, in home port. During these 38 days he married (4 Feb) and on 25 Feb started a 6 months term in the local prison. (more info follows)

"Himalaya" .... 25 February 1859 to 31 March 1860.

The Himalaya was of 3438 tons, an iron screw passenger ship, launched in 1853, purchased by the Navy in 1854 and used as a troopship until 1894. She also carried Armstrong guns to the Second Opium War in 1860.

"Rinaldo" 31 March 1860 to 17 Dec 1864.

The Rinaldo was launched March 1860 and broken up April 1884. She was a second-class sloop with 17 guns, had a Barque rig and a crew of 180. She also had a steam engine which enabled her to travel at 9 knots. George served under three Captains (W Hewitt, JA Dunlop and MH Nelson) who each recorded George's work and attitude as 'V Good'.

One of the Royal Navy's forms show George was married and had been vaccinated for Small Pox.

"Leander" 18 Dec 1864 to 26 January 1865. The *'Leander'* was a 50 gun fourth rate ship converted to screw propulsion in 1861. She sailed to Callo, Port of Lima, Peru and Captain Pratten released George from the Navy, there. George had served his 10 years in the Royal Navy. The Leander carried on to Valparaiso in Chile where they landed parties of men to assist with fighting a large fire in the town. (Ships Papers CW & others)

1859 Gaol and Marriage. The dates for these two events seem to coincide. I am going to suggest that George went AWOL and did not get Navy permission for time off to get married and probably have a short honeymoon.

1859 MARRIAGE: On February 4, 1859 under the name George William Woods, (21) bachelor, mariner, he married by License ELIZA JANE MORTIMORE (18) (known as Jane) with her father William's consent, at St Mary's Parish Church of Alverstoke, Hampshire. Both gave their addresses as ... Gosport. His father John Woods, mariner and her father was William Mortimer, mariner. (Eliza Jane was baptised 19 Sept 1841, mother named Anne.) Witnesses were William Mortimer and Sarah Hobbs. The witnesses and Eliza signed with 'X' marks. George signed the certificate 'George Woods'. The 'William' was not included.
Interesting to note that 2 days before he married, George signed the application for License to Marry form with an "X". (cert CW) The Hampshire Advertiser & Salisbury Guardian newspaper recorded this marriage briefly on Feb 12, 1859 issue. (Segers JF)

> **Gosport** was a major naval town associated with the defence and infrastructure supply of Her Majesty's Naval Base at Portsmouth, across the harbour. (Wikipedia)

WINCHESTER. From the 25th Feb until 22 Aug 1859 George resided in the Winchester Civil Prison. His time on the *'Shannon'* ended on Jan 15 and he must have had shore leave. George was due to join the ship *'Himalaya'* but was sent to gaol instead. George was charged under the *Royal Navy Act 10 & 11 Vic Cap 62*. Our research advises this referred to Naval Deserter's Act of 1847 and suggests he was not authorised to get married. He would not have been charged under this act for theft, burglary, drunkenness or disturbing the peace. This 6 month term seems to have been a disciplinary action, for in the Services you always obeyed, and gained permission to act outside your Naval duties.

We also learnt *'men in ships in home waters, sentenced to imprisonment for civil offences, who were not to be dismissed or discharged from the service, were sent to civil prisons.'*
That is a good sign, that other than this misdemeanour George had a very good record and was wanted back on their ships.
Winchester Gaol was an adult male category 2 prison, located in Winchester town, Hampshire, with a capacity for 700 prisoners ... non Navy and Navy persons. George must have been sentenced to 6 months, as another form shows he received pay for this period of 179 days at 1 shilling and 7 pence per day.
Did Jane visit George in gaol? It was a 30 mile trip, (48km) but she probably did, once, to tell him she was carrying their child.

1859 GEORGE'S SON: George and Jane's son arrived Nov 3, 1859 at Little Beach, Gosport. They named him GEORGE WILLIAM WOODS. George's occupation was noted... 'Seaman, HM Ship Himalaya'. (cert CW)

1865 LEAVING NAVY: At the end of his long service on the *'Rinaldo'*, George travelled on the *'Leander'* to Callao, chief seaport of Lima, Peru, *"where he was put on shore at his own request"*, as his 10 year time with the Royal Navy had expired.

George's marriage must have fallen apart prior to this and Callao was probably a place he had visited before and liked.

1866 Eliza **JANE** Woods married William Harrison (a seaman) on 11 October at Alverstoke, Gosport, in the same church she had married George. Five years later in the **1871 census** Eliza Jane, was a 29 year old **widow**, laundress, had 4 children ... George now 11, William 5, C Jane 3 and Samuel 9 months. All were living at Lower Smith St, St James Court, Gosport, with a boarder named George Newman, 26, unmarried.

1873 Eliza **Jane** Harrison married George Joseph Newman a labourer at HM Dock Yard, on Oct 12, 1873 at Holy Trinity Church, Gosport.

1874 GEORGE DIED.
During the following 9 years we think George lived in the South American area, (maybe on coastal shipping) first landing in Peru and by 1874 he was in Argentina. Here George Woods, recorded as a Naval Gas Fitter, spent some time in the British Hospital at Buenos Aires. George died here aged 40, on Feb 21, 1874.
The Surgeon of the hospital notified the authorities at 'Holborn', England, who registered his death. (cert CW)
The burial records of St John's Cathedral at Buenos Aires show George was buried on Feb 23, 1874, an Engineer from England, and died of Typhoid Fever at the British Hospital. (cert CW)

--oo00oo--

***** George and Eliza Jane Woods' son ....

GEORGE WILLIAM WOODS

1859 Born Nov 3, at Gosport, Hampshire, England.
He may have been baptised George Henry William Woods ?
1886 George married CAROLINE HENRIETTA JANE PERRY
George is recorded as George Henry Woods.
1887 to 1900 Children. George and Caroline had 5 children.... George Oliver Charles DecQ 1886, Olive Violet Lillian MarQ 1888, Dorothy Eleanor DecQ 1892, Kathleen Florence SepQ 1897, Sydney Frank Maurice MarQ 1900. All births were registered at 'Portsea' with this district renamed 'Portsmouth' in 1900.
1901 Census. George 45 stationary engine driver, Caroline 41 (was born Suffolk, Norfolk ?) George 14, Olive 12, Dorothy 8,

Kathleen 3 and Sydney 1, living at 3 Jacobs Terrace and Aylward St, Portsmouth.

1911 census. George 52 boiler riveter at Dockyard, Caroline 50 born Maldon, Essex. Olive 21 dressmaker, Dorothy 18, Kathleen 13, Sydney 11. George and Caroline had been married 25 years, had 5 children with 5 alive 1911 and were living at 125 Talbot Rd, South Sea, Portsmouth with 3 bedrooms and 2 sitting rooms.

The PERRY Family

The **1861 & 1911** Censuses state Caroline was born at Maldon, Essex, England, and this would be.....

Caroline Henrietta Jane Perry was born at Tollsbury, seven mile ENE of Maldon, Essex in the JuneQ 1858.

She was aged 3 in the **1861 census**.

1871 census. Caroline 13, daughter of Oliver Perry, a boatman in RN Coastguard and Eliza Perry; Caroline had six siblings ... Charles 11, Oliver 10, Rosanna 8, Eleanor 6, William 4, Florence 2.

The 1871C advises Charles, Oliver & Rosanna were born at Kessingland, Suffolk; Eleanor at Brancaster, Devon; William & Florence at Burton Bradstock, in Dorset, where they were all living at the time of this census.

(Burton Bradstock is 4 miles SE of Bridport, in Dorset.)

(We thank descendant Patricia Bridgeland for her research. PB)

--oo0Ooo—

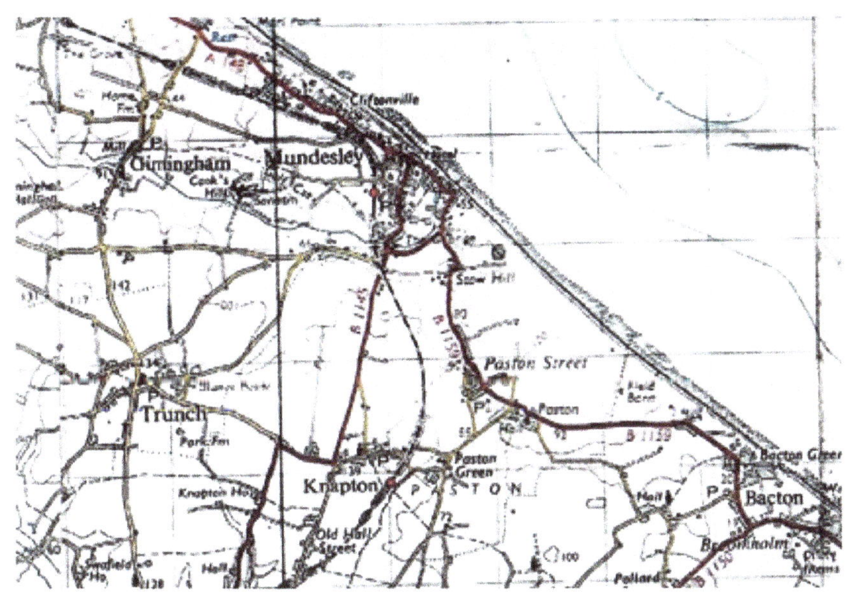

NORFOLK MAP ... The top east corner of the County where our early Woods people mainly lived ... Mundesley, Trunch, Gimingham, and Bacton are visible.

MARY ANN REYNOLDS' family in Norfolk

1st generation

1726 **THOMAS REYNOLDS** baptized 14 Jan 1726 at Metton. Metton is a small town, and a Nolfolk Parish, sitting immediately west of Roughton Parish in northern Norfolk, England. It is 3 mile south of Cromer, on the coast, and 1.7 mile west of Roughton's Parish Church.

St Andrew's the Parish Church of Metton is of 14 century design and heavily Victorianised. (Wikipedia)

1748 Thomas married Feb 28, 1748 **ELIZABETH WOODCOCK** at St Stephens Church, Norwich.

Thomas and Elizabeth had 8 children baptized at Metton .... HANNAH 1752 Dec 18; MARY 1755 May 3; ELIZABETH 1758 Jan 21; **THOMAS 1760** March 9; ROBERT 1762 born Sep 21, bapt Oct 9; MICHAEL 1765 Nov 24; ANN 1767 died June 2; and JAMES 1768 Oct 16:

St ANDREWS, Parish Church METTON, Norfolk.

1726 Thomas Reynolds was buried May 21, 1769 at Metton, Norfolk. Elizabeth was buried ..... (not at Metton before 1812)

--oo0oo--

2nd generation

1760 THOMAS REYNOLDS

Was baptised 9 March 1760 at St Andrew's Metton parish Church, Norfolk, England.

1760
Thomas Son of Thomas
& Elisabeth Reynolds
was bapt March ye 9th

1786 1st marriage by banns, at St Mary's Roughton Church, on 28 February 1786. **MARY HARRISON.** Both were single and of the Roughton Parish. (Mary was baptized on 27 Nov 1760 at Roughton, daughter of Thomas and Mary Harrison.)

They had 3 children ...... Thomas, Mary & John

THOMAS bapt 2 April 1786 at Roughton. He died 1851. Thomas married ROSAMUND CUTLER on July 21, 1808 at Overstand, (2 mile SE of Cromer) Norfolk. In the 1841 census they had 6 children at home. Mary born 1817, George and James 1827, Robert 1829, David 1832, Maria 1838. There will have been more children who were now out working for themselves.

MARY baptised 1787 but died 1787 buried Roughton.

JOHN bapt 18 Mar 1787, bur 19 Sept 1789 at Roughton.

Then wife Mary Harrison Reynolds died 3 February 1788. Thomas (father) then aged 28 and remarried in 1791.

1791. 2nd marriage. Thomas, widower, married **MARTHA PYE** single, at St Mary's Church, Roughton on 14 February 1791. The witnesses were Thomas' brother Robert Reynolds and Elizabeth Bell's brother Samuel Bell. Thomas & Martha signed by X mark.

The PYE Family ....

(Martha was born 23 Jan, bapt 29 June 1769 at Suffield, Norfolk, the daughter of David Pye b1735 and Elizabeth Bell b1737, of the North Repps parish. Elizabeth Bell was the daughter of Samuel and Mary Bell who married, and had 11 children lived and worked in Hanworth and in Roughton Parishes of Norfolk. (JP)

St Mary's Parish Church, ROUGHTON, Norfolk.

The churches round tower is thought to be of Saxon origin but most of the main church body is Victorian.
Roughton is 10.5 miles NE of market town North Walsham.

1841 census Thomas, Ag Lab, 82 and Martha 72 were living at Roughton and had 4 lodgers, none of them their own children.
1846 Father Thomas Reynolds (b1760) died aged 86 and was buried 12 Nov 1846 at St Mary's, Roughton, Norfolk.
1850 Mother Martha Reynolds (b1769) died 22 Sept 1850 (aged 82) was buried with husband Thomas at St Mary's Church-yard.

--oo0Ooo—

Thomas Reynolds and Martha had 9 children

Mary Ann Reynolds born Dec 8, bapt Dec 13, 1791 at St Mary's Church at Roughton, Norfolk. Mary Ann married to JOHN WOODS Nov 18, 1814 at Trunch Church and they had 5 children, fully detailed pages 152 to 168.
MARY ANN REYNOLDS is our Norfolk 3rd generation.

Robertbapt 1792 and Ag Lab, died April 1876. He married Nov 11, 1814 MARIA GOLDHIN 1794-1875, at Roughton. No children with them in the 1841, 51, 61, 71 censuses.

John bapt 16 June 1794 – died 16 Jan 1866. He married Oct 21, 1814 at Roughton to ELIZABETH MAYES 1793 - 1874

They had 9 children ... John 1815-1882, William 1817-1898, James 1819-1819, George 1820-1901, Elizabeth 1822, James 1826-1894, Lawrence 1829-1899, Robert 1831-1832, Henry Herbert Payne 1833.

George bapt Feb 12, 1797 – July 16 1861. He married on March 23, 1818 JANE PERKINS Feb 17 1782-1841.

David born 20, bapt 22 Oct 1799 – died June 23, 1879. Married Nov 5, 1823 to MARY ANN TODD 1803-1873.

James born 16, bapt 10 June 1803- died Jan 7, 1881. He married Dec 27, 1827 MARY PIKE 1808-1844. They had 5 children, Elizabeth 1829, Sarah 1831, Mary 1833, Emma 1838, Susan 1840-1909 at Roughton.

Sarah born & bapt 1 June 1806 – died 1830. She married Oct 31, 1828 JOHN DIXON 1795-1867. child, Jemma 1829.

Elizabeth born 18th, bapt 19 March 1809 – April 1887. She married Jun 3, 1832 to THOMAS PAINTER born Oct 20, 1802 at Roydon & died March 1886 at Roughton. They had 10 children ... Sarah 1833-1903, James 1836-1924, Mary Ann 1837, Robert 1841, Phebe 1843, Martha 1844, George 1848-1929, Ann Elizabeth 1851-1941, Harriet 1853, and James 1857.

Martha bapt 26 Dec 1813 cert – died March 1885. Martha married Nov 25, 1832 to WILLIAM PAUL, fisherman at St Margaret's Parish Church, Overstrand, Norfolk. They had 4 children ... William 1835 married Sarah Ann Cork 12 children, George fisherman, 1838-1894 married MaryAnn ?, Phebe Matilda b1840 married 1863 Thomas Cubitt 7 children, and Elizabeth (Betsy) b1851 married at Siderstrand, Norfolk, to William Hendon and 9 children.

(MARTHA 1813 is Lesley M Walters 3x Gt Grandmother.)

--oo00oo--

The NZ WOODS Family (brief tree on page 128)

JOHN WOODS born 1828 Norfolk.

4th Generation

1828 John Woods was born 1828 a son of John Woods and Mary Ann nee Reynolds and baptized 17 August at the All Saints' Mundesley Parish Church. Father John tried fishing but was mostly employed as an Agricultural Labourer.

For Mundesley photos and details refer back to pages 148-151.

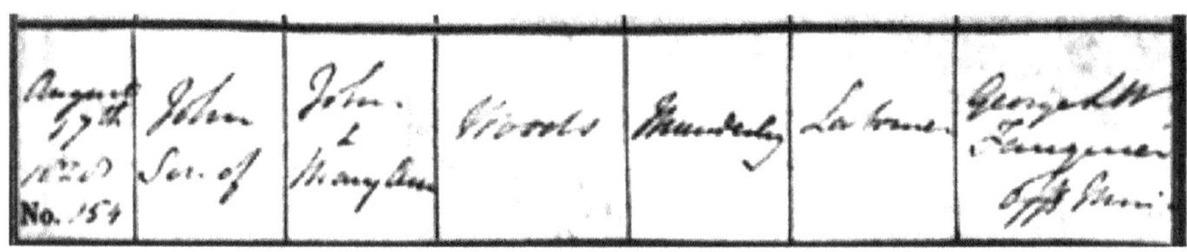

August 17th 1828 No. 154	John Son of	John & Mary Ann	Woods	Mundesley	Labourer	[illegible]

1841 census. John aged 12, was living with his parents in Church Lane, Mundesley, Norfolk, where John senior was a fisherman. No occupation was given for young John.

1846 MERCHANT NAVY.

Aged 18, John Woods enlisted at London, on April 21, 1846, in England's Merchant Navy, as an apprentice and was issued the number 328955.

John's ENLISTMENT form states he was 16 (?) from Mundsley (Mundesley) Norfolk, and was born 25 May 1830. (was 1828) Personal details noted ... Height, growing; Hair, brown; Complexion, fresh; Eyes, grey; Marks, none; (no scars, tattoos, birthmarks etc) and was able to write.

Seems John travelled with a mate as on the same day John Clark 16 of Mundesley also enlisted as given number 328956. (CW)

On the same day (21 April 1846) an **Apprentice Indenture** form was completed. This shows John indentured to Thomas Hamlin & Co for 4 years, which was to expire 21 April 1850. He was to serve on their ***"Duke of Portland"***.

The "DUKE of PORTLAND": A Barque style of sailing ship complete with three masts, having a fore and main masts rigged square and only the mizzen (the aft most mast) rigged fore and aft. (Wikipedia) She was registered at the Port of Greenock, weighed 533 tons, and known generally as a 'packet- ship', taking a few passengers but mostly cargo, until she was converted to a passenger ship in 1850/1 on the England to New Zealand run. She brought four lots of immigrants to NZ.

First Voyage .....

BOMBAY: 'The Spectator' newspaper advises on May 2, under the heading 'East India Shipping', that the *"Duke of Portland"* sailed for Bombay, India on April 23, 1846 from Gravesend, London ... that's 2 days after John enlisted.

Shipping **Schedule G** gave details of the name and number of all who sailed on The Duke that day. Compiled by the master Captain William John Cubitt, there were 25 people on board including the Captain and 'John Woods apprentice # 328955', and his friend John Clark.

Shipping **Schedule A** This was an Agreement to an Act of Parliament in the 8th year of the Reign of Queen Victoria for *'the Captain and several persons whose names were subscribed hereto, to serve in the capacities noted beside their names, on the voyage from London to Bombay from thence to any Port or Ports in the limited Kingdom of Great Britain and Ireland, and the said crew to engage themselves in an orderly, faithfully, honest, careful and sober manner, and at all times to be diligent to their respective Duties and Stations, and to be obedient to the lawful commands of the Master in everything related to the Ship, and the Materials, Stores and Cargo thereof, whether on board Ship, or Boat, or on Shore.'* That was all printed on the form and the Captain also wrote *'It is understood by the undersigned crew that they conform to the regulations of any Port or Ports that the said ship may berth at during the voyage ... no grog allowed but at the option of the Master, small stores in lieu.'*

All agreed to abide by these conditions and signed the Schedule A. Most gave a full signature but 6 men signed with their 'X' including John Woods 328955, whose signature was witnessed by James Davidson the Third Officer. (CW)

This is a little confusing because John stated on his Enlistment form he could write ... then a few hours later he signed with an X which is used by people who could not write.

This first voyage of John Woods must have been both exciting and a trial and jolly hard work. Although young and fit he would need to learn quickly everything he was being taught about working on a sea-going sailing ship ... and learn it as they sailed along.

'The Spectator' newspaper mentions on Sep 12, 1846 that The Duke was at Bombay previous to August 4, 1846. (CW)

On the **back of Schedule A** remarks were added when they enrolled or discharged crew, and on this voyage there were 5 notations which also advised us some places the ship travelled.
1846, August 17 & 18th the ship was in Bombay. (now MUMBAI)
1846, October 15 at Madras (now known as CHENNAI, India.
1847, January 2 at the Port of TRINADAD
1847, February 9 at the Port of St Thomas, VIRGIN ISLANDS
1847, March 6. The Duke arrived home at the Port of Hull, England, and the Schedule C was processed 13 April 1847. (CW)
John Woods had been away from home almost a year and seen a large number of Ports around India and the West Indies.

Second Voyage .....
CALCUTTA: On **May 3, 1847**, Schedule G, a full list of all enrolled was completed by Captain Cubitt, master of The Duke, John Woods and his fellow apprentice John Clark again listed amongst the 26 persons.
This voyage was to Calcutta (now KOLKATA) and Schedule A advises ... *and any other Port or Ports in the East or West Indies and China Seas or for Holland, for a period not exceeding two years, and then to the Post of Delivery in the United Kingdom.* This is the same pre-printed document mentioned during the First Voyage but this time Captain Cubitt has written ... *'No spirits allowed on board or to be bought on board ...'* The document was commenced on **29 April 1847** and signed on 1st June 1847. (CW)

John Woods was one of 4 apprentices on board with the Captain and 23 other men, all about to leave England.

On the back of Schedule A we found 6 events of crew changes.

1847, August 31 at Calcutta
1847, September 3 at Calcutta
1847, September 4 at Calcutta
1847, September 11 at Calcutta
1847, November 3 at Port Louis, Mauritius
1848, January 17 at Madera (Madeira, Portugal)
1848, May 29 After a 13 month trip away, The Duke arrived back at London. (CW)

It is interesting to note Schedule A detailed the wages of the crew ... all except the Apprentices. We do not have the wording of the Apprenticeship document they signed, but it would seem they received no pay, but had guaranteed work, food, clothing and lodgings for the term of their apprenticeship.

Third Voyage .....

NEW ZEALAND 1848, September 9. The *"Duke of Portland"* voyage to New Zealand was quite eventful...........
The Duke left London on **Sept 9, 1848** with Captain Cubitt in control and John Woods as an apprentice. They sat at The Downs until **Sept 11** then proceeded to NZ. (The Downs is an area of sea off the Kent coast, where ships 'parked' until they received favourable winds. It provided sheltered water from rip currents, spring tides or ocean swell. It was a permanent base during the age of sail for warships patrolling the North Sea and a safe, well protected area for anchorage during heavy weather without dragging or snatching.) (Wikipedia)

The Duke had a rather boisterous passage.
On **Sept 29** it experienced a hurricane from the north east which veered suddenly to the south west causing a terrific sea and split many of her sails. On **Nov 9th** the Duke was struck by a violent squall which carried away her three topmasts, main and mizzen top-gallant masts, fore-topsail yard, flying jib-boom, and split

several of her sails. On **Nov 20th** she rounded the Cape of Good Hope and has experienced light winds ever since.

(The New Zealander newspaper January 17, 1849)

AUCKLAND:

1849: The *"Duke of Portland"* arrived at Auckland on **January 15,** with general cargo for this place and Wellington. She brings 23 cabin and 6 steerage passengers for Auckland and 5 cabin and 3 steerage passengers for Wellington.

(Daily Southern Cross newspaper Jan 20, 1849) (CW)

On **January 20, 1849** Captain Cubitt and The Duke sailed from Auckland for Wellington with part of the original cargo, but without John Woods, apprentice number 328955.

(New Zealander Feb 10, 1849) (CW)

On **February 6, 1849** The Duke arrived at Wellington and left for Shanghai on **March 6th 1849.** (arrival, Wgtn Independent Feb 10, 1849 and it's departure, Wgtn Ind March 10, 1849) (CW)

LONDON:

On the ***"Duke of Portland's"*** return to London, Captain Cubitt made out his customary report of all on board as at that date.

328955 John Woods was not there.

He noted John had deserted .... (CW)

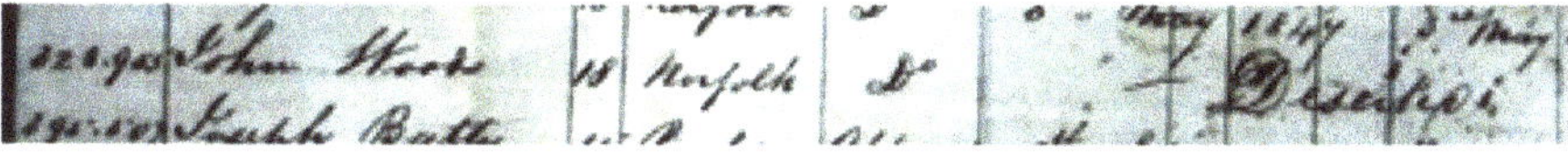

The ship was in Auckland harbour for only 6 days but John Woods (20) managed to safely hide among the population.

--oo0Ooo—

JOHN WOODS in Auckland.

1849 John arrived in Auckland, New Zealand on 15 January aged 20 and we have no proof what he did over the next 3 years but we found him in 1852 as a 'WATERMAN' aged 23.

(We imagine John finding work at the waterfront immediately after The Duke of Portland had left the port)

1852 JURY LIST. John Woods, Gaol St, Auckland ... waterman.
1853 JURY LIST. John Woods, Hobson St, Auckland, waterman.

The **WATERMEN** were an important part of the harbour operations in the early days before even the imposing Queen Street Wharf stretching out from the Commercial Bay reclamation. With mud and shallows between immigrant and cargo ships and the port itself, the boats of the watermen were one of the main ways of conveying items and people ashore.
(Timespanner) (see page 77 for wharves)
So John was a man working on a boat or among boats, especially a boatman who plied for hire. This service necessary for those vessels that drew too much water to be able to tie up to the wharves. Cargo was unloaded from the vessels into smaller boats and conveyed to shore by these watermen. (UE)

1853 MARRIAGE. On 17th February 1853 in Auckland ......
JOHN WOODS 23, married **MARY ANN LOWE** 19, at the Primitive Methodist Chapel. The minister was Robert Ward and witnesses were Joseph Crew and Eleanor Blacklaw .
It is noted on the certificate the Rev Ward married them *by license, according to the rites and ceremonials of the Church of England.* John was noted as ... *a boatman.*
John signed his name and Mary Ann signed with an 'X'.

1853. Marriages in the District of Auckland

MARY ANN LOWE.

Born and baptized in early February 1833, we wonder if she was known as Mary Ann in NZ or simply as Mary.

a … She was baptized as Mary Lowe.

c … She was entered on the *Bolton*'s register as Mary Ann Lowe.

d … Ronald Woods writes about his 'Grandmother Mary'.

e … On the rear of a photo of William (Lowe - Morris) it reads "a brother of Mary Woods".

So, maybe she was known to her family and friends as Mary, but we, New Zealand descendant researchers, have always thought of her as Mary Ann so have continued here using that name.

We have followed Mary Ann from page 21, but what else happened during the 3.5 years after she arrived in Auckland in 1849 from Wellington … until she married in 1853, apart from helping Mum with the younger children and attending church?

--oo00oo--

The PRIMITIVE METHODIST CHAPEL

Sited at the corner of Edwards and Queen St, Auckland.

Earlier on pages 74,75 we detailed activity at this chapel of Ann Lowe (Morris) and briefly mentioned her daughter Mary Ann Lowe (Morris) who married here in 1853 to John Woods.

The Methodist Archivist Mr G Matheson allowed me to view two books in 1993 ... The Register of Members of the Primitive Methodists 1850-1868 and the Edwards Street Baptismal Records 1850 to 1901.

1850 Mary Ann became a member of this Chapel recorded in the year 1st April 1850 to 31 March 1851, very soon after her arrival from Wellington aged about 17. She was a member through to 31 March 1866 and the Register of Members stopped at March 1868. There is no further surviving book to investigate. John and Mary Ann's children ... Martha Ann, Phebe, George, Agnes, William Morris and Henry Joseph were all baptised here, but no record was found for Jessie, John, Jane or Edward? Father John was noted as Boatman, Mariner, and Waterman and 5 different ministers made the baptisms. More detail follows in those children's life records.

"The Rev Robert Ward held his first meeting at 10.30am, January 28, 1849 with 9 attendees. At 2.30pm that day he preached in the town in the open air to about two hundred attentive hearers. From here he preached and held prayer meetings for the public in offered private homes. On March 16, 1850 the first Primitive Methodist Church opened by Rev Ward with services three times that day and he recorded the afternoon and evening attendances were overwhelming with even the aisles filled and some could not get in." (part P.M. in Auckland)

1851 "In 1851-2, new officials and workers received were **Miss M A Morris,** (this is our Mary Ann Lowe) Messrs. G Tilly, J England, C Partington, A Campbell, D McClusky, T Cheeseman and R Stone. The Rev J Long arrived in 1859 and in his final year (1862) the Sunday School Hall was erected.

(selections from *Primitive Methodism in Auckland 1849-1913*)

METHODIST CENTRAL MISSION

1913 Photo showing the Church in the background and the Sunday School hall and Goodwill Store (Op Shop) underneath.

The book *Fifty Years of Primitive Methodism in NZ* mentions on page 147 ... **"Amongst the early workers in the Sabbath School, Mary Ann Morris, now Mrs Woods, is spoken of as having rendered valuable service"** (T, CW)

--oo00oo—

JOHN WOODS continues ... John Woods was living in Auckland from 15 January 1849 and we strongly believe Mary Ann's mother Ann brought her 6 youngest children to Auckland via coastal ship, early in 1849 from Wellington. (p73) Did that coastal vessel require the services of a waterman to transfer passengers to land? Is this perhaps how John 20 and Mary Ann 17 met? John Woods insisted on using the C of E ceremonial rites for his marriage to Mary Ann, so we do not think he was a regular member of the Primitive Methodist Chapel where Mary Ann spent much of her time. In 1850 Mary Ann became a registered member of the Auckland Primitive Methodist Church. Ronald Woods wrote that his grandmother was quite illiterate because there were no schools in the early 1800s. (RW)

CHILDREN: John and Mary Ann Woods had 10 children .....
Martha Ann 1853, Phebe 1855, Jessie 1856, George 1859, John 1861, Jane 1863, Agnes 1866, William 1868, Edward 1870, and Henry Joseph 1875.

We will detail these children's lives, marriages and events, following John and Mary Ann's chapter.

OCCUPATION:
John Woods was recorded on various records as ....
Waterman, Mariner, Seaman, Master Mariner, Boatman, Lighterman, and as Skipper (Captain)
This NOTICE in the New Zealander newspaper appeared **30 August 1854**

NOTICE.

IN consequence of the high price of Provisions and materials, we, the undersigned Lightermen deem it necessary to raise the price of Cargo to 5s. per ton, from the date hereof.

Charles Robinson
John Lander
John Bennett
James Copeland
Donald M'Clain
Joseph Neill
John Woods
James Elliott
Charles Philpotts
David Kell
George Short
Henry Stevens
Thomas Short
John Copland
James Cranch.

HOME: The electoral rolls for 1853, 1854, 1855, 1856, 1857 and 1858 all advise John Woods and family lived in **Hobson St,** Auckland, probably in the residence John had before he married. At least three, maybe 4, of his children were born at this address.

1859. CHAPEL ST: Between 1859 and 1862 John does not appear on the Electoral Rolls, but we have found John took a **LEASE** on a property in Chapel St, Auckland in 1859.

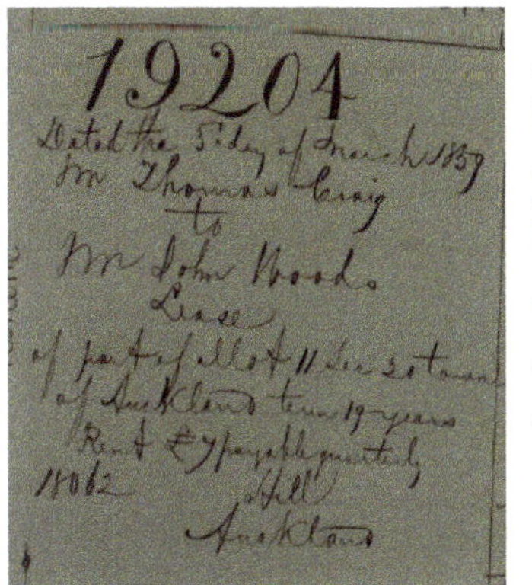

19204
Dated the 5th day of March 1859
Mr Thomas Craig
to
Mr John Woods
Lease
Hill
Auckland

Auckland
Deed Book 11D
pages 938-9.
DEED 19204
dated
3 March 1859

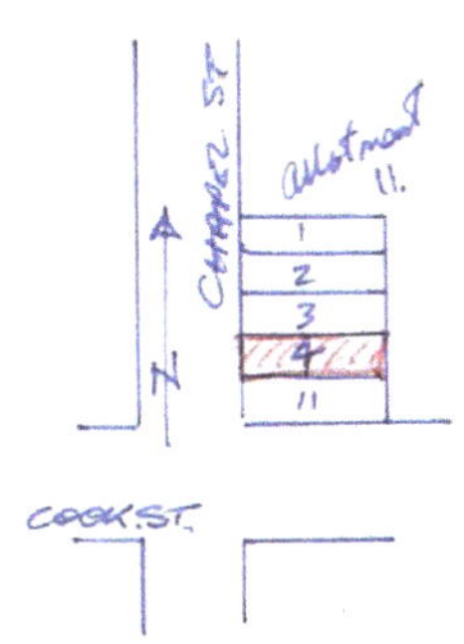

In long legalese this basically states that Mr Thomas Craig, a builder, leased the property (land and premises) known officially as Chapel St, Lot 4, Allotment 11, of Section 30, Auckland … to John Woods, boatman, for 19 years, at 7 pounds rent per year, with quarterly payments of 1 pound 15 shillings each on 1st of January, April, July & October, and was signed in the presence of James Hill, clerk of Auckland.

The land measured 105 feet 6 inches deep, by 25 feet wide facing Chapel Street. (approx 32 x 7.6 meters)

The premises mentioned was a four roomed cottage.

John and Mary Ann's son George born in 1859, and six more siblings after him, were probably all born in this house. (T, CW)

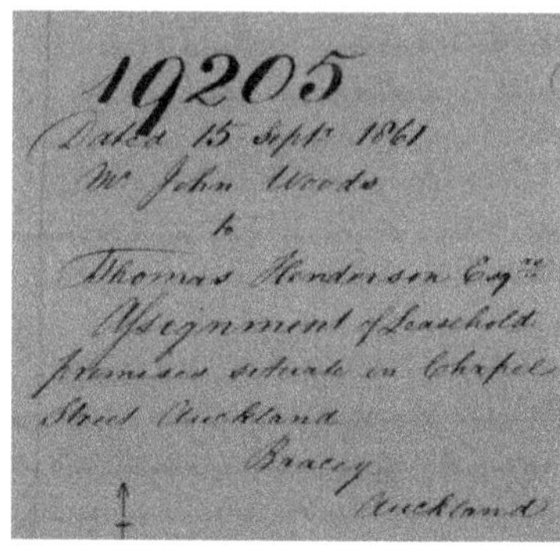

19205
Dated 15 Septr 1861
Mr John Woods
to
Thomas Henderson Esqre
Assignment of Leasehold
premises situate in Chapel
Street Auckland
Bracey
Auckland

Auckland Deed Book 12D part 1, pages 223-4-5,
DEED 19205
dated 15 September 1861.

This is a Mortgage agreement where Mr Thomas Henderson Esquire (Merchant) lent John Woods (Boatman) 110 Pounds until 1 July 1865, with lot 4 Chapel St as security. Repayment of 10 pounds per year in equal quarterly payments, and if John Woods defaulted Mr Henderson could enforce power of sale on 1 July 1865. John had to insure the premises for 100 pounds against loss and damage by fire. John signed this agreement.

This property remained in this Woods' family for 40 years.

John Woods died while at this address and Mary Ann moved to live with her retired brother William Morris in 1899. (RW)

1859 CHAPEL Street FORMATION.
Within four months of John taking up the Chapel Street house the newspaper *Southern Cross,* on 12 July 1859, advises ....

PUBLIC NOTIFICATION by John Williamson,
Superintendent of the Province of Auckland.

Whereas a majority of the persons occupying property liable to be rated ... having a frontage onto Chapel St, between Victoria St and Cook St (that's 2 blocks) ... have represented to me that they are willing to be specially rated for the purpose of forming and metaling that portion of Chapel Street ... I therefore order and direct that an equitable sum of one shilling and sixpence for every foot of frontage be levied. The said rate is to be paid on the first day of August next. The schedule provided → lists the names of those liable and the amount payable by each such person.

(condensed version T)

THE SCHEDULE

	Feet.	£	s.	d.
Thomas Sansom	49	3	13	6
David Anderson	25	1	17	6
John Havil	100	7	10	0
John Lilewall	120	9	0	0
Daniel Lockwood	110.	8	5	0
Hugh; Macky	66	4	19	0
John Wilson	48	3	12	0
Henry Dodd	29	2	3	6
John McInnis	56	4	4	0
Connell & Ridings	84	6	6	0
Edward Wilson and William Stephenson	56	4	4	0
William Rose	57	4	5	6
James Rutherford	57	4	5	6
Charles Stephenson.......	22	1	13	0
James Rutherford	34	2	11	0
Robert Bain	14	1	1	0
Andrew Anderson and John Dutch	24	1	16	0
Thos. W. Marsh	77	5	15	6
Frederick Bowers	70	5	5	0
Andrew Anderson and John Dutch	42	3	3	0
Joshua Robinson	32	2	8	0
Connell and Ridings (for Mrs. Hobson)	84	6	6	0
George Vaile	56	4	4	0
Henry M. Jervis (estate of late Richard Binns)	57	4	5	6
S. & J. R. Vaile	57	4	5	6
John Jearard	28	2	2	0
Wm. B. Montgomery	28	2	2	0
John Higgins	57	4	5	6
John Probert,........	152	11	8	0
Alfred Boon	44	3	6	0
John Goodwin	30	2	5	0
Richard Smith	56	4	4	0
William Rattray	114	8	11	0
Edmd. Mahoney	66	4	19	0
John Campbell........	25	1	17	6
Chas. Morrison	25	1	17	6
James Copeland	25	1	17	6
John Woods	25	1	17	6
Peter Beck	60	4	10	0

Chapel St is not receiving guttering and tar-seal ... just being levelled out and having gravel spread on it. (T)

SHIPPING. John used a number of small boats working as a Lighterman or as a cargo carrier around the Auckland harbour and its nearby ports.

These newspaper reports call him either Wood or Woods.

We do know John was ***Master of the cutter Tartar in 1867*** and was ***Master of the cargo boat, the cutter Diamond in 1882***.

As we go through the years of John Woods' life we will record the trips and cargo he carried.

1858, 8 February

This advertisement appeared in the Daily Southern Cross

…………

THE MONDAY'S REGATTA.

THE cargo boat "TEASER" is open to sail any boat, or vessel, that sailed in the Race, won This Day by the Tryad, for 5, 10, 15, or twenty Pounds. The Tryad herself NOT excepted.

Persons willing to take this up, may apply at the Commercial Inn, Auckland.

JOHN WOODS.

February 8th, 1858.

1858, 10 July.

Auckland Town Fire. The Osprey Inn was the source of a fire that started about 2am and destroyed many wooden businesses and 50 houses and the Commercial Hotel. Strong north-westerly winds pushed the fire through Shortland St, part Queen St, High St, O'Connell St, and Vulcan and Chancery Lanes. Henderson & Macfarlane rebuilt the Commercial Hotel this time in brick and parts of it still stand today. As a result of this fire the NZ Insurance Company was formed in 1859. "Papers Past" has a full account of this event from the Taranaki Herald, 24 July 1858.

The area that burnt down was close but did not involve Elliott St where Ann Lowe/Morris lived, nor did it involve Hobson Street where John and Mary Ann Woods and children were living at that date, but there must have been lots of black smoke and ash throughout the lower part of town and lots of anxious thoughts and discussion within our family.

John Woods must have often popped into the Commercial as the 1858 February article above suggests, and we believe Thomas Henderson had a 'shipping office' within his Hotel.

1860, 31 January

The TWENTIETH ANNIVERSARY of the COLONY

Yesterday, being the twentieth Anniversary of the foundation of the Colony, the day was, as usual, observed as a general holiday, all place of business being closed. Our citizens freely availed themselves of such amusements as their peculiar predilections suggested to be most agreeable. A 'party' on board one of the ships in the harbor, a picnic to the lake, water excursions up the river, a sail up and down the harbor, being among them; but the center of attraction, and that which promised the greatest amount of amusement and jollification, was, unquestionably ... THE REGATTA.

The newspaper continues to describe the day ... then advises the result of 11 races held on the water.

The seventh race for **Open Cargo Boats was won by WOODS on TEASER 11 tons.**

John won the Twenty pounds first prize.
Daily Southern Cross newspaper.

1860, 2 February

A notice appeared recording 7 men who were *'duly licensed to act as Lightermen at the Port of Auckland, under the 17th Clause of the Customs Regulation Act 1858'*
John Woods was one of these men. (The NZ Gazette)
Also reported on 2 February in The New Zealander newspaper.

1860 JURY SERVICE. John Woods, Chapel St, Boatman.

CUSTOMS.

THE undermentioned persons have been duly licensed to act as Lightermen at the Port of Auckland for the year ending 31st December, 1861 :—

Bennett, John
Casey, Jeremiah
Clark, George
Combes & Daldy
Copland, James
Edwards, John
Harris, Christopher Atwell
Kell, David
Macfarlane, Daniel
Philpot, Charles
Robinson, Charles
Short, George Henry
Wadham, Henry John
Woods, John

WILLIAM YOUNG,
Deputy Commissioner
of Customs.

Custom House, Auckland,
21st March, 1861.

1861, 21 March

A notice in the NZ Gazette shows 14 men licensed *'for the year ending 31 December 1861'* as Auckland port, and repeated in The New Zealander 20 April 1861 ....

1861-1864 NZ WARS

These battles between the English immigrants and the Maori were essentially over land ownership and occupation, and do not seem to have involved John Woods at all. We have found no record of John volunteering or being conscripted into the wars. During this time John was providing an essential service to Auckland town on its wharves and waterways. The battles were fought near New Plymouth, through the Waikato and ended at Tauranga. At no time did the war reach into Auckland.

1862. John renewed his license for the year ending 31 December.
1863, 7 Feb. John Woods renewed his Lighterman License for year ending 31 December along with 12 others.

1864, 16 Jan. John Woods of Queen St Wharf renewed his license.

1864, 30 September An advertisement in the 'Tenders' column of The New Zealander, was addressed to LIGHTERMEN. *Tenders are required for the Carriage of Lighthouse material to*

Tiri-tiri Island. For particulars apply this office, where tenders will be received until Saturday, October 8, 1864. (Marine Board Office)

We believe John Woods never owned his own boat but worked for many years for Henderson & Macfarlane helping on their cargo boats or skippering them. The company would have decided whether to tender and whether their boats could handle this work. There were many small cargo boats on the water.

1864 Photo of AUCKLAND HARBOUR

Taken by D M Beere from Smales Point this shows a boat yard in the foreground, Queens Wharf extending from the shoreline and North Head and Devonport in the background. We are advised this photo was taken in January 1864 on Regatta Day. There are many one, two and three masted boats on the water and some tied to both sides of the wharf. Was John sailing that day? (Auckland library Sir George Grey Special Collection ID 5-383)

1865, 9 February
John Woods went from helping passengers and carrying small cargo to the wharves ... to short trips to villages scattered around the Auckland harbour. On this day the *Ship's Arrival* section of the newspaper advises .... ***Mirander, cutter, Woods, from Mercury Bay with 17,000 feet of timber.***

1865, 25 February. John Woods renewed his license for year to 31 December 1965 along with 17 others.

JOHN WOODS' BOATS.
Photo of an unnamed CUTTER in full sail.

A **LIGHTER** was otherwise known as a Barge or Scow ... a medium sized flat bottomed boat designed to be sailed in shallow water and usually rowed and sailed by the man or men in charge of it. The daily activity of these Lighter boats was not mentioned in the newspaper's Shipping News.

A **CUTTER** was a small sail boat with either one or two masts and sails, and a large deck for carrying passengers and cargo of various forms over greater distances than lighters. Every time one of these cutters left the Port of Auckland or returned to the Port of Auckland, that vessel and contents were recorded in the newspaper's Shipping News, as were the sea-going ships travelling to Auckland from all around the world.

1865 GAS LIGHTING. The streets of Auckland were first lit by gas lamps in 1865. Before this the residents stumbled about the streets in the evening relying on the moonlight. (A)

1866 AUCKLAND DIRECTORY. Entry reads ....
John Woods, boatman, Chapel St, Auckland.

1866 ELECTORAL ROLLS. The entry reads, *John Woods, Chapel St, Dwelling, Householder in Auckland West, Ward #2.*
For 1866, 1867, 1870 to 1876 all the entries are the same.

1866 SHIPPING ACTIVITY (ex DSthC & NZer newspapers)
Jan 24, Woods, *Mary Ann* from Maketu.
Jan 27, Woods, *Mary Ann* sailed for Thames with sundries.
Feb 21, Woods, *Mary Ann,* from Tairua with 16,400 feet timber.
March 5, Woods, *Mary Ann,* for Tairua with sundries
March 7, Woods, *Mary Ann* to Tairua with sundries.
March 13, Woods, *Mary Ann* ex Tairua with 14,500 feet timber.
March 16, Woods, *Mary Ann,* to Tairua with sundries.
April 10, Woods, master, *Mary Ann,* arrived yesterday from Tairua with a cargo of timber.
May 14, Woods, master, *Mary Ann,* sailed on Saturday evening for Tairua Saw Mills, with a large cargo of stores, 13 head of cattle, 1 horse, 1 dray, etc and 2 passengers.

May 18, Woods, master, *Mary Ann* arrived from Tairua Saw Mills with a cargo of timber and several passengers.

June 21, Woods, *Mary Ann* 21 tons, sailed for Tairua with 1.5 tons potatoes, 1 ton flour, 5 bags sugar, 1 box candles, 1 tierce beef and 2 passengers.

A large article immediately after this June 21 entry, advises owners of a **Cargo Boats and Watermen's boats.** ***Inspection*** *of all will be held by order of the Acting-Collector of Customs and new rules would be enforced... each boat to have its name legibly painted to its stern and a cargo boat to be provided with a proper size dingy to carry the same name. An annual license fee of 2 pounds per annum would be imposed.*

June 25, *Mary Ann* returned from Tairua.

July 6, Woods, *Mary Ann* cutter, from Mercury Bay with timber.

July 13, Woods, *Mary Ann* 21 tons, from Tairua in ballast.

July 27, Woods, master, *Mary Ann* from Tairua Saw Mills with 19,000 feet timber.

July 30, Woods, master, *Mary Ann* sailed for Mercury Bay with sundries and 2 passengers.

Aug 10, Woods, master, cutter *Mary Ann* from Mercury Bay with 16,200 feet sawn timber and 1 passenger.

Aug 28, Woods, *Mary Ann* from Wangapoa with 14,000 feet timber and 2 passengers.

Sept 1, Captain Woods, the cutter *Mary Ann* sailed for Wangapoa via Mercury Island with a full cargo of merchandise and 5 passengers.

Dec 21, The cutter *Mary Ann* took a cargo of sawn timber to the Tamaki from Wangapoa Mills. (In one part of report Woods was in charge and in another Mr Heath was captain ?) (T, CW)

The *Mary Ann* was captained by Heath on Oct 6, Oct 23, Nov 2, Nov 16, Nov 29 and Dec 11 and probably Dec 21.

Where was our John Woods during the 7 months, Sept to Dec inclusive of 1866 and the first 3 months of 1867 ... there was no reported activity by John Woods in the shipping news?
(We think he was operating one of Auckland's Lighters .... T)

1867 SHIPPING ACTIVITY

April 6, Woods, master, *Mary Ann,* cutter, arrived from Wangapoa with sawn timber and 4 passengers.
April 13, Captain Woods, *Mary Ann* from Wangapoa with sawn timber and discharged into the schooner *Queen* and the cutter *Glimpse* for Canterbury and the schooner *Joanna* for Timaru.
April 30, Woods, *Mary Ann,* from Thames with sundries and passengers.
June 10, Woods, *Mary Ann* from Waikawau, Thames with sawn timber.

1867 April 25: ACCIDENT ON BOAT.

SERIOUS ACCIDENT.—An accident of rather a serious nature befel one of the cargo boatmen in harbour yesterday afternoon. It appears that whilst the cutter Tartar was alongside the barque A. H. Badger, transhipping wheat, the master of the boat, John Woods, suddenly missed his footing, and fell into the hold. Just at this moment a sack of wheat came sliding down the plank, striking the poor fellow on the side, and breaking his thigh bone close to the hip joint. Woods was at once taken on board the barque, and medical assistance was promptly at hand.

This cutting from The NZ Herald

The **Auckland Hospital Records** show John Woods spent 48 days in their care. He told them he was 40 (b1827) and his religion was Church of England.
He was there from 24 April to 11 June with *'traction of femur'*. The thigh-bone, and longest thickest bone in a human skeleton.

--oo0Ooo—

1867 *TARTAR.* This is the first mention of John Woods and the *Tartar* cutter, which John was to spend 8 years operating, through to about 1875. The Tartar was built in 1847, was of 15 tons, and one of the boats owned by Henderson & Macfarlane.

HENDERSON & MACFARLANE

Thomas Henderson and friends Catherine, Henry and John Macfarlane arrived from Scotland on the ship *'London'* in 1842 and built up a very large business in the Auckland district. They operated the Circular Saw Shipping Line successfully trading in Australia, America and China, and had at least five cutters ... the *Tartar,* the *Teazer,* the *Tryad,* the *Harvest Home* and the *Alabama,* operating on the Auckland harbour. Thomas owned the Commercial Hotel in Shortland St, Auckland, bought many acres of bush covered land from the Maoris and operated timber mills inland in the area of Auckland that today bears his name 'Henderson'. They had many other enterprises operating too.

> Thomas Henderson married Catherine Macfarlane and it was he who lent John 110 pounds in September 1861. We think that money was to help John buy the Chapel Street house. We wonder if Henderson & Macfarlane named the Mary Ann after John's wife, as it may have been new, and they needed a name. John spent a couple of years sailing the cutter. Was it just a co-incidence? (T)

1867 SHIPPING continued

The earlier mentioned *MaryAnn* entries of **April 30 and June 10** are incorrectly recorded as skippered by John Woods ... as he was resting in Hospital, not out sailing the seas on those dates. Someone else must have been captaining John's boat.

We are advised that a broken femur can take from four to six months to heal. Say April 24 to early November.

Did John sail immediately after leaving Hospital on 11th June ? We doubt it. What did the family do for money ? No ACC then.

June 11, June 17, July 3, July 8 The cutter *Mary Ann*, Woods, master ... brought sawn timber up from Tairua Mills & Thames.

John may have been the registered Captain of the *Mary Ann* but probably someone else was on these four trips also.

July 6, ACCIDENT TO THE *TARTAR*

"As Messrs. Henderson & Macfarlane's cargo boat *Tartar* was coming down the creek laden with timber on Thursday night last, she was in the absence of any wind caught by the strong ebb tide, and drifted right amongst a large clump of Pohutakawa trees, resulting in the carrying away her mast and bowsprit, besides other damage. The *Tartar* was bought down the river yesterday in tow of the *Teaser*, for repairs etc. " (NZ Herald)

No captain is mentioned. This is one month after John was released from hospital after breaking his leg ... so, was someone else in charge of the *Tartar* that night ?

We think this may be about the time John returned to his job .....

Dec 12, *Tartar,* cutter 10 tons, Woods, left for Kauwareranga, Thames, with 11,181 feet of timber.

Dec 18, *Tartar,* Woods, arrived from Thames, with 6 hammers, 2 packages of bacon and 1 cask pork.

Dec 20, 1867. NZ Herald, **FOUNDERING OF THE *ALABAMA***
"It is our painful duty to chronicle the foundering of another of our small coasters, by which a seaman William Walling, or more commonly known as "Gipsy Bill" has lost his life. The deceased was a seaman on board the cutter *Alabama,* a vessel of about 20 tons belonging to Messrs. Henderson and Macfarlane. The *Alabama* was a regular trader to the Thames (peninsular) and had made several successful trips to the diggings. On Tuesday morning at about 12 o'clock, the vessel sailed from Shortland", (Two small towns, Grahamstown and Shortland became the township of Thames, when the authorities decided they should become a single identity in 1874) ...... "Suddenly a squall from the S.W. struck the vessel and she immediately turned over and filled. In a few moments she sunk in five fathoms of water and the three persons on board William Trail the master, William Walling and William Hamilton a passenger were thrown into the water" ..... "We understand the owner of the *Alabama* will dispatch at daybreak this morning the cargo boats *Tartar* and *Teaser* with appliances for raising the sunken vessel." (selected comment. T)

Dec 24, 1867. "The cutter *Tartar* arrived in harbour last evening with the body of the unfortunate man William Walling, who drowned on Tuesday last by the capsizing of the cutter *Alabama*. The body of the deceased was conveyed to the dead-house and an inquest will probably be held today. The *Alabam*a has been successfully raised, and is being towed by the *Teaser,* which may be expected in this morning. The body of William Walling was found on Chamberlain's Island." (NZ Herald)

John Woods boat was the *Tartar,* was he involved in this?

--oo0Ooo

1868 SHIPPING ACTIVITY.

This is a condensed account of a busy year for John Woods and the *Tartar*. We have found 35 records of them leaving or arriving back in Auckland with cargo, with destinations of Thames, Tookey's Flat, Shortland, Henderson's Mill, Hotsprings, Waiheke and Orewa. Many trips to some of them. The *Tartar* carried bullocks, a wagon, half ton of hay, a large amount of sawn timber, and coal, thousands of shingles, pumpkins, a lot of firewood, 2 horses, bags of flour and bran, many biscuits, palings and bricks. Eight times John was 'in ballast', meaning he left port empty but came home laden with cargo. (T,CW)

1869 SHIPPING ACTIVITY.

This condensed account of John Woods and the *Tartar's* activities follow closely the previous year 1868. The newspapers reported 35 trips to Shortland, Thames, Tookey's Flat and Henderson's Mill, carrying sawn timber, bricks, shingles, coal, firewood, bushels of lime, and palings, and 8 trips in Ballast.
However mid- year John's boat the *Tartar* was sunk.

From the Daily Southern Cross of 5 July 1869.....

"A severe gale started about 4pm on June 27 and raged all day 28th coming from the north-west and created much havoc with the shipping vessels ... where a number of cutters broke from their moorings ... the fishing cutter *Catherine* drifted ... the cutter *Fly* broke from her moorings and drifted under the stern of the brigantine *Fanny,* where the force of the waves soon smashed her to pieces ... another waterman's boat drifted onto the wharf and had her gunwale smashed ... The schooner *Martha* and the cutter *Julia* also fouled and did each other a large amount of damage ... where one man had his arm broken fending a boat from a pile ... the ship *Percy* dragged her anchors 300 yards ... the barque *Coorong* drifted towards the wharf ...

the cutters *Tartar* and *Wahapu* were seen to fill and sink, the former with her cargo on board ... the cutters *Eliza, Triad,* and *Teazer* sank in Freeman's Bay during Monday ... at 10pm the wind had considerably abated, and men were enabled to go see what damage had been done to their several vessels, and make all secure for the night ..."

Poor old John Woods and his mates of Henderson & Macfarlane shipping had quite a nasty experience.

1870 SHIPPING ACTIVITY.

On the 18 February 1870 the newspapers NZ Herald and Daily Southern Cross detail almost word for word an inquiry into the Collision between the *SS LUNA* and the cutter *Tartar.*

George Mundle was in charge of the *Luna* at the time and stated.... "In coming up the harbour from the Thames, about 9pm, approaching the North Head, the man on the look-out cried out, "A vessel right ahead". The *Tartar* at that time had no lights or signal light whatever. I was quite close when I saw her. It was a bright moonlight night, and difficult to distinguish a vessel's sails. Immediately I stopped the engines, and altered her course. I put the helm to starboard to save the cutter from being cut in two. We struck her on the starboard quarter. I lowered a boat immediately and went to the cutter's assistance. He got safely to shore. E Collins, E Felton and John Sparks also spoke on behalf of the *Luna.*

David Manning said... I am a seaman ... master of the *Tartar,* I hold no certificate. I started from Queen St Wharf, bound for Motutapu Island in ballast. There were two of us on board. I was off the North Head about a quarter of a mile. The wind was baffling. About a quarter of a mile off I saw both lights but did not change my course until the steamer was close to me. I sang out to them three or four times, as loud as I could. When I saw

she was coming too close, I shoved the helm down, and ran forward. The steamer *Luna* did strike me on the starboard quarter. I had no lights on my vessel at the time because the night was so clear you could see a vessel four miles off. Assistance was rendered to me and I got ashore.
A passenger on the *Luna,* Mr John Murdock, a storekeeper at the Thames, recollected someone calling from the Tartar before any notice was taken by the Luna. **John Woods**, a seaman on board the cutter *Tartar* confirmed the statement made by D Manning was correct in every particular. He believed the steamers course was altered because the Tartar's course was altered and he seemed to be still steering towards us.
The conclusion of the court... According to the regulations for preventing a collision at sea, when two vessels, one a steamer and the other a sailing vessel, are meeting in such a way as to involve risk of collision, the steamer must keep out of the way of the sailing vessel. However, in this case it would appear that, owing to the master of the *Tartar* neglecting to use lights required by regulations, the cutter was not seen in time to avoid a collision. The party found infringing the regulations was deemed to have caused the accident." (abbreviated T)

The master of the *Tartar* was found guilty of this accident. Why was John Woods not the Master of the *Tartar* that night? The Shipping News seems to have decided to no longer report in newspapers, the activity of Auckland's coastal trading cutters. There is nothing to record for 1871 but John Woods was probably fully occupied unloading the larger ships in port and bringing the cargo to the wharves, as captain of the *Tartar*.

1872 SHIPPING.

8 February. "The dingy of the cutter *Tarta*r went adrift in harbor this morning as she was beating up. The dingy drifted towards

the *Watchman*, (off Cape Colville) but was recovered by a boat putting from a vessel alongside the wharf. (Auckland Star)

1873 SHIPPING.

8 February, "By mid-day the weather had strengthened to strong gale force and accompanied by frequent showers of rain. A heavy swell set in with the flood tide, and in consequence of the spray dashing over the wharf many places of business on the west side of the wharf were compelled to close their shops. At the Queen St wharf the greatest amount of damage was done. The schooners *Charybdis* and *Ivanhoe*, lying on the east side of the wharf, were exposed to the full force of the gale and considerable damage was done to themselves and the wharf by their bumping against it. About 4pm the new twin *SS Lily* cast off from the wharf where it had been safely moored during the day. It proposed to anchor in the stream between the wharf and the breakwater. However, owing to the strength of the gale, she was forced to immediately drop anchor, and on her swinging round her stern came into contact with the schooner *Charybdis*. The force of the collision smashing in the stern of the *Lily* and doing considerable damage to the schooner. Eventually the *Lily* got away under steam to a berth at the breakwater, but not before she had fouled the cargo boat *Tartar* belonging to Mr G Henderson, carrying away her bowsprit and doing other damage." The newspaper report continues with many other accidental damage to the areas drains, buildings etc. and can be read in full detail in the Daily Southern Cross issue. (T)

1874 SHIPPING.

17 April. A short item in the Daily Southern Cross mentions the *Tartar*. "The **cargo boat *Tartar*** has been engaged by the Government for the required communication between the

quarantined ship *Dorette* and the authorities in Auckland. The boat made her first trip yesterday morning."

There are numerous items re this quarantine on Papers Past.
14 April. Auckland Star. A full list of 350 passengers.
15 April. Auckland Star. "*Dorette* arrived 14th with large batch of immigrants and has been placed in quarantine in consequence of Scarlet Fever having been prevalent. Not expected to be any serious detention as the 8 cases (children) were of the mildest type and no appearance in the last 10 days."
16, 20, 24 April. Lots of discussion with many agencies about procedures and requiring the *Dorette* to fly the Yellow Flag.
25 April. The *Dorette,* clipper ship from London, could leave the Quarantine Ground at Motuihi in Auckland harbor.
27 April. Cargo discharged from the *Dorette.*

1875. 10th CHILD. On January 11, John and Mary Ann Woods 10th child, **HENRY JOSEPH** (HARRY) was born in Auckland.

1875 SHIPPING.
6 July. Sundays Gale. All newspapers reported results of a fearful westerly gale which stuck Auckland on Sunday, and culminated in a succession of heavy squalls between midnight and 3 am Monday, after which the fury of the gale abated.
A huge amount of detail is given but "again Geo Henderson was most unfortunate. The *Teaser* sank, the *Harvest Home* lost its bowsprit and port bulwarks, the ***Tartar*** drifted alongside the breakwater, stove in her stern and went down, the *Triad* also came to grief but she is not much damaged." The NZ Herald on the 8th July, said "the *Tartar* has become a complete wreck." (T)

The *DIAMOND.* We think about July 1875 John found work on the cargo boat *Diamond* which was owned by Captain John

Shearer (Shera) and Mr Utley. In April 1881 we found the owner had become Edward Clare, who also acted as Captain. The *Diamond* was the cargo boat John worked on until his death.

1876 January 5. CHILD'S DEATH.

On Wednesday afternoon January 5, a little girl named Maggie Brown aged 12 (daughter of Mr Brown, driver of the Whau and Mt Albert) came to her death by drowning in the Whau Creek. Briefly, "Maggie with her little brother went to the creek to play in a flat bottomed boat that had been washed up to the bridge by recent floods. Maggie put her brother into the bow of the boat, took off her own clothes and began to push the boat down the steep slope of the mud-flat to the water, and just as she got to the water's edge it shot off into the water pulling the unfortunate girl forward with such violence she fell face down into the water, and vanished. The girl's mother and others searched for Maggie but without success.

About 5 o'clock, **Mr Woods, boatman**, who happened to be up the creek at Mr Archibald's brickyard, some miles below where the accident occurred, discovered the body floating down, and secured it. Information was sent to the Police who soon arrived. It is to be hoped that the sad end of Maggie Brown will act as a warning to all boys and girls who play on boats in the water."

An Inquest was held 6th. (Daily Southern Cross 7 & 15 January)

--oo0oo—

1877 CHAPEL STREET:

19 May 1877 Some comments from the minutes of the Auckland City Council meetings.

On this date, council set "Rates for the City" at 1 shilling in the pound or ratable value of each property, payable 1 June 1878.

John Woods' rates were based on value of 15 pounds.

4 December 1878 A petition was received from the residents of Chapel Street in reference to the condition of the footway. The surveyors report thereon was read. It was moved that the Town Clerk write informing the petitioners the work will be proceeded with as quickly as possible.
27 August 1879 The surveyor to prepare a report and estimate for kerbing, channeling, and asphalting Chapel St.
25 October 1879 Surveyor recommends tenders be called for Chapel St works, at once.
10 December 1879 Two tenders received for Chapel St work. The tender from A Wooley & Brewin was accepted.
15 January 1880 Wooley & Brewin's account was received and approved for payment.

> From this we learn that Chapel St was a sea of dust and/or mud and maybe pot-holes in the loose gravel, for our John, Mary Ann and family to walk upon until mid-November 1878 when they and fellow residents had had enough and sent the petition to council. It might have taken a year to happen but then they were walking on asphalt footpaths and roadway and water on the street was controlled by curbing. Must have been a great Christmas present for the street's occupants in 1879.

20 January 1880 The Council approved an extra Rate of ½ penny in the pound of rates value of each Auckland property, fixed for Library use.

1879 LARCENY CHARGE

4 July. We find John Woods kept bad company, as the NZ Herald and Auckland Star report throughout July.
"Two of the hands on the cutter *Diamond,* named John Woods and Robert Sargent, were apprehended last night by the Water Police, on a charge of having in their possession a coil of rope

belonging to the owners of the schooner *Marmion*. The schooner was berthed alongside the wharf and on Tuesday at dusk the rope in question was coiled up and close to the windlass, but on Wednesday morning it was missing and was not seen again until found in the possession of the prisoners. They were charged with having in their possession 70 fathoms of rope, value 20 shillings, the property of William Johnstone. Mr Laishley appeared for them and pleaded not guilty. Sub-Inspector Pardy asked for a remand until the return of the schooner's captain from the Kaipara. The prisoners were remanded until the 14th inst. Bail in own recognizances, 40 pound, two sureties in 20 pound each.

15 July. Mr Pardy applied for a further remand as the captain still had not appeared. Mr Laishley strongly objected to a further remand as he felt there was not a slightest chance of the Captain returning, however, the case was further remanded one week.

21 July. Mr Pardy again asked for an adjournment as the principle witness, the schooner Captain had not appeared even after being twice subpoenaed. Mr Laishley asked for a dismissal of the case, especially of the man Woods, holding as he did certificates from different people, who had known him for twenty years, and had given him an excellent character.

The prisoners were discharged.

NZHerald **24 July** Under a charge of Disorderly & Drunkenness, Robert Sargent was fined five shillings and costs. (3 days later)

--oo0oo—

About 1882/3 **CHAPEL ST** was renamed **LOWER VINCENT ST** and in 1993 the name was changed again to **FEDERAL STREET**.

--oo0oo—

PHOTO of .... MARY ANN WOODS
and son HENRY JOSEPH (HARRY)
estimated taken about 1880
(Harry 4 to 5. Mary Ann about 45)

1882 JOHN WOODS DROWNED on Wednesday 13 September.

1882 DEATH NOTICE for John Woods.
"On September 13, by drowning in Auckland Harbour, John Woods, aged 52. The funeral will leave his late residence, Lower Vincent St, tomorrow (Sunday) September 17, at 1pm. Friends will please accept this intimation" The Methodist Rev W. S. Potter officiated.

(NZ Herald 16 Sept 1882)

The DROWNING REPORT
14 September 1882 Selection from NZ Herald & Auckland Star.

BOAT ACCIDENT IN THE HARBOUR
TWO MEN DROWNED

Shortly after 8 o'clock last night, a cry of "Help" was heard by persons on the wharf, from someone in the water between the Queen St and Railway Wharves. The cry was heard by Damian O'Connor, waterman, when he was at the northern end of Queen St wharf. He ran up to the steps, took his boat and in company of Mr H Parker of H. M. Customs headed in the direction of the cries but could see no traces of either boat or men. Sergeant Martin and Constable Macdonald also proceeded in a small boat and searched all around for some time between the wharves without success. Mr O'Connor, the waterman, states that shortly before the cry for help he had assisted a man named John Woods, master of the cargo boat *Diamond* and his mate, a wooden-legged man, to get into a dingy from Mr Fallon's reclamation wall, for the purpose of going off to their vessel, which was at anchor about 200 yards from the eastern side of the wharf. Both men, being in an intoxicated condition were expostulated with and advised by Mr O'Connor, the waterman, not to attempt going across in that condition. *(Note .. the state of drunkenness was denied in following newspaper reports.)*

Woods would not be reasoned with and both men having got into the dingy commenced to pull across to their cutter. He believes they must have upset the boat, the water being slightly rough and when Mr Parker boarded the *Diamond* and searched, he found no trace of the men having been on board.
It was concluded that they had managed to capsize the dingy and all had gone down. *(The Herald was the morning paper and the Star the evening paper and that day the 14th the Star made no comment about drunkenness but said)* ... O'Connor and others who saw Woods and his mate leave the wharf are of the opinion that they were sober and well able to take care of themselves. The Herald advises ... Woods was a man of about 60 years of age, and leaves a wife, with a large family but they are for the most part grown up, and able to do for themselves. It is stated that Woods had lately given way to drink, and that he had a very narrow escape from drowning a few days ago over at the North Shore. The Star advises Woods was about 56 and the other person lost was known as Musgrave, a single man of about 30 years who was an excellent swimmer and Mr Buckland whom he boarded with was astonished he met his death by drowning. Musgrave was about five foot seven in height, with only one leg.

The Star advises John Woods' body was recovered on the 14th shortly after 2 o'clock by the Water Police who were dragging the area. He was conveyed to the Morgue and was identified by a son. He was wearing a full suit of tweed clothes and a strong pair of boots. His hat was the only missing article. The search for Musgrove was resumed but he was not found.

15 September 1882 Selection from NZ Herald & Auckland Star.
Again both newspapers continued with this drowning story.

The Herald amended two items... John Woods lived in Lower Vincent St and not Drake St as they first thought... and secondly they received some representations by those who saw John Woods shortly before the accident and advised their readers John was not under the influence of liquor, at least not sufficiently intoxicated not to be able to manage the dingy.

About 6pm four Maoris came up from Orakei and bought the body of Musgrave to the Water Police. They informed that the remains had been found near to Paul's settlement, lying on the beach, evidently left by the receding tide earlier in the afternoon. The Maori named Te Parata was entrusted with the duty of conveying the body to Auckland and giving particulars to the Police. The body was taken to the morgue and identified as William Musgrave. William had lost a leg through a train running over it at Onehunga. The Coroner's Inquest was set to be held at 2pm in Gleeson's Hotel.

JOHN WOODS INQUEST

1882 The Star covered the Inquest in its 15 September issue.

New items to be revealed included ...

Mr Damian O'Connor became Daniel Connor.

Dr Goldbro', coroner, presided and a jury of 13 men with James Hamilton being foreman. Sergeant Martin for the Police and evidence was taken in relation to John Woods. Daniel Connor stated the deceased came to the waterman's house at a quarter past seven on the 13th and asked witness if he had seen his dingy. He said "No". He said "Someone has stolen it." Witness said he would look for it and didn't think it was far away and he did find it. John felt the paddles and said they were his. The dingy was half full of water and he told Musgrave not to go. I did not think Musgrave was a fit man to go with the wooden leg. Witness and Mr Tucker the butcher walked away down the wharf and saw the two men shove off towards the *Diamond* cutter. They went to the end of the wharf and heard the cry for help. Woods was a steady man. It was a stupid act to go out in the boat when she was half full of water. I went out next morning with the deceased son and brother-in-law and after an hour of dragging brought up John Woods. It was about 800 yards to the *Diamond*. Woods and Musgrave were on good terms, I advised the deceased to bail out the boat. She would carry 6 or 7 people safely. Sergeant Henry Martin stated he knew John Woods and heard the evidence of Connor and agreed with it all. He was present when Woods was found. He was by Mr William's fish shop at the time of the accident. The wind was blowing in the opposite direction which prevented him from hearing the cries for help. The dingy had not been found but one of the paddles was found by the side of the cutter and the other on the deck of the cutter and I surmise that when standing up, it was put there with the intention of going on board. He thought the men had stood upright, and upset the dingy. The coroner, addressing the jury, said it was perfectly useless to call further evidence as it was evidently an accident.

The evidence for William Musgrave was exactly the same. The men were evidently not drunk. Had they attended to the advice of Mr Connor, an experienced waterman, the catastrophe might have been avoided. The foremen and the jury concurred with the remarks of the coroner, and a verdict of **accidental death by drowning** was recorded.

> The actual Inquest papers, complete with all juror's names, differ minutely but the above and the details given by the newspapers are mainly accurate.

The Auckland Weekly News carried the story on 20 Sept. (T)

--oo0Ooo--

John Woods death certificate says he was 50 years old, born in Norfolk, son of George Woods a farmer, and married 23 years. (William Musgrave was 40, single.) The coroner was 'informant'.

Someone in the family gave the coroner some incorrect details but no harm done.

--oo0oo—

The HEADSTONE over John Woods' grave at Auckland's Grafton Cemetery, Karangahape Road, details 5 occupants

ANN CROCKER
18 Nov 1868, ~~55~~ (63)

HENRY MORRIS
11 May 1852, 5yrs

S.R.H. MORRIS
27 Feb 1868, 21 mths

JOHN WOODS
13 Sep 1882, 52

MOSES CROCKER
27 Aug 1895, 80

Please refer to page 84 for every word on this headstone.

--oo0oo--

JOHN WOODS. Turns out there were a number of men with this name living in Auckland and in other parts of NZ during the years our John was alive. Most records do not give ages or addresses, so it's quite easy to think all activity mentioned in the 5 newspapers recorded only our John Woods activity. But not so. There was a JW a doctor. Another JW a Lieutenant on a regularly visiting ship, another stole a revolver at Waiau, another JW arrived from Victoria, Australia, a single miner, one JW went to school at Oxford, ChCh, and between 1874 and 1877 5 John Woods married in NZ, there was a John Woods living in Howick who run up a string of drunkenness and vagrant charges and died of alcoholic poisoning in 1871 at Coromandel, and he had a son JW. The drowning of our JW mentions alcohol, in so far as he and his mate had had a couple but could still safely row a dingy. Our John worked hard on his boat shifting many often heavy items onto and off his boat and I am sure at the end of each day he had 'a couple' on the way home. However, I am not convinced that this contributed to the overbalancing of the boat and being thrown into the sea at 7.15pm. Probably just bad luck they both tried to leave the boat at the same time and that one did not wait until the other had climbed aboard after placing his oars on the deck. (T)

--oo0Ooo—

Mary Ann Woods' life continues ....

After Sept 13, 1882, Mary Ann Woods was a widow, and her life carried on for another 36 years. She would have been happy to have most of her children nearby.

1883 Mary Ann (50), listed in the Directory at Lower Vincent St. In 1890 and each year to **1898** MAW was listed at Lower Vincent St with brother William Morris and son Harry HJ Woods (15-23).

1893 NZ WOMEN Get To Vote ... Mary Ann was never listed.

1896 MRS JOHN WOODS was recorded in Wises NZPO Directory as living in ... Lower Vincent St.

WOODS FAMILY HOME MOVEMENTS

By 1896, the Chapel/ Lower Vincent/ Federal St home of John and Mary Ann Woods was first occupied in March 1859, then purchased in September 1861, with 7 children born, 10 children raised, father John dying, one child had died and 7 had married, leaving Mary Ann 61 and sons Edward , and Harry 24. Then son Edward married May Marsh in Dec 1896, and May moved into the Woods home and their son Edward (Eddie) was born there in Feb 1898.

In 1899 Mary Ann and Harry Woods. moved to live with her brother William Morris at 8 Canada St, Newton, Auckland in 1899. (Canada St is now Kawaka St) (RW)

About **1914** Mary Ann moved to live for a while with daughter Jessie Gow, then to Pah Road, Mt Roskill home of her daughter Jane and John Haslett where she lived out her final years. (RW)

OUTDOOR CUPPA on the steps at Pah Road ... next page .....

L to R **Ivy Woods (daughter son John) daughters Jessie (Gow) and Jane (Haslett) with Mary Ann.**

1900, December 20
AGED PENSION

When Mary Ann Woods was aged 67 she was approved to receive the full New Zealand Pension of 18 pounds. (CW)

NZ Herald newspaper copy

→

A SITTING of the Old Age Pensions Court for Eden County was held yesterday, Mr. H. W. Brabant being the presiding magistrate. The Deputy Registrar represented the Department. His Worship awarded pensions to the following for the full amount of £18 :—John Keenan, Sarah Chambers, David Watt, Katene Reweti, Hannah Jensen, Mary Ann Woods, Emma Dunne, and Rini. Lesser : The following amounts were awarded to the undermentioned :—Neil Beaton, £17 ; Ann Cooke, £15 ; Joseph G. Phipps, £14 ; and Sophia Elizabeth Hodson, £6. The list contained 37 cases, which were all disposed of before the Court adjourned at six o'clock. In one case of the claim not being entertained, the joint properties of husband and wife were sworn at £798. There were three native applications. Mr. King reported the death of one. Mr. Brown, native interpretor, appeared on behalf of the Government. By the instructions of the investigating magistrate all matters were got through for the two remaining cases, and full amounts ordered in both.

1902 DIRECTORY

In this year Mary Ann's son, **Edward Woods** (Mill Hand) and family, occupied the Lower Vincent St house.

1902: Mary Woods (no Ann mentioned) was living at Canada St, Newton, Auckland.

1908 PHOTO: The Chapel/Lower Vincent St Home.

Vincent St runs up to the right. Lower Vincent St (was Chapel St) is center foreground and the 'Kia Ora' building is on Cook St. The two-story building on the corner of Cook and Lower Vincent Streets was a Grocery Store run by A T Harris from about 1882 to 1901, then taken over by James Mercer. The house beside it, with pyramid shaped roof was the **home of John and Mary Ann Woods and family.** Two houses towards the photo's lower border was the home of John & Mary Ann's son William Morris Woods aged 25 from about 1893. He was still living there in 1902 aged 34. Wises Directory. (CW)

(Photo taken in June 1908 by Henry Winkelmann from the tower of St Mathew's Church. (Auckland Library's Sir George Grey Special Collection ID-2-W1018)

1918 ... MARY ANN WOODS DIED

On 16 November 1918 Mary Ann Woods died aged 85, at her daughter Jane's Pah Road, Mt Roskill home. She was buried at Waikaraka Cemetery, Auckland. (row 65, plot 3360)

Ronald Woods was nearly 6 when his Grandma Mary Ann died, and in 1964 he said he could still *'remember the old lady feeding him blackballs off Aunty Jess's sideboard.'* (RW)

Mary Ann's headstone reads ……

In loving memory
of
MARY ANN
relict of the late
JOHN WOODS
died 16th Nov 1918
aged 85 years.

"Peace Perfect Peace"

--oo0Ooo—

1925 PHOTO Chapel / Lower Vincent St .. the WOODS' Home

In this photo the cameraman was standing across Cook St, which runs left to right down towards Queen St and looking up Lower Vincent St toward St Mathew's Church tower on the left. It shows the Grocer's shop, which had burnt down, has been cleared away and **John and Mary Ann Woods' family home** now is the first on the right. An amazingly small 4 room cottage for all those children and where most of them were born. (CW)

(Photo taken 1925 by J D Richardson. Auckland Library's Sir George Grey Special Collection ID-2-W1018)

--oo0Ooo—

The lives of
JOHN & MARY ANN WOODS' 10 children follows ......

JOHN and MARY ANN WOODS 10 children

Martha 1853, Phebe 1855, Jessie 1856, George 1859, John 1861, Jane 1863, Agnes 1866, William 1868, Edward 1870, Henry 1875.

--oo0Ooo—

1..... MARTHA ANN WOODS born on Nov 27, 1853 in Hobson St, Auckland, (registered 1854/2369) was baptised by the Rev R Ward at the Primitive Methodist Church in Auckland on Dec 18, 1853. Her father John Woods was noted as 'a Boatman'.

(No photo of Martha has been found. T.)

1878 Martha married **WILLIAM ROBERT TURNER** Aug 1st, at Onepu, Avonside, Christchurch. Rev R Tout officiated.

(Auckland Star 21 August 1878)

William R Turner and Martha lived firstly in Christchurch where all 8 of their children were born.

1909 In this year they moved to Tauranga where Robert bought 420 acres of land at Kaimai 'to improve', and a 1.5 acre plot on the corner Selwyn and Elizabeth Streets in Tauranga, where he built a 1500 square foot home. A description of this appeared in the newspaper. (Bay of Plenty Times Feb 21, 1910)

1916 This Electoral Roll shows the family were living in Selwyn St, Tauranga.

1918 Their daughter **LILLY** died at Tauranga Jan 25, 1918. William and Martha moved to Palmerston North in 1918 where William farmed at Kairanga.
When William retired their final address was 46 Featherston St, Palmerston North.

Martha and William had 8 children they named ....

Hilda Mary b1879, married Robert Bampton but no children.
Leonard Mountain b1880, married Florence Cawthron Shirtcliffe and had 6 children ... Jeffrey Leonard, Brian Arthur, Joan Lilian, Gordon John, Noeline, Dorothy Florence.
Lillian May (Lilly) b1881, died single Jan 25, 1918, aged 36, at Tauranga.
Edwin Robert Corless b1882, married Thelma Ellen Small.
Charles William b1883, married Anna Marie Cecelia Peterson.
Beatrice Maud b1885, died Dec 15, 1904, single aged 20.
Herbert Edgar b1888, (Bert) married Hilda Gertrude Lancaster with 2 children ... Patricia Joyce, William Lawrance (Bill).
A brief-tree follows for the Lancasters on page 225.
Stanley Campbell b1889, married Annie Dickinson and had 7 children ... Marion, Jack, Edwin, Robert, Jean, Margaret and, Graham.

See Family Tree pages 226 to 230

WILLIAM & MARTHA TURNER'S headstone at Palmerston North Cemetery.

1919 WILLIAM DIED on 17 June 1919 aged 77 and left a Will he signed in Tauranga on 5 March 1910 ... The Public Trust was to convert everything into cash and invest it, with income to go to his wife Martha and daughters Hilda and Lillian at one third each, until Martha died, then equally divided amongst all his surviving children. Two daughters Beatrice and Lillian, died before their father, so would not have inherited.

William had been involved in the A&P Association, Arbour Society, Literary Society and on the Public Library Committee. His obituary advises he was an 'enthusiastic worker' for the Baptist Church. (SK)

1937 MARTHA DIED on 21 May 1937 aged 83, at her son Charles residence at Kairanga.
William and Martha are buried together at the Terrace End Cemetery, Palmerston North. (Wesleyan Block 52, plot 36)

Martha's Will (dated 4 April 1925) was short ... she left her *'daughter Hilda all my personal effects together with whatever money I die possessed of'*. This Will was witnessed by ......
Martha's sister Jessie and her husband Frederick Meikle.

M. A. Turner.

Martha's signature on her 1925 Will.

--oo00oo--

The TURNER family:

1st generation

John Turner married Elizabeth Mountain = son William.

2nd generation

William Turner married Sarah Stockdale = son Robert.

3rd generation

Robert Turner, born Mar 19, 1819 at Leeds, Yorkshire, England, *(baptised at St Peters, Leeds 29 Aug 1919*) on Jan 10, 1839 at Leeds, Robert married **AGNES ANN CORLESS.** (cert vol 23 page 345) *(Agnes was born to Robert and Helen Corless 22 June 1816 at Leeds and baptised the same day at St John's Roman Catholic Poulton Le Fylde Church, in Lancashire.)* **They had 3 children ....**

4th generation

1839 MARY ANN TURNER was born at Leeds, England, on November 5, for Robert and Agnes,

1840 TRAVEL: On September 14, Robert 21, Agnes 24, and wee daughter Mary Ann 9 months, boarded the *'Slains Castle'* sailing ship at Graves End, London and arrived Port Nicholson, Wellington, New Zealand on Jan 25, 1841.

1842 WILLIAM ROBERT TURNER was born on Aug 17, for Robert and Agnes, in Nelson, New Zealand.

1844 AGNES ANN TURNER was born on Jan 17, Robert and Agnes' at Akaroa.

Children William and Agnes was baptised by Roman Catholic Bishop Pompallier at Akaroa on April 4, 1844.

c1846/7 Robert and Agnes' family moved to Australia, but returned to Lyttleton, NZ in Dec 1850 on the ship *'Woodridge'*. They lived at Sumner, Christchurch where William farmed. Another visit to Australia to join in the gold rush but not successful and they returned to Sumner. Daughter Agnes told her children, that as children they spent part of their school days in Australia and used to pick up nuggets of gold in the gutters after rain at Ballarat, and look under stones for snakes to kill with sticks. They returned to NZ and the goldfields of Gabrielle's Gulley near Dunedin, but soon returned to Christchurch. At some point Robert and Agnes returned to Australia where they lived and later died ...

Agnes died on Feb 26, 1868 buried at Yan Yean, Victoria, and **Robert died** in 1899 at Hotham, Victoria, Australia.

--oo0Ooo—

More on **<u>Robert and Agnes Turner's three children</u>** ....

1... Mary Ann Turner born 5 Nov 1839 in Leeds UK, married Dec 17, 1855, Victoria, Australia, to **George Nankivell.** He was a Cab Proprietor and in 1903 they lived at 40 William St, Balaclava, Melbourne.
Mary Ann and George had 11 children ... Agnes Ann, Avice, Mary Ann, William Robert, George Wesley, John Edgar, Selina, Edwin Frank, Henry, Mary and Arthur George Turner.

Mary Ann died 30 Aug 1931 and was buried at Maldon, (36km south of Bendigo) aged 91. George died in 1908.

2... William Robert Turner born 1842, married **Martha Ann Woods**, as mentioned earlier starting on page 220 in this book.

3... Agnes Ann Turner b1844, married May 4, 1865 to her brother Williams' wife Martha's uncle, **George W D Morris**. Agnes and George Morris had 10 children and their life story starts page 100 of this book.

--oo0Ooo--

(Most of the content above is from notes made by Mrs Hilda Ford (nee Turner) & the Jane *(Woods)* Hazlett's family bible ... all shared by Arthur Dudley Morris and Brenda Emus ... with Ship details and NZ BDM items confirmed from Ancestry and other internet sites, and the book 'White Wings' by Henry Brett. (T)

--oo0Ooo–

Brief-tree for <u>The LANCASTER family</u> (refer Herbert Turner)
1st generation
John Lancaster married Jane Turner in Lancashire, England.
2nd generation
Stephen John Lancaster born 5 Nov 1859 NZ, married Sarah Ann Eagle, daughter Robert and Hannah Blanche Puttenham.
Stephen & Sarah had 11 children ......
3rd generation
Thomas born 1860 married Elizabeth Bowler.
Stephen Robert 1862 married Catherine, Isabella, Ethel.
Sarah Jane 1864 married James Donald.
Hannah Mary 1866 married Thomas William Lewer.
Ernest Samuel 1867 married Kate Brunger.
Arthur 1869, married Arabella Bowler. Had 6 children including **Hilda Gertrude Lancaster who married Herbert Edgar Turner.**
Emma Effie 1872 married Walter Bazire Messenger.
Amy Alice 1873 married William Fry Newcombe.
Ada 1875 married William Henry Young.
Henry John 1877 married Agnes Marry Whitbread Edwards.
Phoebe 1879 married Charles Nicholas Cathie.

(We are grateful for the research of Adam Turner.)

--oo0Ooo-

MARTHA ANN WOODS married WILLIAM ROBERT TURNER . FAMILY TREE
they had 8 children ... Hilda, Leonard, Lillian, Robert, Charles, Beatrice, Herbert & Stanley

HILDA MARY TURNER
born 4 Aug 1879
died 28 July 1976 (97) bur Timaru
married 1911 no issue
ROBERT BAMPTON
born 1878
died 7 Sep 1932 (54) bur Burwood, Christchurch
HILDA married JAMES WILLIAM FORD
James died 1949 (72) no issue

LEONARD MOUNTAIN TURNER
born 16 June 1880
died 29 Jan 1961 (80)
married 1920
FLORENCE CAWTHRON SHIRTLIFFE
born 7 June 1895 Waimea South
died 27 Dec 1976 (80)
bur Mangere, Lawn C plot 55

6 children named ....
Jeffrey, Brian, Joan, Noeline, Gordon and Dorothy.

JEFFREY LEONARD TURNER
born 9 Sep 1921
died 25 Aug 2011 (90)
bur Snapper Rock, Auckland
married
ELSIE IVY
born
died
5 children ...

GLORIA TURNER

ROSS TURNER

ELIZABETH TURNER

DEREK LAWRENCE TURNER

DAVID JOHN TURNER
Jan 1955 to 16 July 1955
buried Putaruru

BRIAN ARTHUR TURNER
born 20 Sep 1922
died 22 May 1985 (62)
married 7 Oct 1950
DULCIE MARGARET HARVEY
born 15 March 1932
died 12 May 1997 (65)
Both buried Matamata.
9 children ...

GWENYTH MARGARET TURNER
m ... COPE = 3 children

OWEN DOUGLAS TURNER
m ... PICKIN = 2 children

COLIN LEN TURNER
m ... WEHIPEHANA = 2 children

BRUCE CHARLES TURNER
m ... GREGORY = 3 children

BEVERLEY TURNER

ROSEMARY TURNER
m ... SOLLY = 1 child

STEWART TURNER
m ... CHAMBERLAIN = 2 children

NORMAN TURNER
m ... JENNINGS = 3 children

MAURICE BRIAN TURNER
b 6 March 1963 Matamata
m 18 Nov 1995 Wodonga, Australia
RUTH AULMAN
2001 Stephen Joseph Turner
2003 Naomi Elizabeth Turner

Leonard & Florence continued

JOAN LILIAN TURNER
born 13 Sep 1923
died 31 Dec 1997 (74) buried Masterton
married 1955
KEITH KING DONOVAN
born 19 Dec 1921
died 23 Sep 1993 (72)
both buried Riverside Cemetery, Masterton, Lawn C/B34-35

NOELINE MONICA TURNER
born 1927
died 1 Oct 1949 (22) buried Putaruru, NZ

GORDON JOHN TURNER
born 5 May 1929
died 9 Nov 2007 (78)
married 10 Sep 1949
PHYLLIS JUNE PERRIN
born 23 June 1931
died 26 Sep 2013 (82)
buried at Tokoroa plot 309
5 children ...

BARRY TURNER
born

GRAHAM ALLAN TURNER
born

ANNETTE TURNER
born

SHARON MIRIAM TURNER
born

JANINE MAYE TURNER
born

DOROTHY FLORENCE TURNER
born 3 Dec 1934 (Dot)
died 26 Feb 2013 (79)
married 19 Dec 1953
JOHN DAVID BATEY
born 2 May 1929
died 18 Feb 2003 (74)
bur Manukau Gardens

Dot and John had
3 children and
10 grandchildren

MARK DAVID BATEY
born
m CAROLYN DIANNE CURRIE
5 children ... Nicole, Kelly,
Janelle, Simon & Jayden

KIM NOELINE BATEY
born
married ... ? ... GIBBONS
Kim had 2 children ...
Jenna & Rachel

CHRISTOPHER JOHN BATEY
born
married
3 children ... Shayne, Troy, Kayne

LILLIAN MAY TURNER
born 8 April 1881 & died 24 January 1918 (36)
remained single .... buried at Tauranga

ROBERT next page

EDWIN ROBERT CORLESS TURNER
born 2 Aug 1882
died 1978 Christchurch
married
THELMA ELLEN SMALL
born 2 Nov 1905
died 7 Oct 1992

CHARLES WILLIAM TURNER
born 4 Nov 1883
died 11 Nov 1954 (71)
married 1908
ANNA MARIA CECELIA PETERSON
born 1888
died 8 January 1968 (80)
buried Palmerston North, KG-M8/35

BEATRICE MAUD TURNER
born 29 Jan 1886
died 15 Dec 1904 (19) bur Burwood, Christchurch, NZ

HERBERT EDGAR TURNER (Bert)
born 13 Jan 1888
died 13 March 1981 (93)
married 8 June 1921 P/Nth
HILDA GERTRUDE LANCASTER
born 21 June 1898
died 5 Nov 1982 (84)
both Crem Palmerston North, NZ

3 children ... Norma, Patricia and Bill

NORMA RUTH TURNER
born 16 Feb 1925
died 24 Feb 1926 (1)
bur Terrace End, Palmerston North.

PATRICIA JOYCE TURNER
born 25 July 1927
died 17 Jan 2010
m 1951 Palmerston North
THOMAS O'BRIEN DEVINE
(Tom) born 18 May 1927
died 9 Jan 1973
bur Aramoho, Wanganui, NZ

5 children ... Kathleen, Mark, Jane, Ann and Paul.

KATHLEEN MARY DEVINE
born 3 March 1953
died 20 Aug 1970 Wanganui.

MARK JOSEPH DEVINE
born 25 Aug 1954
died 12 May 1963 Wanganui.

JANE PATRICIA DEVINE
twin b 29 Oct 1956 Wanganui
died 24 Oct 1998 Wanganui
partner ...
2 children ...

Nishi Rose Devine
b 21 Jan 1984
d 27 Dec 1987 Wanganui

Tommy Devine
b
d

ANN LOUISE DEVINE
twin b 29 Oct 1956 Wanganui

PAUL THOMAS DEVINE
born 1952 or 1958
died 1983

Bert and Hilda continue	WILLIAM LAWRANCE TURNER known as BILL. born 31 January 1931 died 20 September 2001 (70) married 11 July 1959 MARCIA IRENE O'HARA born 16 April 1934 died 19 July 2010 (76) buried Palmerston North 3 children ...	ALAN TURNER born GREGORY PAUL TURNER born SUSAN TURNER born
STANLEY CAMPBELL TURNER born 13 May 1889 died 31 Oct 1978 (89) married 1900 ANNIE DICKINSON born 28 March 1891 died 13 May 1938 (47) both buried Cheviot, Canterbury 7 children ... Marion, Jock, Edwin, Robert, Jean, Margaret & Graham.	MARION TURNER born 12 May 1909 died 1 Nov 1941 (32) married ATHOL JACKSON born died 1 child ...	GRAHAM JACKSON born 1933 died 27 Jan 1965 (32)
	JACK TURNER (Jock) born 1911 & died 4 Sep 1916 (5) buried Burwood, Christchurch, NZ	
	EDWIN TURNER born 1913 & died 25 Sep 1916 (3) buried Burwood, ChCh, NZ	
	ROBERT TURNER born 12 Sept 1918 died 25 May 1963 (44) buried Tokoroa. married ALISON ELIZABETH McEWEN born 5 children ... Ian, Grant, and	IAN DAVID TURNER born 29 April 1947 died 2 July 1969 (22) GRANT ROBERT TURNER born 2 Nov 1948 died 2 Aug 1970 (22) Father & 2 children buried Tokoroa .... TURNER born ...... TURNER born ...... TURNER born
	JEAN TURNER born 25 Nov 1920 died 8 Dec 2009 (89) Tauranga married JACK EVANS born 1 June 1925 died 13 July 1978 (53) both buried Tokoroa plot H67 4 children ...	PETER G.... EVANS born married DIANNE A ... ? born BARRY J.... EVANS born married RAEWYN D... ?

Stanley & Annie continued

Jean & Jack continued

RAEWYN born ...

MAUREEN DAWN EVANS
born
married
KEVIN GEORGE RYAN
born
2 children ...

- Lisa .... Ryan
  born
- Jason Patrick Ryan
  born

JUDITH EVANS
born

GRAHAM TURNER
born 6 July 1922
died 18 Feb 1943 (21)
NZ Army Accident
buried Putaruru Cemetery

MARGARET TURNER
born 13 Nov 1924
died 5 Feb 2000
married
RICHARD EVANS
born 1920
died 22 Dec 1993 (73)
bur Tokoroa RSA plot 49

3 children ... Pamela and Kenneth and Christine.

PAMELA GAYE EVANS
born
died 16 Nov 1946

KENNETH EVANS
born
married with 2 sons
....
born
= 2 sons

CHRISTINE DIANNE EVANS
born 9 Dec 1955
died 6 Oct 1980 (25)
Bur Putaruru plot 2/74

b = birth
m = married
d = death date

Original Tree gathered by Gwyeth *Woods* Broadbent 1999, plus some 2019 additions
Unless noted event happened in New Zealand

Martha and William's son Leonard's headstone at Mangere, Auckland

Martha and William's son Charles' headstone at Palmerston North, NZ

Martha and William's granddaughter Dorothy's headstone at Manukau Gardens, Auckland

Martha and William's grandson Jeffrey's headstone at Snapper Rock, Auckland

Martha and William's grandson Brian's headstone at Matamata.

Martha and William's grandson Gordon's headstone at Tokoroa.

2….. PHEBE WOODS was born in the Hobson St, Auckland home of John and Mary Ann Woods, on May 14, 1855 and was baptised June 3, 1855 by the Rev R Ward at the Primitive Methodist Church in Auckland.
Her name was spelt Phoebe on her marriage and death certificate, but on her headstone, property title, election rolls and a gifted bible, it was always spelt PHEBE.

Phebe's mother Mary Ann nee Lowe, was aged seven when she came to New Zealand on *'The Bolton'* with her mother Ann nee Griffiths and father Griffith Lowe, landing at Wellington in 1840.

1872 … PHEBE WOODS 17.5 yrs, married JOHN THOMAS aged 21, Flour Miller, on 31 December. The newspaper wrote ……..

THOMAS—WOODS—On January 1, at the Whau Presbyterian Church, by the Rev. David Hamilton, John Thomas, of the Star Mills, to Phoebe Woods, of Auckland. This being the first marriage celebrated in the Whau Presbyterian Church, the Rev D. Hamilton presented the newly-married couple with a handsomely-bound Bible, and the settlers of the district presented an album bearing an appropriate inscription, as a token of esteem and in commemoration of the first wedding celebrated in the church.

DAILY SOUTHERN CROSS 22 JAN 1873

(The newspaper recorded a wrong marriage date.)
Phebe gave birth to 15 children known as …… Mary, Arthur, Albert, Alfred, Frederick, Jessie, John, Percy, George, Syd, Elsie, Jack, Charles, Bertha and Roy. (Five of these (underlined) died very young.

The Whau Presbyterian Church opened for Easter 1860 and was renamed in 1935 ... St Trinians, Avondale. (CW)

"The THOMAS family." (1993 book by T N Price), details **John Thomas & Phebe's** family from ... 1700 to 1993 in Devon, England and in NZ complete with descendant details ... together with **Uncle George Thomas & Polly's** life and descendants.

"WILLIAM THOMAS & Family" (2001 book by T N Price) details John's brother ... **William & Eliza Thomas'** family.

DEVON: Situated in the north of Devon, England are the small villages of Berrynabour, Bittadon, West Down and the larger town of Illfracombe. All are known to feature in the Thomas family beginnings, but West Down is the village and district in which they spent the greatest amount of time ... from 1730 to 1991. The West Down village is seven miles south of Ilfracombe.

Phebe's husband John Thomas had an older brother William and younger sisters Joanna, and Elizabeth.

JOHN THOMAS senior (left) aged 25, arrived at Wellington 1854, and by 1859 had moved to Auckland, was living beside the Oakley Creek at Whau (now Waterview, Auckland) and operating The STAR FLOUR MILL ... A grain grist mill.

--oo0Ooo--

John (who married Phebe) arrived in New Zealand aged 4, with his brother William aged 6, and his parents **John Thomas and Jane nee Coates** from north Devon, England and with **Uncle George Thomas** who later married Jane Morris ... known as Polly. She was a half-sister of Phebe's.
(Polly's Lowe/Morris' life is detailed pages 123-126 in this book)

The STAR FLOUR MILL:
Father John unfortunately died 5 April 1865, aged 36.

Son John and his brother William, now 14 and 16 worked the flour mill with help from Uncle George and others. Then a fire destroyed the mill, but it was rebuilt in 1873, and sold in 1876.
Phebe and John with three children moved to the South Island where John, with his brother William, operated the

Thomas Bros Nursey at Allenton, then near the town of Ashburton, but now a suburb of the town.
Brother William later returned to the North Island, had the Terrace Nursery at Ngawapurua and in 1898 had the 88 acre Riverview Farm at New Lynn and later operated The Queen Mary Brickworks from this land on the western banks of the Whau Estuary at New Lynn, in Auckland.

John (& Phebe) opened a **Grain & Produce Store** in Havelock St, Ashburton, fed mostly from the Allenton Nursery, and where his children and grandchildren were employed for many years.
In the photo above are John & Phebe' sons Percy, Roy & Alfred.

RETIREMENT: In 1908 John and Phebe left Ashburton, leaving the business to their children, and retired to live in the Coromandel township, purchasing just out of town in Rings Road, a large home previously occupied by the Kaponga Mine Managers', Hodge and Argall.

This home still exists in 2019 and is the roadside residence of the "Coromandel Cottages" motel complex.

Phebe and John Thomas celebrated their **Golden Wedding Anniversary in 1922** at Coromandel.

Another photo of
PHEBE THOMAS nee WOODS
Taken 1900 at Christchurch, aged 45.

John died March 4, 1928 aged 76 and
Phebe died June 23, 1934 aged 79.

They are buried together in the Methodist section of the Coromandel Cemetery .....
"I sung unto the Lord a new song"

Seven sons and daughter Elsie survived them.

--oo0oo--

PHEBE and JOHN THOMAS' Family in 1907

L to R rear ... SYDNEY, PERCY, ELSIE, FREDERICK, GEORGE,
L to R front ... JACK, JESSIE, JOHN and PHEBE, ALFRED, CHARLES and young ROY in front.

The writer's grandfather was son Percy.
Daughter Elsie remained single.
Daughter Jessie died aged 28, 1907.
Son Charles died in WW1, Nov 1916.

The other 7 children all married and raised good sized families as the following brief THOMAS FAMILY TREE shows.

--oo0Ooo--

JOHN THOMAS 56

PHEBE THOMAS nee WOODS

The THOMAS FAMILY of Devon, England and New Zealand

Generation						
1st Generation	**WILLIAM THOMAS born c1700** married c1729 **HESTER ?** 2 children ...					
2nd Generation	**JOHN THOMAS born 1730** married 1755 Ilfracombe **ELIZABETH HARRIS 1730 twin** 4 children ...	ELIZABETH b 1732				
3rd Generation	**CHARLES 1766** married 1794 West Down **ANNE HEDDON 1772 - died 1799** 3 Children ...	WILLIAM 1756	ELIZABETH 1757	ANN 1774		
	Charles 2nd married 1800 **JULIAN HEDDON (sister of Anne) b1768** **8 children ...** Anne 1801, John, Robert, Charles, George, Mary, Hester, and Grace 1813					
4th Generation	**WILLIAM 1797** married 1821 Ilfracombe **ELIZABETH LEWES (Lewis)** 6 children ...	ELIZABETH 1792	JOHN b & d 1799			
5th Generation	**JOHN** **to NZ**	**WILLIAM** died young	**ELIZA** died age 18	**ELIZABETH** lived Devon	**GEORGE** **to NZ**	**RICHARD** died at 10

see following page for descendants of **John Thomas** and **George Thomas** in New Zealand.

The THOMAS FAMILY continued ... in New Zealand

5th Generation	JOHN THOMAS born 1829 Devon arrived NZ 12 Feb 1854 *"Duke of Portland"* married 1848 Ilfracombe, Devon JANE COATES born 1823 Devon 4 children ... Joanna b1852 & died in Devon Elizabeth born 1859 NZ (untraced) PLUS 2 sons		GEORGE THOMAS 1837 Devon arrived NZ 25 May 1855 *"Sea Snake"* married 1860 Auckland, NZ JANE 'POLLY' MORRIS b1842 12 children ...
6th Generation	WILLIAM 1848 m 1870 Auckland ELIZA McKAY 1850 14 children ...	JOHN 1851 m 1872 Auckland PHEBE WOODS 1855 15 children ...	SELINA ANNE 1861 m Roland Hill ELIZA JANE 1862 died 1878 at 16 years ELIZABETH 1864 m George Henry Harper MARY ANN 1866 m Thomas John Stewart (Tom) JOHN (Jack) 1867 m Isabella Mary Stewart WILLIAM 1869 m Bertha Winnifred Bicknell GEORGE 1871 m Mary Ann 'Minnie' Morgan RICHARD HENESY 1873 died 1875 at 2 years HESTER (Esther)1875 m Joseph Searle Kimber (Joe) EDWARD ERNEST 1877 m Cecila Mary Stewart ALFRED SAMUEL 1880 m Magarita (Maggie) Burke HILDA JANE 1883 m Roderick Forrester Lewis
7th Generation	ELIZABETH JANE 1871 m William Sowry ELIZA 1872 m Herbert Sowry JOHN COATES 1875 m Alice Mary James Alice died 1909 Jack remarried to Rose Myrtle Cameron WILLIAM HENRY 1877 m Mary Elizabeth Close MARY ANN 1880 m Leonard Alfred Gardner ARTHUR GORDAN m Elsie Rose Wilmhurst ALBERT PETER 1885 m Ethel Violet Ladbrook ELEANOR ROSE 1887 BEATRICE m Harry Dove ETHEL ISABEL 1888 m Ernest Lorenzo Hawken GEORGE ALEXANDER died 1891 at 6 weeks EDITH MAY 1892 m Arthur Dove ALICE AGATHA 1893 died 1894 at 10 mths WALTER JAMES 1894 died 1917 at 22 IVY GLADIS 1896 died 1896 at 2 mths	MARY JANE 1874 died 1878 at 4 years ARTHUR HAMILTON 1875 died 1875 at 3 mths ALBERT JOHN 1876 died 1876 at 9 mths ALFRED EDWARD 1877 m Sarah Ann Cates FREDERICK WILLIAM 1878 m Margaret Jane Page JESSIE ELIZABETH 1879 died 1907 at 28 years JOHN WOODS 1880 died 1881 at 5 mths WALTER PERCIVAL 1881 m Elsie Maud Stevens GEORGE BERTRAM 1882 m Susan Page JAMES SYDNEY 1884 m Muriel Miles Segers PHOEBE ELSIE 1886 died single 1971 (85) JOHN HENRY (Jack) 1887 m Edith Elizabeth Martin CHARLES ERNEST 1888 died France WW1 1916 BERTHA MAUD 1890 died 1891 at 8 mths ALEXANDER ROY 1901 m Margaret Rose Brown	

These **41** children of William, John and George produced many descendants for New Zealand.

3..... JESSIE WOODS was born on 12 November 1856, in the Hobson St, Auckland home of her parents John and Mary Ann Woods.

1876 SINGER: We know Mary Ann Woods' family attended the Edwards St Primitive Methodist Chapel and *The Daily Southern Cross* newspaper records on 29 August 1876. *"A musical entertainment was given at the Edwards St Schoolroom in aid of the trust funds of the Chapel."* There was a chorus, recitations, piano solo and solo singers. Amongst these *"'The Anchor's weighed' sung by Miss Jessie Woods."* We believe this is probably 'our' Jessie and she performed at least 10 times as Miss Woods, as recorded in this newspaper over the 3 years 1874 to 1876 when she was 18 to 20 years old. Jessie married in 1877. There were 3 other Edwards St outings and others performed for Good Templar evenings.
It is interesting to note Jessie's daughter Floss, referred to as 'Miss Flossie' (16) sang at events while living at Whitianga during 1895. The Observer paper... *"At Mrs Leonard Lee's benefit concert ... Miss Flossie Gow has a very pleasing voice, and I think as she gets older she will have a powerful one. She also has a good style of singing, excepting that she does not give her words clearly." (!)* Others who contributed songs included *Mrs Gow (Jessie) and Mr F Mickle (Meikle)."* Flossie did marry a Fred Meikle in 1898 ... and this is probably where they met?

1877 Jessie aged 21 married **NATHANIEL GOW** on 24 July at the Primitive Methodist Church, Alexandra St, Auckland.
Nathaniel became a shoemaker and a community worker.

Jessie and Nathaniel had 5 Children they called ......
Floss 1879, Ralph 1881, George 1885, Ray 1892 and John 1894.

1879 Nathaniel and Jessie's first child was born 26 Feb at Auckland. Named Jessie Florence she was known as Floss.

1881 4 June NZ Herald advises … *"at her residence, Archhill, the wife of Nathaniel Gow, a son."* This is son Ralph, and implies son Nathaniel and Jessie were living at Nathaniel seniors home.

1885 Jessie & Nathaniel's son George was born at the home of his grandmother in Lower Vincent St, Auckland, on 4th June.

1886 About 1886, Jessie & family moved to live in Whitianga.

1887 7 Dec NZ Herald. Nathaniel Gow was gazetted a member of the Licensing Committee for the Mercury Bay district.

1890 3 Jan, Auckland Star. *Ralph, aged 8, son of Nathaniel Gow, shoemaker of Mercury Bay, was thrown from a horse he was riding. Unconscious for some days after the accident, he is now progressing favourably and is expected he will be all right.*

1892 Nathaniel and Jessie's fourth child Nathaniel Ray, known as Ray, was born in Whitianga on 8 December.

1893 FIRE (Auckland Star 29 Aug) Richard Kennedy faced 2 charges … with having on 9 June wilfully set fire to the shop of Nathaniel Gow, situated in Whitianga, Mercury Bay and with having set fire to some paper and rubbish under the door of the shop. A very long report …. Basically, Nathaniel locked up his shop at 20 to 11 pm. As he was going home he remembered he had left behind a leather bag and returned for it. When about 30 yards from the door he saw someone striking a light down near the ground. A man seemed to be blowing at something.

Nathaniel got closer and recognised the man. Seems a few months earlier Nathaniel had to choose between 2 men for a ferry licence for the County Council. He gave the work to the other man. The Jury, without retiring, found the prisoner guilty. The prisoner was sentenced to 3 years penal servitude.

1893 Nathaniel Gow was elected onto the School Committee.
1899 Nathaniel re-elected to the School Committee.
1900 Election of Mercury Bay School Committee .... Messrs Gregor Alex Hodge (Chair), William Conway, Harry Sullen, William Patterson, Abraham Trelesse, Robert P Hodge and Nathaniel Gow. 26th NZH & Auckland Star 27 April 1900

1894 Jessie and Nathaniel's fifth and final child John Cameron was born 28 April 1894 and was known later as Jack.

1894 Nathaniel, now a JP presided over the Inquest of a child who accidentally drowned in Waiweka Creek. (30 Aug NZH)

1897 On 20th March an evening was held in Whitianga for the Roman Catholic Church Benefit. Although Protestant the Gow and Meikle families willingly aided this function by singing songs. Mr Meikle twice "Very Suspicious" & "When the tide comes flowing in" and Mrs Gow (Jessie)"Children's Voices"and Miss Gow (Floss) "Tit for Tat". (Programme RT)

1898 Nathaniel JP, presided over a Slander Case (19 Sept NZH)

1898 First child FLOSS married

The marriage of Miss Flossie Gow, only daughter of (Jessie &) *Mr Nathaniel Gow, JP, of Mercury Bay, to Mr Frederick William Meikle, second son of Mr William Meikle, JP, of the same place, was solemnised on a recent date* (10th) *in the little non-sectarian church.* (The Whitianga Union Church) *Long before the bride arrived with her father the church was filled to standing-room. The bride's dress was of white silk lustre, trimmed with white satin. She wore a handsome bridal veil and orange blossoms, and carried a lovely bouquet. The ceremony was performed by The Rev Harrison, Church of England minister, of Coromandel. The bridesmaids were cousin Miss Baildon of Auckland and Bertha Henderson. Mr A Meikle was Best-man. After the service the Church Committee presented the couple with a Bible. On arriving outside the church to get into their buggy they received a shower of rice from their many friends. After an excellent wedding breakfast, served at the bride's parent's residence, Mr & Mrs Meikle were driven to the wharf where they departed to honeymoon at Rotorua. The SS Murital was gaily decorated with flags.*

(abridged NZ Herald 15 Sep 1898 & The Observer 24 Sep T)

Their wedding certificate shows Floss was 19 and Frederick 28 an Engineer. Fred's father was William Meikle and mother Grace nee Hook. Floss' parents were Nathaniel Gow, a storekeeper and Jessie nee Woods. The witnesses were Arthur Edward Meikle and Julia Currie Baildon nee Gow. (cert RT)

Flossie and Frederick had 5 children …

Ross 1899, Vera 1901, Clyde 1903, Bruce 1906 and Keith 1911.

1900 *A case of immense interest was heard at Whitianga on the 18th & 19th before Mr Nathaniel Gow and Wm Meikle, JP's.* (Floss' father and her father-in-law) *The charge was one of shooting a bullock with intent to steal the carcase. Hector McKay (claimed it was his bullock), against William B Nicholson, the latter of considerable means, ex Hotel owner, a Gumtown farmer, who recently opened a butcher shop in the town. Mr David Peebles was Nicholson's butcher and he shot the beast.*

NZ Herald 24 Sept.

1901 NZH 6 July. A Statement appeared in the paper for The Big Beetle Gold Mining Co (no liability) operating at Kapowai, Thames County, offices at Whitianga. Document confirmed the shareholding in the company where 100,000 shares at one shilling were offered. 50 people took up shares including Wm Meikle 4275 and Nathaniel Gow 950. The document was signed by Frederick William Meikle, manager and Nathaniel Gow, JP.

1904 Jessie and Nathaniel Gow returned to live in Auckland.

1905 Directory: Nathaniel, bootmaker and Jessie, and son Ralph, draper, were living at Prospect T'ce, Mt Eden.

c1908 PHOTO of 4 GENERATIONS

L to R: **Jessie, Mary Ann Woods, Vera and Floss.**

Vera was born 1901 ... Mary Ann died 1918. Guess Vera 6 to 8, so, photo taken about 1908.

1908 Shortly before 5pm a horse harnessed to a spring-cart (trap) bolted down New North Road towards Kingsland, and frightened more by a passing tram, rushed onto the footpath at Violet St, knocking down a man named Nathaniel Gow, who was walking in the same direction. Dr Girdler found the man was only semi-conscious, had sustained slight injuries to the head, arm and thigh. The horse belonged to Alexander Blaney who had left it in a paddock for a few minutes to pay an account in an adjacent office. Bystanders were unable to give any reason why the horse bolted. Auckland Star 20 Feb 1908

1908 Nathaniel Gow, bootmaker, was a witness called to the Inquest of George McCausland 71, who died in hospital about 4pm, after his own horse and spring-cart, ran over him on the New North Road, Kingsland, Auckland. It seems he made a habit of sitting on the shaft and had slipped off it. Nathaniel testified he had seen deceased about half past one in Eden T'ce, about a quarter mile from the accident scene. The deceased had been sitting on the nearside shaft and appeared quite sober.

Auckland Star 8 Dec 1908

1910 Son RALPH married. (Observer 29 Oct & AStar 19 Nov)
On 19 October at St Pauls Church, Ralph, eldest son of Nathaniel Gow, Esq, of Prospect Terrace, Mt Eden... to Lillian Gertrude, only daughter of Mrs A M Robinson, Liverpool St, Auckland and eldest granddaughter of the late Chas Barnes, tailor, Auckland.
The Rev CAB Watson officiated and as the contracting parties had been members of the choir for several years they were given a choral service. The bride was given away by her brother Charles Robinson. The chief bridesmaid was Miss Rebe Houghton of Wellington and Miss Lallie Pelley (Petley) of Coromandel. Ralph's brothers George and Ray were best-man and groomsman. The groom presented his wife with a

cheque, and the bridesmaids with gold locket and chain, and an enamel and gold bracelet respectively. *(abridged T)*

1911 Directory and 1914 Directory: Living at Prospect Terrace, Mt Eden were ... Nathaniel Gow, bootmaker and Jessie Gow domestic duties; and George Gow, fitter.
Nearby in Rocklands Avenue were Ralph and wife Lillian Gow.

1912 Son GEORGE married. *On 18 Dec at St Matthews Church, Auckland, George Drummond Gow, second son of Nathaniel Gow Esq of Mt Eden, married Ada Eunice Lelilia (Letitia?) Nicholas, only daughter of Mr Alfred Nicholas of this city.* AStar 1 Feb 1913

Eunice, born 1890, was the daughter of Alfred Edwin Nicholas and Henrietta Ellen Grove, m 1888 NZ. (BDM)

George and Eunice had 1 child named **Jean Eunice Gow b1914.**

1913 Son Ray was playing hockey for Mt Eden Second Eleven. On 14 June he was on a sick-list and commentator thought his services would be greatly missed. On 16 June Mt Eden beat United 4-1 ... Ray Gow scored 1 goal, Alexander 2, and Bartlet 1.
("Hockey Hits" Observer 14th and NZ Herald 16th)

1914 Son Ralph's mother-in-law remarried *on February 28, at the Baptist Tabernacle, Auckland. Mrs A M Robinson nee Barnes, married William Perifer of Manutuke, Gisborne. The reception was held at the residence of the bride's daughter* (Mrs Gow ... Lillian) *and after the usual toasts the happy pair left on a tour of the Hot Springs district. Mrs Ralph Gow wore cream voile over silk, white and gold hat ... Mrs N Gow (Jessie) wore black toilette.* No other Gow family was mentioned in the report but many other people were mentioned.
Observer 7 March 1914

1916 WW1 Son Ralph answered a recruiting drive for men to fight overseas. The Auckland Star 16 Aug, shows Ralph Gow, clothier of Mt Albert, was accepted after all necessary testing. Ralph's enlistment paper dated 3 Oct 1916 shows he had married in 1910, worked for Hallenstein Bros, Queen St, a clothing salesman, he had volunteered for the 22nd Reinforcements and had served about 2 years prior in No 3 NZ Engineers, and had last resided at Ewington Ave off Dominion Rd, Mt Albert.

1916 Directory. Ralph, clothier asst, of Rocklands Ave, Mt Eden.

1916 WW1. sons Ray Gow, marine engineer, and John Cameron Gow, salesman, were both listed on "The 1916 1st Reserves Index" and show both of them of Prospect T'ce, Mt Eden.

1917 10 Sept Auckland Star. Isabella Gow (Nathaniel's sister) married William Baildon in 1867 and they celebrated their Golden Wedding Anniversary in 1917. (A number of the comments in this newspaper are typed throughout this history.)

1917 WW1 & 1920: George Gow enrolled for WW1 in 1917 and his address was Bishop St, Epsom. The Electoral Roll for 1920 states he was an Engineer living at Bishop St, Epsom.

1918 NATHANIEL died. The Death notice advises he died aged 62 on 22 July, dearly be-loved husband of Jessie and youngest son of Nathaniel C Gow. The funeral will leave his late residence 16 Prospect T'ce, Mt Eden ... for Waikaraka Park Cemetery. (NZH) In Jessie's obituary in 1934 it mentioned that Nathaniel, while at Whitianga, became Chairmen of the County Council and The Hospital Board in that area. (NZ Herald 27 Sep 1934)

1918 Nathaniel's Obituary *"...the family arrived in Auckland on the 'Ganges' in 1863. Mr Gow has been in bad health lately, and really never recovered from an accident that happened some years ago, when he was knocked down by a pony and trap in Eden Terrace. Deceased is survived by his widow, 4 sons and one daughter (Mrs F Meikle). Mr Ralph Gow is in camp, another (George) is in the Railway Dept, the third (Raymond) is an engineer in the employ of the Union SS Co, and the fourth (John) is farming."* (24 July Auckland Star)

1918 Jessie's mother Mary Ann Woods died 16 November.

1919 Son Ray married. Ray Nathaniel Gow married Maggie Noble Buchanan (Rita) on 24 September at St Georges Church of England, Takapuna, Auckland. Reception was held at the 'Inverness' rooms 222 Victoria St (now Lake Rd) in Takapuna. Ray and Rita had 1 child named **Margaret Jessie Gow b 1924.**

1919 Oct. Challenge to Nathaniel's Will.
An order under the Family Protection Act, providing for maintenance of a widow, was made by Mr Justice Stringer at the Supreme Court this morning. The submission of the plaintiff, Mrs Jessie Gow was that she was entitled to reasonable maintenance from the estate of her late husband, Nathaniel Gow, bootmaker of Auckland. No provision had been made for her in his Will, of which the Public Trustee was executor. It was explained that the plaintiff's five children, who were all beneficiaries of his Will, raised no objection to provision being made for their mother, who at present was dependant on them. After some discussion his honour made an order for a payment to the plaintiff of 2 pounds a week, and empowered the Public Trustee resort to the capital for the purpose and to sell the real property in the estate if and when he considered proper. Costs were allowed to both parties out of the estate. Auckland Star 11 October 1919

1919 Oct 22. SALE Advertisement by Smith & Halcombe for sale by auction of 195 Dominion Road, Auckland ... centrally situated residential property ... First Class freehold property ... 8 roomed dwelling-house with all conveniences, bathroom, hot & cold water, porcelain basin. Insured for 400 pound ... land containing 27 perches being Lot 13, DP 1927, part Allott 12 of Section 10. A splendidly situated property. NZH 22 & 29 Oct

1919 Electoral Roll: At 16 Prospect T'ce, Mt Eden were .... Nathaniel, bootmaker (?) and Jessie Gow; and Ralph, Dominion Rd clothier and Lillian Gertrude Gow married; and John Cameron Gow, rope-man. Living at Bishop St, Epsom were George Drummond Gow, engineer, & Ada Eunice Letitia Gow.

1920 Son JOHN married. John (Jack) Cameron Gow married Ruby Tillie (or Lillie) Hill on 26 February 1920 at the Congregational Church, Mt Eden, Auckland. Ruby was born in Australia on 24 September 1894.
Jack and Ruby had a child they named ... **Dulcie Gow b 1921.**
Jack lived at Ihumatao Road, Mangere, Auckland.

1923 .. 1926 .. Auckland Directories:
Jessie Gow was living at 16 Prospect T'ce, Mt Eden ... alone.

1924 Son George married. George Drummond Gow's second wife was Edna Bertha Clayton. They married 12 January 1924 at the Methodist Church in Gisborne, NZ.

George and Edna had 2 children ......
Phyllis Olga Gow b 1924 and Ailsa Winifred Gow b1934

1928 & 1935 Electoral Rolls: George Drummond Gow and Edna Bertha Gow were living at 16 Prospect T'ce, Mt Eden.

We feel around 1927-28 Jessie moved to live with son Jack.

1934 JESSIE DIED at her son Jack's residence in Montgomery Rd, Mangere, on 22 Sep 1934, (77) and survived by all her children.

Nathaniel & Jessie's headstone at Waikaraka Park Cemetery.
(Area 3, B11, Lots 18 & 18A)

Jessie's Obituary reads ...
The death at her son's residence, Mangere of Mrs Gow, removed one who was born in Auckland 77 years ago. She was the daughter of Captain John Woods, a well-known mariner in Auckland's early days, and was married at Alexandra St Church to the late Mr Gow, whose father Nathaniel C Gow arrived in Auckland in the ship 'Ganges' in 1863 and was one of the first elders of St James Presbyterian Church. She and her husband resided for about 25 years at Mercury Bay, where Mr Gow was Chairmen of the County Council and The Hospital Board. They returned to Auckland about 30 years ago and lived at Mt Eden where Mr and Mrs Gow were closely associated with the Mt Eden Congregational Church. The sons are Messrs Ralph Gow of Sydney, John Gow of Mangere, George and Ray Gow of Auckland. Mrs F Meikle of Tauranga is the only daughter. There are 8 grandchildren. The internment took place at the Waikaraka Cemetery at Onehunga, Auckland. (NZH & AStar 7 Sep 1934)

Jessie's son Ray, for many years tended his parents' gravesite and his Great Grandmother Ann's gravesite at Grafton Cemetery, Symonds St, Auckland. (CW)

The GOW FAMILY BRIEF TREE ……………………. 3 generations

JOHN GOW cb1781 married MARGARET CAMPBELL

2 children

NATHANIEL CAMERON GOW b1815
married
MARGRET DRUMMOND
9 children

MARGARET GOW died aged 2.5 years

JANET GOW
married JAMES CRAWFORD
? Children

MARGARET DRUMMOND GOW
married HENRY CURTAIN
6 children

ISABELLA GOW
married WILLIAM BAILDON
10 children

JOHN DRUMMOND GOW
married JANE K DONALDSON
5 children

JULIA GOW
married THOMAS BOOTH
5 children

NATHANIEL GOW
married JESSIE WOODS
5 children

JAMIMA GOW
remained single

MARY GOW
married JAMES A SNEDDON
2 children

Family details pages 252 - 256
This family came to NZ in 1863
and lived at first in Auckland.

MARGARET GOW b1820
married
ROBERT CLARK
4 children

JANET CLARK
married ARCHIBALD CURRIE
10 children

MARGARET CLARK
?

ISABELLA CLARK
?

NATHANIEL CLARK
died aged 3

Family details pages 257 - 258
This family lived in Scotland.

The GOW family from Scotland .... 3 generations.

1 JOHN GOW born c1781, Caithness County, Scotland.
1799 Aged 18 John enlisted in Rothesay & Caithness Fencibles, army regiments formed to defend against a possible invasion at the time of the French Revolutionary Wars.
1800 John Gow left the Fencibles and joined the 1st Battalion, 79th Regiment of Foot on 7 July. He fought in the Napoleonic wars in Egypt, become Corporal 6 Oct 1805 and Sergeant in 1807 at the Peninsular Campaign, but was not involved at the Battle of Waterloo. In 1809 his regiment was in Portugal.
1811 John was recruiting Sergeant at Aberdeen in the 79th, 2nd Battalion and 25 Feb 1813 promoted to Quartermaster Sergeant.

1812 John Gow married MARGARET CAMPBELL August 3.
We have found John and Margaret Gow, had two children ....
1815 Son ***Nathaniel Cameron Gow*** was born in Edinburgh and daughter ***Margaret Gow*** born in **1820** at Mauritius.

Son Nathaniel's 1815 baptism record reads ... ***John Gow, Sergeant in the 79th Regiment in Canongate and Margaret Campbell his spouse, had a son born 7 March 1815 and baptised 19th March at Canongate Church,* (photo) *they named Nathaniel Cameron Gow.*** *The 2 witnesses were local grocers.*

The **79th Regiment of Foot, 2nd Battalion** was formed on 3 April 1805 at Stirling and in June moved to Dundee. It was also known as **The Cameron Highlanders.** John must have had great respect for his Army group and of its commander Lt Col Nathaniel Cameron, as he gave those names to his son.

The 2nd Battalion of the 79th Regiment (infantry) supplied drafts to the 1st Battalion and did not go abroad.

Uniform of the 79th Regiment of Foot in 1815

British Army Muster (Pay List) Book 1812-1817
Quarter Master Sergeant John Gow of the 79th Regiment of Foot, 2nd Battalion, received 2 shillings and sixpence per day, for 31 days, 25 May to 26 June 1815, amount issued 3 pounds 17s & 6d. Total should be 7 pounds 17s & 6d. Maybe there were deductions for food, tax, etc.

1815 After receiving his son in March, John seems to have been transferred to Dundee where a document shows .....
John Gow 79th Regiment of Foot, 2nd Battalion, started a Muster on 24 May 1815 which ceased 4 January 1816.
Another document states that the 2nd Battalion was disbanded at Dundee on 25 December 1815. (Some Christmas present !)

1816 John Gow now joined the **82nd Regiment of Foot** and served throughout Ireland until the Regiment embarked for Mauritius Island in the east African sea, in Jan 1819. They birthed at Port Louis on 23 June 1819.

1820 Daughter Margaret was baptised at Mahebourg, Mauritius on 7 April 1820. (She stated she was born at "East Indies/British subject" in future Scotland censuses ... but this not accurate.)

1822 John Gow died at Mauritius 12 August 1822.

We believe it was a health problem that caused John's death, as the 'History of the 82nd Regiment' records ... *"Nothing worthy occurred 1820,1821,1822."* After John's death, wife Margaret and her 2 children returned to Scotland and the town of Paisley.

--oo0Ooo—

2 NATHANIEL CAMERON GOW, born 1815 in Edinburgh, married 2 Nov 1839 at Paisley Low Church of Scotland, to MARGRET DRUMMOND born 24 March 1819, and (she died 15 Nov 1906 in NZ) Nathaniel became a shoe maker. Shoe makers tended to move into a town, provide everyone with shoes or boots, then moved to the next closest town to make as many boots and shoes they needed, then move on again.

Nathaniel C Gow and Margret had 9 children ...

MARGARET born 10 Mar 1840 but died 22 Oct 1842, aged 2 ½.

JANET born 26 June 1842, married 16 Feb 1865 Auckland, NZ to James Crawford.

MARGARET DRUMMOND born 1844 – died 6 Sep 1934, married 27 Aug 1867 NZ, Henry Curtain (born 1841 London – died 25 Jan 1922 Auckland) They had 6 children ... James 1868, Nathaniel Gow born 1873, Julia 1875 – 1956, married 1901 Alfred Augustus Creamer 1875-1950, William Drummond born 1878, Arthur 1880 – 1951, married 1920 Clara Edith Woolley, Jemima Caroline born 1886 married 1909 George Moore.

Margaret and Henry are buried Waikumete Cemetery. Auckland

ISABELLA born 15 Nov 1846, died NZ 19 April 1933, married 1867 William Baildon born 1837 Huddersfield, England and died 1917 NZ. They had 10 children ... George 1868 – 1946, married 1893 Maggie (Peggy) Kerr died 25 Jul 1925, Caroline (Carrie) 1870 – 1940, married 1892 John Farrell 1868-1938, John William 1873 – 1963, married 1900 Elizabeth (Lizzie) Shelford 1877 - 1901,

Joseph 1875 – 1953, married 1902 Irene Ferguson 1880 - 1968, Julia Currie born 1878 married 1915 Lawson Benson, Nathaniel Cameron Gow 1880 – 1947, married 1904 Elizabeth Edgar Ellis d 1949, William Frederick 1883-1885 (2), William born 1885 killed in France 1918, Frederick Joseph 1888 – 1968, married 1919 Gladys May Townsend 1895 - 1990, Harold Leslie 1892 – 1972, married 1922 Elsie Linda Morrison born 1901.
(ex NZ BDM and Isabella's Obit in Auckland Star 12 Apr 1933)
JOHN DRUMMOND born 17 June 1850, died 26 April 1922, married 11 Oct 1882, Jane Kennedy Donaldson born 11 Aug 1884 – died 12 Oct 1945. They had 5 children ... John Alexander 1884-1960, married 1914 Beryl McAllister Williamson 1894 - 1979, Nathaniel Cameron 1885 – 1957, married 1915 Violet Blanche Stuart Blair, Margaret Donaldson 1888 – 1973, married 1917 William Edward Robinson 1881 - 1967, Isabella Baildon 1888 - 1963, Mary Drummond 1894 - 1971.
John and Jane are buried at Waikumete Cemetery, Auckland.
JULIA CURRIE born 2 Jan 1853, died 5 Nov 1896, married 1880 Thomas Booth in NZ. Julia and Thomas had 5 children ... Albert Sutcliffe 1884 – 1884, Emma 1887, William Cameron 1888, Margaret Drummond 1894- 1894, Arthur 1896.
NATHANIEL 1855 (our 3rd generation) married **Jessie Woods.**
JAMIMA born 26 Feb 1858. NZ Electoral Roll 1919 described her as 'Spinster'. Jamima Gow died 7 Aug 1922 in NZ.
MARY born 22 June 1861 – died 5 Mar 1890 (29) Auckland, married 6 Dec 1886, James Alexander Sneddon born 2 Jan 1864 died 14 May 1939, Auckland = 2 children. James married 1904 Isabella Elizabeth Clark. They had 1 child.

All nine of Nathaniel C and Margret Gow's children were born in Scotland.

The first 4 children were born at Paisley, then 2 born at Barrhead and the last 3 born at Neilston, all towns close to each other in the Parish of Renfrewshire, about 10 miles south west of Glasgow City, Scotland.

Scotland's 3 censuses in 1841, 1851, 1861 provide the names of and the location born for these children of Nathaniel CG and Margret. In 1841 the family lived at 30 Storie St, Paisley, 1851 at Arthurlie House, Barrhead and 1861 at Main St, Neilston.

In 1861 Nathaniel, shoe-maker, is noted as employing 3 men.

(During these censuses Nathaniel C Gow was aged 26, 36, 46. Some details are from other Genealogy trees and Mrs William Baildon's Golden Wedding news item ... 9 Sept 1917 A Star.)

1863 The **family travelled on the *Ganges* to New Zealand.** They first farmed at Awhitu Peninsular on Auckland's west coast, then in 1869 moved to 12 Home St, Arch Hill, Auckland town.

1869 When the St James Presbyterian Church, Auckland minister was Rev R F Macnichol, his Elders were Nathaniel C Gow and Thomas Richardson.

1876 Auckland Directory shows Nathaniel C Gow at Newton West, a Bootmaker of Victoria St, Auckland.

1877 When St James Church held its Annual Meeting 100 people attended, including Nathaniel C Gow.

1887 Nathaniel C died *17 Nov at his residence in Archhill aged 72, an Elder at St James and left a large family and 30 grand-children. Respected by a large circle of friends.* (Auckland Star. T)

1906 Nathaniel Cameron's wife Margret died 15 Nov aged 87.

They were buried together at Waikumete Cemetery, in the Presbyterian section A part 3, plot 7, at a 1 pound fee.

--oo0Ooo—

3 NATHANIEL GOW born 1855, married on 24 July 1877 in Auckland to **JESSIE WOODS**.

Pages 240 to 250 record what we know of their life.

They spent about 18 years in the Whitianga area and when they left Nathaniel (who spoke Maori fluently) was presented with this Maori carved CANOE BAILER for services to various Coromandel Maori groups. (MM)

--oo0oo—

<u>**Nathaniel Cameron Gow had a sister MARGARET GOW.**</u>

Margaret was born on Mauritius Island in 1820 and returned to Scotland, where aged 26 she married ROBERT CLARK.

Robert was born 1808 at Kirkintilloch, Dumbartonshire, Scotland and died in 1858.

Margaret and Robert Clark had 4 children .....
JANET born 1844 at Campress, Stirlingshire, Scotland, married 15 June 1866, Archibald Currie and had 10 children.
In the 1891 census her mother Margaret Gow aged 70 was living with them at Dumbarton town. Janet died 21 Sep 1899 at Netherbank, Dumbarton. Archibald was a carrier, born 13 Sept 1843 at Killintilloch and died 10 Dec 1919 Dumbarton.
MARGARET was born 1846 at Kirkintilloch.
ISABELLA was born 1849 at Kirkintilloch.
NATHANIEL b 15 Oct 1856, died aged 3+ on 7 Feb 1860 at K.

In 1858 Margaret (born 1820) was aged 38 with four children, when her husband Robert died.
In 1866 her daughter Janet married Archibald Currie.
In 1870, 22 August, Margaret married again, to JOHN MOTHERWELL (1810-1882) a widower, at Cadder-west, Lanarkshire, Scotland.
The 1871 census shows Margaret and John living with two of his children. Her 4 children had left home.
In 1881 Margaret 62, John Motherwell 71, living on their own at 26 Cumberland Lane, The Gorbals, Glasgow.
In 1882 husband John Motherwell died.
In 1891 Margaret 70 living with daughter Janet Currie.
In 1901 maybe inmate Maryfield Poor House, Dundee.
In 1903, Margaret died 17th January, at the Dumbarton Combination Poorhouse. The certificate shows son-in-law Archibald Currie informed the authorities. (T)

--oo0Ooo--

Jessie's Great Granddaughter-in-law Peggy Meikle has compiled an impressive historical document on her **Gow, Richardson, Meikle and Woods** families, which at this time is unpublished.

Most of these files were donated to the Mercury Bay Museum.

We are grateful of the assistance and sharing of knowledge from the family for this record, especially the John Gow's naval records. T. (PM, MM)

--oo0Ooo—

photo L to R: **IVY WOODS, JESSIE (Gow), JANE (Hazlett) and MARY ANN WOODS** taken before 1918, at daughter Jane's Pah Rd, Auckland residence. (Mother, 2 daughters and a granddaughter)

The WHITIANGA residence of Floss and Fred Meikle.

Page 260... The Whitianga Residence photo, is a postcard from Floss & Fred to her sister Martha, care of their mother Mary Ann Woods, at Canada St, Auckland, saying how sorry they were they could not get down to meet up with the visiting Martha.

(Probably taken about 1907 ... 3 children visible with Floss)

Floss and Fred Electoral Rolls

1914 Floss and Fred (engineer) at Whitianga.

1938 Floss & Fred at Devonport Rd, Tauranga.

1947 Fred died 29 April at the Choral Hall, Airedale St, Auckland. He lived then at 1 Stirling St, Remuera. His death certificate also refers to him as *"a retired Theatre Proprietor aged 76, born at Whitianga, NZ and his parents were William Meikle and Grace nee Hook. He was buried at Waikaraka Park Cemetery in Presbyterian section. His wife J F M, (Floss) a widow was age 66 and all five of their children were still alive"*.

The Choral Hall still exists in 2019 at 5-7 Symonds St, Auckland and now part of Auckland University. (T)

1949 Rolls. Floss – widow, 37 Shore Rd, Remuera, Auckland.

1958 Floss died 23 May at Nelson, NZ. (78)

--oo0Ooo--

JESSIE WOODS married NATHANIEL GOW .... FAMILY TREE
they had 5 children ... known as Flossie, Ralph, George, Ray and Jack

JESSIE FLORENCE GOW
b 26 Feb 1879
Auckland, NZ (FLOSS)
d 23 May 1958 Nelson
m 10 Sep 1898 Whitianga
FREDERICK WILLIAM MEIKLE
b 5 Sep 1870 Whitianga
d 29 April 1947 Auckland
bu Waikaraka, Auckland

5 children .... Ross, Vera, Clyde, Bruce, Keith

ROSS NATHANIEL MEIKLE
born 2 June 1899
died 2 March 1970
bur Waikumete, Auckland
married 10 Sep 1930
AMY ELLEN DAWICK
born 17 July 1910
died 24 Nov 1982
no issue

VERA FLORENCE MEIKLE
born 7 May 1901
died 25 Feb 1972
married 1926
DENIS AQUILA IVORY
born 9 June 1892
died 20 March 1960
bur Tauranga, NZ

2 children ...
Suzanne and Michael

SUZANNE MARY IVORY
born 29 March 1928
died 18 Dec 1995
married 1948
BERNARD WILLIAM DONOVAN
born 15 Sept 1921
died 16 Aug 2000

4 children ...
Patricia, Mary, Clare & Michal

PATRICIA ANNE DONOVAN
b 19 Aug 1949 NZ (twin)
m 24 June 1972 Canada
CHRISTOPHER JOHN TRUMBULL
b 19 Nov 1945 Australia

= 5 children ...
Michael, David, Richard, Antonia and Nicholas.

Michael Donovan Trumbull
b 22 April 1977 Australia
m 3 Oct 2009 Vanuatu
Dawn Marquette Tingwell
nee Mangum
= 1 child ...
Cooper Clifton Trumbull
b 8 April 2009 Australia

David Anthony Trumbull
b 10 Jan 1979 Australia
m 12 Nov 2005 Australia
Kate Darling Horrocks
b 9 May 1979 Australia
= 2 children ...
Finn Felix Trumbull
b 9 Aug 2008 Hong Kong
Leo Samuel Trumbull
b 13 Nov 2010 Australia

Richard Aquila Trumbull
b 2 Feb 1980 Australia

Antonia Nancy Trumbull
b 6 April 1982 Australia

Nicholas John Trumbull
b 24 Feb 1986 Australia
m 27 Jan 2018 Australia
Annika Jean Martz
b 4 Nov 1985 Australia
= 2 children ...

Flossie & Frederick cont..	Vera & Denis continue	Suzanne & Bernard continue	Nicholas and Annika = 2 children ... *Joshua David Trumbull* *b 22 Jan 2017 Australia* *Charlie James Trumbull* *b 29 Nov 2018 Australia*
			MARY MEIKLE DONOVAN b 19 Aug 1949 NZ (twin) m 22 June 1968 NZ BRUCE WILLIAM BOWLER b 16 July 1946 NZ = 2 children ... Liesel and Rebekah
			Liesel Mary Bowler b 20 Dec 1968 NZ m 10 Nov 2001 Australia Glenn Rowan Wightwick b 9 June 1966 Australia = 3 children ... *Thomas Ian Wightwick* *b 14 April 2003 USA* *Katherine Mary Wightwick* *b 16 Feb 2005 USA* *Samantha Lyn Wightwick* *b 10 Dec 2007 Australia*
			Rebekah Kathleen Bowler b 9 Sept 1970 NZ m 26 Aug 1995 Australia Steven Russell Gillibrand b 16 Nov 1966 England = 2 children ... *Jessica Suzanne Gillibrand* *b 9 Oct 2000 Australia* *Georgia Mary Gillibrand* *b 8 Oct 2002 Australia*
			MARY 2nd marriage ... 27 Sept 1986 Australia PETER HOWARD ADELSTEIN b 8 Oct 1946 Australia = 2 children ... Juliet Ivory Adelstein b 3 Sept 1987 Australia Nadia Anne Adelstein b 20 Dec 1989 Australia
			MARY 3rd marriage ... m 4 June 2004 Fiji GRAEME FOGELBERG b 10 Dec 1939 NZ

Flossie & Frederick cont.. | Vera & Denis continue | Suzanne & Bernard continue

CLARE DONOVAN
b 13 April 1952
m 8 Jan 1972 NZ
ALEXANDER KIRK
b 22 May 1950 Scotland
= 3 children ...
Gretchen, Samuel & Oliver

Gretchen Kirk
b 18 Aug 1977 NZ
m 11 Aug 2007 Port Douglas
Gerald Mark Gordon Joe
b 13 Feb 1978 NZ
= 2 children ...
Lachlan Gordon Joe
b 1 Feb 2009 NZ

Ethan Alexander Joe
b 16 Sept 2010 NZ

Samuel Alexander Kirk
b 25 May 1979 NZ
partner
Helen Rachel Lamb
b 14 July 1972 NZ

Rachel's son ... Laurence
John Welshman Duckham
b 19 Feb 2006

Oliver Kirk
b 12 July 1981 NZ
m 11 Nov 2016 USA
Reanna Jayne McNeilage
b 7 Jan 1982 NZ
= 4 children ...
Lennox Kingston Kirk
b 3 Nov 2009 NZ

Loukas Bella Kirk
b 9 Aug 2013 NZ

Freja Sabine Kirk
b 31 Dec 2015 NZ

Rafton Kohl Kirk
b 3 May 2018 NZ

MICHAL JOSEPHINE
DONOVAN
b 1 Jan 1955
m 24 Feb 1979
THOMAS HUGH PIERARD
b 10 July 1958

= 4 children ....
Alexandra, Rachel,
Miriam and Francis

see next page ....

Flossie & Frederick cont..	Vera & Denis continue	Suzanne & Bernard continue	Michal & Thomas continue
			Alexandra Ivory Pierard b 22 Aug 1980 partner James Marks b 21 Aug 1978 = 2 children ... *Rupert Pascoe Marks* *b 29 April 2011* *Theodore Francis Pierard Marks b 16 April 2014*
			Rachel Clare Pierard b 10 April 1983 partner Mohammad Sadra Saffari b 20 Aug 1981 Iran = 2 children ... *Ranui Hafez Pierard Saffari* *b 16 March 2015 NZ* *Elia Matin Saffari* *b 13 Nov 2017 NZ*
			Miriam Michal Pierard b 21 June 1986
			Francis Louis Thomas Pierard b 16 May 1990
			MICHAL'S 2nd marriage m 27 July 1997 NZ DENNIS JOHN HORTON b 23 Aug 1943 NZ
		Suzanne secondly married 21 Oct 1960 WILLIAM GEORGE BIRNIE born 14 Dec 1916 at Ashburton NZ died 1 May 1994 at Tauranga NZ = 1 child .. Rachel	RACHEL IVORY BIRNIE b 10 Aug 1962 m 14 Nov 1987 PETER GERARD TRANTER b 1 April 1951 = 3 children ... Stephanie, Jessica, William
			Stephanie Michal Tranter b 22 Aug 1990 m 16 Jan 2015 Marcus Eugene Cheval b 24 July 1990 England = 2 children ... *Levi Eugene Cheval* *b 6 Aug 2016* *Brodie Peter Steven Cheval* *b 23 May 2019*
			Jessica Rachel Suzanne Tranter b 27 Oct 1993
			William next page .....

Flossie & Frederick cont..	Vera & Denis continue	Suzanne & William continue	Rachel & Peter continue
			William Peter Lemonnier Tranter b 31 Dec 1998
		MICHAEL DENIS IVORY born 18 Jan 1931 NZ	
	CLYDE WILLIAM MEIKLE born 7 Aug 1903 died 18 June 1976 m 20 April 1935 EDNA ROSE MURRAY born 6 April 1912 to William Murray who married 1908, NZ, Rose Anna Smelt England. Edna died 12 April 1944 | CLYDE secondly married in 1947 IRIS ZENA DARE CRAIG born 1 Feb 1910 died 17 Nov 1976	MURRAY CLYDE MEIKLE b 18 Sept 1938 NZ m 1 Sep 1967 London HARRIET CHAPMAN -ANDREWS born 12 Sept 1939 Devon, England 2 children ...	KATHERINE JANE MEIKLE b 8 Dec 1968 Seattle, USA married 1996, London DANIEL TARRANT-WILLIS b = a daughter SADIE ROSE TARRANT-WILLIS born 12 Dec 2003, London | Katherine secondly m 3 May 2012, London GILES ASTON ALASTAIR MURRAY SCOTT MEIKLE born 24 May 1973 Cambridge, England.
	BRUCE GOW MEIKLE born 15 Nov 1906 NZ died 15 Aug 1975 married 21 March 1942 PEGGY DORIS RICHARDSON b 10 July 1921 England 4 children ... Pauline & Judith, Jennifer, Shirley	PAULINE MARGARET MEIKLE born 6 April 1943 died 17 March 1993 m 21 OCT 1978 IAN ROBERT FRANKLIN born 6 Sept 1944 = 2 children ...	ANNETTE MARGARET LILIAN FRANKLIN b 13 Aug 1981 JOHN ROBERT BRUCE FRANKLIN b 1 Aug 1983
		JUDITH DIANE MEIKLE born 9 Nov 1945	
		JENNIFER KATHLEEN MEIKLE born 26 Sept 1947 married 28 Dec 1974 DONAL BURNETT LEADBEATER born 29 May 1939 died 12 June 1989 2 children ... | Jennifer secondly married 2007/8 SELWYN CALLIS b	TONI KATHLEEN LEADBEATER b 12 March 1977 KIM SARA LEADBEATER b 12 Aug 1982 m 2007/8 PAUL ROBERTSON b 2 children .... Violet Robertson b 28 Nov 2011 Hugo Robertson b 12 July 2014

Flossie & Frederick cont..	Bruce & Peggy continue	SHIRLEY CHRISTINE MEIKLE born 13 Oct 1954 married 24 Oct 1976 LESLIE MAKEPEACE MEGGET (Les) born 31 July 1946 2 children ... Katrina & Bruce	KATRINA JOY MEGGET b 12 March 1977 BRUCE LESLIE MEGGET b 12 Aug 1982 m 25 Jan 2009 AIMEE SIM b 2 children ... SOPHIE ELIZABETH MEGGET b 15 Oct 2011 OLIVER JAMES DANIEL MEGGET b 5 Feb 2014
Jessie (Floss) Gow a widow aged 68 second married FRED ARTHUR THOMPSON retired clergyman, a widower of Tauranga	KEITH FREDERICK HOOK MEIKLE born 22 Aug 1911 died 18 Feb 1982 married 13 Sept 1939 NZ KATHLEEN LILIAN MARY SNELL born 7 Apr 1908 died		
RALPH JOHN GOW born 1 June 1881 died 12 April 1971 Australia married 19 Oct 1910 LILLIAN GERTRUDE ROBINSON born Australia died 1977 Australia			
GEORGE DRUMMOND GOW born 4 June 1885 died 29 April 1973 married 1912 ADA EUNICE LELILIA NICHOLAS born July 1890 died 1 child ... Jean	JEAN EUNICE GOW born 25 Aug 1914 died Feb 2003 married 1935 NZ FREDERICK BENJAMIN STONEX born 4 Sept 1908 died 14 May 1980 NZ = 2 children ... Noeline & Diane	NOELINE STONEX born died married .... DE LIEV born died DIANE STONEX born	
George 2nd married on 12 January 1924 EDNA BERTHA CLAYTON born 7 Nov 1902 died 26 Nov 1994 2 children ... Phyllis and Ailsa	PHYLLIS OLGA GOW born 30 July 1924 died 5 Oct 1999 Australia married 20 Jan 1945 WESLEY SPENCER GILFOYLE born 21 May 1920 died 7 May 1969	BARBARA JANET GILFOYLE born 7 May 1946 m 10 Nov 1966 NZ WILLIAM DAVID JAMES DOWN born = 4 children ...	JAMES ROBERT BRUCE DOWN b 18 March 1969 JUSTINE BARBARA DOWN b 26 May 1971 m 4 Aug 1994 OLIVER THOMAS JACK born

George & Edna continue	Phyllis & Wesley had 7 children ... Barbara, Wayne, Christopher, Mark, Shelley, Bryn and Finlay	Barbara & William 4 children ... James, Justine, Sara and Gareth	SARA MELISSA DOWN b 6 March 1973 GARETH EDWARD DOWN b 29 Nov 1976
		WAYNE STEVEN GILFOYLE born 27 May 1947 married 26 July 1969 ANNE FRANCES HARRIS b 21 Jan 1944 in Australia 5 children born NZ	MICHELLE LOUISE GILFOYLE b 20 Nov 1971 KATHERINE ANNE GILFOYLE b 26 July 1973 WESLEY STEVEN GILFOYLE b 16 April 1975 ANDREW SPENCER GILFOYLE b 28 April 1979 NICOLAS JOHN GILFOYLE b 12 March 1981
		CHRISTOPHER DRUMMOND GILFOYLE born 28 June 1949 m 28 July 1972 NZ PAMELA JEAN RIDDELL born 25 Dec 1952 = 2 children ...	SELINA ROCHELLE GILFOYLE b 6 Nov 1973 HAYLEY PAMELA GILFOYLE b 14 July 1976
		MARK JOHN GILFOYLE born 29 May 1952 died m 22 Feb 1980, NZ BARBARA VAN LOON b24 Jan 1957 Holland = 2 children ...	LUKE ZANE GILFOYLE b 12 July 1984 ASHLEY MARK GILFOYLE b 20 Sept 1986
		SHELLEY BRIAR GILFOYLE born 6 Sept 1958 m16 Aug 1980 Canada ROBERT JAMES MARKS b 5 June 1957 Canada = 3 children born in Canada	KELSEY BRIAR MARKS b 20 Dec 1985 TYLER JAMES MARKS b 12 March 1988 TANNER SPENCER MARKS b 10 Jan 1991
		BRYN ANDREW GILFOYLE born 15 July 1960 married 13 April 1995 NZ FRITHA TAGG born	
		Finlay next page	

George & Edna continue

Phylis & Wesley cont...

FINLAY DUNCAN GILFOYLE
born 6 Feb 1964 NZ
married 10 Feb 1990 Australia
NICOLA JENE ROLLS
born 12 Aug 1967 NZ
1 child ...

CAITLAND JENE GILFOYLE
b 23 Nov 1994 Australia

AILSA WINIFRED GOW
born 8 Oct 1934
died 2 March 2001 NZ
married 26 Nov 1955
BRIAN GEORGE KING
born 27 March 1931
died 10 June 1993
= 3 children ...
Warren, Murray & Garry

WARREN GEORGE KING
born 14 Oct 1957
married 1 Dec 1978
MARGARET VIVIAN McKENZIE
born
= 2 children ...

EMMA MARGARET KING
b 15 April 1980 Australia

DANIEL GEORGE KING
b 13 Feb 1982 Australia

MURRAY CLIVE KING
born 8 Sept 1959
died 30 June 1974 (14) New Plymouth

GARY EDWARD KING
born 6 Sept 1962
married 17 Nov 1984
LORAYNE SUE WILSON
born
= 2 children ...

RHIANON EVE KING
b 29 Aug 1978

LORELIE CAITLYN KING
b 4 June 1990

NATHANIEL RAY GOW
born 8 Dec 1892
died 3 Dec 1974
married 24 Sept 1919
MAGGIE NOBLE BUCHANAN
born 8 Feb 1893
died 18 Nov 1961
1 child ...

MARGARET JESSIE GOW
born 26 July 1924
died 24 May 2012 (87)
bur Waikaraka Cemetery, Auckland

JOHN (Jack) CAMERON GOW b 28 April 1894
died 10 March 1981
married 26 Feb 1920
RUBY TILLIE HILL (Rita)
b 24 Sept 1894 Australia
died 13 July 1989 NZ
1 child ... Dulcie

DULCIE JOAN GOW
born 29 April 1921
died 2006
married 25 Jan 1947
ROSS CLENDON HOWARD
born 4 July 1923
died 2005

3 children ... Christine, Rosalind and Tim

CHRISTINE CLENDON HOWARD
born Feb 1948
lived Queensland in 1977
married Feb 1970 NZ
GIOVANNI BRUNO TONETTO
born 1934 Italy

= 2 children ...

MICHAEL ANTONY TONETTO
b 2 Nov 1972

DANIELLA CHRISTINE TONETTO
b

ROSALIND ANNE HOWARD
born

Tim next page ....

Jack & Rita continue	Dulcie & Ross continue		
		GRAEME TIMOTHY HOWARD (Tim) born 2 Nov 1958 married SHIRLEY born 2 children	Gemma Howard b c 1994 son .... Howard b

b = birth
m = marriage
d = died

Original Tree by Peggy D Meikle 1998, with some additions
Unless noted, event happened in NZ.

4….. GEORGE WOODS the 4th child for John and Mary Ann Woods was probably born in the Chapel St house, Auckland, and arrived on 9 April 1859.

1859 His mother was heavily pregnant with him when she and John took out the Lease on the Chapel St property signed 3 March 1859. We believe, Mary Ann, John and George's 3 older sisters would have moved in straight away.

The family were to live in this home for many years. George was baptised by Rev J Long at Primitive Methodist Church, Auckland on 2 June 1959.

George remained single, and became a shoemaker.

Chapel St was renamed Lower Vincent St in 1882/3.

1884 George died at the Lower Vincent St home of his parents, 14 June 1884, aged 25 of 'Bright's Disease'.

George was buried in the plot next to his father's grave at the Symonds Street Grafton Cemetery, Auckland.

--oo00oo--

5..... JOHN WOODS (junior) was born at the Chapel St home on 29 December 1861 in Auckland.

In 1884 John reported the death of brother George and noted his own address as Lower Vincent St, Auckland.

The Electoral Roll 1887 lists **John Woods junior, Chapel St, Bootmaker,** along with Robert Woods, Bootmaker.

John married **SUSANNAH KNEEBONE** (Susie) on 11 June 1889 at Primitive Methodist Church, Auckland.

Photo of SUSANNAH
Susie was born 22 October 1862 at sea on board the *Ida Zeigler*, en-route to NZ.

From 1895 the family lived at 8 Alderley Rd, Mt Eden, while operating a shoe-makers business at Dominion Road, Auckland. (RW)

John and Susannah had two children they named **GEORGE ALBERT** born 5 May 1890 and **IVY MAY** born 10 July 1891.

1895 Deed 8A/623 shows John Woods had the property 8 Alderley Road, Mt Eden, transferred into his name on 30 October 1895. When John died in 1934 the property changed from deed R58-6710 to CT 593/296.

1910 John's Uncle William (Lowe) Morris died and his Will required John Woods junior and John Haslett to be Executors.

1913 SUSANNAH died 24 March 1913 aged 50 and was buried at Waikaraka Park Cemetery, Auckland.

Sometime after Susannah's death husband John and son George went to live with daughter Ivy at Eltham. (RW)

1934 JOHN WOODS Died: John Woods died aged 73 on 6 July 1934 at the residence of his son-in-law Charlie Morrison at Eltham, Taranaki and was buried at Waikaraka Cemetery, with Susie. Area 1 Block K plot 31+31B:

--oo00oo—

Son GEORGE never married and later died at Eltham. (RW)

PHOTOS: Rifleman George in full WW1 uniform 1917, 'J' Company, Army number 40407. (Hardware Assistant)
And .... George in later life at Eltham.

1951 George received half the residue estate from his Aunt Jane Haslett.

1960 George Albert Woods, retired salesman, died 23 May 1960 at the home of his sister Ivy Morrison in Eltham, NZ.

George signed his Will 11 October 1957 and his trustees (Ivy & Charlie) were *"to convert his property to money"* and his residue estate (valued under 2500 pounds) bequeathed to Ivy *"for her own use and benefit absolutely.*

Daughter IVY MAY WOODS was engaged to a son of her Aunty Phebe ... Charles Earnest Thomas, when sent to fight in WW1. Charles was killed in France aged 27, on 12 Nov 1916.

above. JOHN WOODS with CHARLES THOMAS and IVY, on front steps of John Woods' home at 8 Alderley Rd, Mt Eden. ←

1929 On 18 April 1929 Ivy married ALEXANDER CHARLES MORRISON (Charlie) a farmer of Eltham, Taranaki, NZ at the Knox Presbyterian Church at Eltham. There were no children.

Daughter IVY ←

CHARLIE MORRISON at Pah Rd, Epsom. →

1951 Ivy received half the residue estate of Aunt Jane Haslett.

1973 Charlie died 4 Aug 1973 and left all his estate to wife Ivy.

1978 Ivy died 15 August 1978, a resident of Eltham but died at Stratford, Taranaki. Ivy signed her Will on 20 November 1964. The Guardian Trust was instructed to divide her residue estate equally between 7 different Church groups and Charities, as originally nominated by Charlie in his Will if Ivy predeceased him. There were no bequeaths to any individual person. (CW)

Charlie and Ivy were buried together at the Eltham Cemetery, plot 19 block 3.

--oo0Ooo—

The KNEEBONE FAMILY:

Susie, born 1862, was the daughter of CALEB KNEEBONE (12 Feb 1838 – 8 Feb 1907) & HANNAH TRUSCOTT (16 Nov 1836 – 11 April 1926)
Both born in Cornwall, England.

Susie had 8 siblings … Edith 1861, Edward 1865, Annie 1867, Jane 1869, William 1871, Laura 1873, Mary 1875 and Frances 1877.

Waikaraka Park Cemetery headstone for John and Susie Woods (CW)

Eltham Cemetery headstone for Caleb & Hannah Kneebone.

6..... JANE WOODS was born in the Chapel St home in Auckland City on 10 October 1863.

1883 Jane married JOHN HASLETT on 24 January 1883 at the home of Nathaniel Gow, Arch Hill, Auckland by a Primitive Methodist Minister. John and Jane had no children.

John was born in 1855 at Drumory, near Belfast in Ireland, a son of John Haslett, a farmer and Mary Ann McLanaghan. John Haslett senior died 14 August 1896 aged 77 and is buried at Purewa Cemetery, Auckland, with his other son James Hopner Haslett who died 5 January 1894 aged 37.

Jane and John Haslett's 63 Pah Road, Mt Roskill, home.

A number of photos were taken on these front steps ... including a couple showing sisters Jessie and Jane, mother Mary Ann and niece Ivy Woods and her future husband Charlie Morrison.

"Jane was known as Aunty Jinnie and her husband was a carrier and became a wealthy man" advised Ronald Woods. *"They lived in a 'swish' house in Empire Road, Epsom."* (RW)

Jane & John Haslett's home at 26 EMPIRE Rd, EPSOM. (CW)

1910 Jane's Uncle William (Lowe) Morris died in 1910 and his Will required John Haslett and her brother John Woods to be Executors.

1918 Jane's mother Mary Ann Woods spent her final years living at the Pah Road home and died in 1918. Sometime after wards Jane and John Haslett moved to Empire Road, Epsom.

1899 John Haslett is mentioned as helping Jane's Uncle William (Lowe) Morris, find a new home in Canada St, in March 1899.

1928 **John Haslett died** on 8 March 1928.

The Auckland Star of the same date wrote …

DEATH OF OLD BOWLER.
Mr. John Haslett, of Epsom, who died at the annual reunion of veteran bowlers on the Auckland green yesterday.

"The annual veterans' bowling tournament, which was taking place at the Auckland Green this morning, came to a tragic termination after barely an hour's play,

Mr John Haslett, of Empire Road, Epsom, and the doyen of the Carlton Bowling Club, dying suddenly as result of a heart attack.

Mr Haslett, who was 77 years of age, had been under medical attention for heart weakness for a considerable time, but his death came as a tragic shock to his many friends who were on the green.

John Haslett was born in the neighbourhood of Belfast, Northern Ireland and came to NZ in 1862. He was a carrier in Auckland, a well- known and greatly respected person, and was Chairman of the Mt Roskill Road Board for a lengthy period until he retired 5 years ago.

The NZ Herald, the next morning displayed a photo of John in his bowling hat. They also noted that John arrived in New Zealand in 1862 on the *"Indian Empress"*, and he was one of the

survivors of the old Victoria Rifles. The Death Notice of burial arrangements confirmed John lived at 26 Empire Road.
John's Will was created on 10 November 1924 and he left all his *household furniture, plate, linen, china, & other effects of a like nature* to wife Jane. Everything else, after all debts paid, he gave to his Trustee's to manage and for his *wife to have the use, occupy and enjoy, to receive rents, profits and income from these residue items of his estate, for the term of her natural life.*

There was one bequeath .... *Trustees to invest 200 pounds and the net income to be used to clean, renovate, repaint and keep in good order the grave and tombstone of my parents and brother at Purewa Cemetery and that for Janes' mother Mary Ann Woods at Waikaraka Park Cemetery.* (What a wonderful consideration. T)

John's Will continues for 4 more pages, detailing many actions and bequeaths to be made upon the death of his wife Jane.

--oo0Ooo--

1951 Jane died aged 87 in Auckland 20 September 1951.

Jane's Will was signed on 7 August 1950 and she made numerous bequeaths to friends and family. Her executors were brother Harry (Henry Joseph Woods) a retired mercer and Keith Thomas Poole, Auckland solicitor.

She left her piano and chesterfield suite to friend Minnie Eileen Vincent, all else was to be converted to cash.
She gave 100 pounds to the Presbyterian Leslie Orphanage, also 100 to the Methodist Orphanage, Mt Roskill.

Family received ... 500 pounds to niece Elsie Thomas, Coromandel, 200 to brother Edward (Ted), 250 pounds to niece Ila Findlay, wife of Henry, Kaitaia Store Manager, and 250 pounds to nephew Ronald Woods, Auckland Chemist.

As well as taxes, funeral and headstone and other expenses she allowed executor KT Poole to deduct professional charges.

The residue of her estate to be divided equally between niece Ivy May Morrison and nephew George Albert Woods.

Their burial plot at PUREWA CEMETERY, Auckland. Block A, Row 10, plot 17.

John Haslett's parents occupy plot 16 beside them.

--oo0Ooo--

7 ..... AGNES WOODS, the seventh child of John and Mary Ann Woods, was born in the Chapel St, Auckland home on 7 July 1866 and baptised by Rev W Colley at Primitive Methodist Church on 27 August 1866. Her birth was registered by her Step-grandfather Moses Crocker. Later if life she was also known as "Aggie".

(AGNES ... CW)

1892 AGNES married 16 May 1892 at the Auckland Registry Office, to **PATRICK McLEOD PETLEY**. They had 8 children.

Lila 1892, Arthur 1894, Nelly 1897, Jenny 1899, Winnie 1902, Vera 1904, Dorothy 1907 and Patrick 1912:

At first father Pat worked as a miner in Coromandel, and after his accident became a Fruitier and then a Grocery storekeeper.

The PETLEY family .....

Patrick (Pat) was born 5 July 1869, a son of John Alexander Charles Petley and Mere Kingi. On Pat & Agnes' wedding certificate, John was a 'surveyor'. John born c1819 at 'Seven Oaks', lived at Riverhead, Kent, England. He came to NZ on the *'Racecourse'* arriving 11 June 1847. At the time of the 'Maori Wars' he was made Captain of the 58th Regiment on 15 March 1848.

Mere Kingi was born at Opotiki c1830, daughter of Wiremu Kingi, a chief of the Ngati Awa tribe and a white woman. John and Mere married 14 Dec 1858 and had 6 children ... Harriet 1856, Jack (John Alexander Charles junior) 1858, Mary Allen c1860, Gladwin Henry 1864, Charles 1866 and **Patrick McLeod Petley** in 1869.

John died 8 Dec 1871 and Mere died 6 June 1916.

HOMES. Pat and Agnes' moved from Auckland to Tairua for the 1892 birth of Augusta (Lila), to Whitianga 1894 for Arthur and were living in Coromandel for the birth of Nellie in 1897. All the following children were born at Coromandel.

1895 Entertainer. The Whitianga *Mercury Bay Observer* of 15 June shows Pat was amongst the entertainers at Mrs Leonard Lee's fund raiser. The report includes .. *'Mr Pat Petley gave the character song 'Get Your 'Air Cut' with all the drollery imaginable, which convulsed the audience, It would be a smart fellow to beat Pat in that line.'* Also mentioned were ... *Miss Flossie Gow has a very pleasing voice ... Mrs Gow, and a Mr F Mickle contributed songs.*

1897 Comedian. *"The Coromandel News & Peninsular Gazette"* reported on a benefit concert in their issue 9 Nov 1897. Patrick Petley was described as a comedian and performed at many benefit evenings held in the Caledonian Hall. On this occasion following the Coromandel Town Band, there were several soloists, a violinist, recitations and dancing. Then to quote from the newspaper *"'The Band Played On' and this item was given by our local comedian Mr Pat Petley and was thrice encored, the recall items being an imitation of Bland Holt,* (an excellent clown in pantomime) *and a recitation expressive of something ludicrous."*

1902 Pat's Shocking Accident. *The Auckland Star & The Thames Star* both reported this accident on 20 January 1902. Combined we learn... *"Patrick was fishing with family and friends on the shores of Coromandel harbour, near Little Passage. He was in the act of throwing a plug of dynamite into the water, when it exploded in his hand, causing severe damage to his hand and the side of his neck. At the hospital his right hand had to be amputated at the wrist. He has a* *wife and young family dependant on him and they are not in good circumstances. General sympathy was expressed for Petley's family, he being a general favourite and well known throughout the district."*

1902 Tender. Pat looked for some other employment and placed a tender of 52 pounds per year, for contract of Coromandel Wharf Lighting. A Ben Gatley offered 45 pounds but Council decided to retender hoping to get more. NZ Herald 22 April.

1902 Song. On July 28 the *NZ Herald* records a benefit evening at the Caledonian Hall, Coromandel for the Volunteer Fire Brigade, where Pat Petley appeared on the programme. This time he sang *"When we went a-Hunting ... encored", then a sketch Mr Petley & Mr French, and later a song and dance Mr Petley.* A busy night.

He had been working as a miner but from this time the Electoral Rolls show his employment as "Fruiterer, and Grocer."

1908 Electoral Roll. There were only 2 Petley's listed on the Thames Roll ... Patrick Petley, fruiterer and Agnes Petley domestic duties, of Coromandel.

In 1908 the family were living in Coromandel where Patrick was a Fruiterer and in this year Agnes' sister Phebe and her husband John Thomas decided to leave his Christchurch business in the hands of his sons and retire to live in Coromandel. Although Agnes was 11 years younger than Phebe they must have been 'close'. It seems John put some money into Patrick's business about 1912 and it became a Grocer shop in Coromandel. Our photo shows the shop near the Kaponga St bridge at the northern end of the town with the name ... "THOMAS & PETLEY". John & Phebe's Thomas' daughter Elsie had a Haberdashery shop in the same main street Coromandel. For a while the Petleys also lived at the Mount in Tauranga.

(T, ex death notice, RW)

1909 NZPO 'Town Directory' lists Patrick Petley, fruiterer.
1912 NZPO 'Town Directory' lists Pat at Coromandel, grocer.
1920 NZPO 'Town Directory' Pat is a grocer at Coromandel.

1920 Photo of the THOMAS & PETLEY shop. (RH side) Comments page 283. Photo from The School of Mines and Historical Society's booklet of "Coromandel Trade & Businesses Index ... 1900 to 1940"

KAPANGA ROAD, COROMANDEL ABOUT 1920.

1924 In the Trade Directory, Storekeeper, Patrick Petley is listed.

1925 & 1926 The entries for Patrick in the NZPO Directory imply he had 2 businesses operating ... one at 24 Disraeli St, Grey Lynn, Auckland and the one in Coromandel. However in 1926, aged 57, Patrick only had the Grey Lynn grocery business.

1928 John Thomas died. (maybe the loan was called in then)

1929 No Directory mention of a Petley shop anywhere.

Between 1928 and the early 1940s Agnes and Patrick are thought to have lived at Waihi or Mt Manganui.

1936 *Bay of Plenty Times* 19 March article. *The Catholic community at Mt Manganui arranged a dance in the Peter Pan Hall in aid of Church Building Fund.* Many people attended including *Mrs Pat Petley dressed in black silk.*

1937 *Bay of Plenty Times* 23 December, advert .. *Pat Petley's Motors, in Waihi, sends clients and friends Christmas Wishes.*

1938 Pat Petley's Motors, Waihi, (Ford Agent) advert for *Mechanic, First Class, wanted urgently ... take charge of workshop, top wages to right man.* NZ Herald 27 Jan 1938

1938 Many general adverts for 'Fords' at Pat Petley's Motors. Business phone number 117. Waihi Daily Telegraph 17 March

1938 *Mr Hugh McInally had established a car painting and duco plant at Pat Petley's Motor's premises.* WDT 25 June

1938 *The High School Old Boys Assn Football Club function. The 2 medals presented by Mr Pat Petley were won by Mr Moffat (junior) and Mr Jarvis for the seniors.* WDT 27 Oct

1938 *The Mt Manganui branch of the Labour Party held an evening at Peter Pan Hall ... Music was supplied by Murray Garriodes Band and extras by Mr Pat Petley and Mr G Lindopp. Mr & Mrs Pat Petley of Waihi were guests of Mr & Mrs Petley senior.* BofPT 1 Nov

1938 WDT 8 December. *Pat Patley's Motors in Seddon St, Waihi are local agents for Hawke Motors, Te Aroha who have 100 used motor vehicles for sale.*

1939 Mr McInally still at Pat Petley's Motors. (adv) WDT 25 Feb

1939 BofPT 17 Feb, Personal Notes .. *Mrs Pat Petley is visiting Te Aroha and Auckland.* (Daughter Lila lived in Te Aroha and daughter Winnie was in Auckland.)

1939 NZHerald 28 Feb: *Book-keeper wanted, male or female, take sole charge garage and office. Pat Petley's Motors, Waihi.*

1939 NZHerald 1 April *... For Sale.. Speedboat 'Scram' apply Pat Petley, Mt Manganui, Tauranga.* Also listed in 6th and 8th April.

1940 BofPT 9 October: *Mt Manganui Yachting Club Annual meeting, officials elected included Pat Petley, as Vice Commodore.*

PATRICK McLEOD PETLEY.

1941 BofPT 14 May: *Mt Manganui Yacht & Power Boat Club End of Season function. Mr Pat Petley recitations.*

1942 BofPT 1 July: *Members of Lady Galway Guild raised money for the Patriotic Fund. Included in the list of competition winners Mr Pat Petley won a cheque.*

Early 1940s. Agnes and Pat retired to Takapuna to live near their daughter Jenny, with daughter Winnie living just a ferry ride away across the harbour in nearby Ponsonby.

1942 Auckland Star 19 Dec: *"Glad & Charl & Pat Petley send Christmas and New Year Greetings to all Auckland Yachtsmen."*

1943 WDT 14 July: *Pat Petley's Motors.. wanted ... Office Girl.*

1945 AGNES DIED aged 78, on 27 April 1945 at her home at 7 Ngaio Road, Takapuna, North Shore, Auckland.

1946 PAT DIED aged 77, on 23 January 1946 at the Mater Hospital, Mountain Road, Auckland.
The Death Notice adds ... *formerly of Coromandel and Tauranga.*

Patrick McLeod Petley's WILL *".. to divide the remainder amongst my sons and daughters, Lila Mulvihill, Arthur, Jenny Drummond, Winifred Gray, Vera Barker and Patrick* junior *in equal shares."*

C Little & Sons, undertakers, interred them at Auckland's Birkenhead / Glenfield Cemetery ... Old portion, Anglican section, Block 2, Plot 031, in the extreme north-western corner of this cemetery. (T)

Their headstone is divided in two sections, and very faint ....

IN LOVING MEMORY OF

AGNES	PATRICK
beloved wife of	beloved husband of
PATRICK PETLEY	AGNES PETLEY
died 27 April 1945	died 23 January 1946
aged 78 years	aged 77 years

"AT REST"

--oo00oo—

LILA, AGNES, & ARTHUR PETLEY

The PETLEY HOME, PILOT BAY, Mt MANGANUI with family L to R.... Phyllis, Ray, neighbour, Agnes, Rita, Ken, Colin, Pat & Arthur. Arthur is Pat & Agnes' son, the others are 5 of Arthur's 8 children. (GB)

--oo0Ooo—

AGNES and PAT had 8 CHILDREN ......

1 **AUGUSTA MARY** (known as Lila & Larley) born 15 June 1892, went to the Convent School from 21 October 1990, married 25 Jan 1916 to Thomas (Tom) Henry Mulvihill. They first lived at Whitford, Auckland, then at Te Aroha. Lila had a shop "Lila's Hat shop". Tom was Postmaster at Te Aroha. Tom died 25 October 1968. (81) Lila/Larley died 30 August 1969 (80) at her home at 9 Brick St, Te Aroha and they were buried at Te Aroha Cemetery. Lila is on her headstone and death notice but she is Augusta on her birth & death certificates.

Lila and Tom had one child Elizabeth (Betty) Leon Mulvihill born 5 July 1917 at Mt Eden, Auckland. Aged 26 she married (1) Frank Crist and (2) aged 37 married Thomas Edmund Foley who died 11 Dec 1973 (59). Betty died 8 July 1987 (70). Both buried at Te Aroha, Cemetery.

2 **ARTHUR GLADWIN** (Artie) born 12 July 1894 at Whitianga, died 9 April 1976 at Wellington & was buried at Korori Cemetery. Arthur went to a local school from 5 December 1900 to 16 December 1909, then joined his father at the grocery shop. Arthur later became a jeweller in Wellington.

1915 Arthur was listed as a member of the Coromandel Band.

1916 Arthur married Alice Maud Bowater. Alice's parents owned a timber mill at Westport. Arthur travelled to France for WW1 and was gassed but survived. After the war he went to Westport and worked as a watch repairer. He also opened "Petley's Emporium". His children Joyce and Ken both worked for their father at Westport.

Arthur and Alice had 8 children, the first, Joyce, was born at Mt Eden, Auckland and the other 7 at Westport. Later, Arthur and Alice moved to Upper Hutt where Arthur and son Ken manufactured jewellery and they were the first to make seamless rings.

Arthur and Alice's 8 children were named ... **JOYCE, VELDA, PHYLLIS, COLIN, KEN, RITA, RAYMOND and BARRY.**

3 **NELLY** born 11 Aug 1897, lived 5 months and died of dysentery & convulsions on 24 Jan 1898, buried at Coromandel.

4 **JEAN ALMA (Jenny)** born 1899 married 19 Sept 1918, to WILLIAM SCHOLFIELD. Secondly married ART DRUMMOND

who was in charge of Auckland Power Board's generators on the North Shore. Jenny and Art adopted a girl named VALMAI. Jenny is known to have played the piano very well.

5 **ELSIE WINIFRED** born 9 March 1902 (Wynn or Winnie) married in 1920 ERNEST PARKER GRAY, who worked for the Telephone Exchange at Ponsonby. They lived at 87 Clarence St, Ponsonby, Auckland.

Winnie and Ernie had 3 children ... a daughter c1921 and 2 sons born c1929 and c1932. One son became a builder.

Sisters Jenny and Winnie were involved in a railway crossing car crash at Cadmans Road, Paeroa on 20 August 1960 in which Winnie (58) died instantly from her injuries and husband Ernie was badly injured. It seems they were travelling to Te Aroha to visit her sister Larley. Ernie was driving and being deaf did not hear the bells. Several hundred people visited the crossing afterwards. For days after The Hauraki Plains Gazette, The Hauraki Plains Council and The Thames Sub-branch of Federated Farmers expressed concern at their meetings of the speed of railcars approaching crossings. (GB & RW)

6 **VERA** born 8 April 1904 at Coromandel, started school 10 May 1915 at a local school but moved to the convent school later. Vera married twice.

(1) 19 Dec 1923 to INGLIS IVAN LITTLEWOOD at Auckland. Ivan was born 20 Oct 1903 at Taupiri, and later farmed there. He died 23 April 1955. Ivan's mother was the daughter of a Maori Chief and they gave him a hill at Howick. Ivan went to South Africa with the Kiwi League team 1922-23.

Vera and Ivan had 5 children ...

NORMA, IVAN, PEGGY, DESMOND and REX.

Vera was a capable artist and had pictures everywhere.
Vera and Ivan separated about 1932-33.

The children stayed with their father until he died, then went to live with Auntie Winnie.

(2) Vera married FREDERICK CHARKLES BARKER 7 April 1943. Vera died at 1063 Whangaparaoa Rd, North Shore, Auckland, on 3 Nov 1989 of Cerebrovascular Accident and was buried at Waikumete Cemetery, Auckland.
Fred kept horses at Te Atatu and had his own racetrack. He drove trotters and wouldn't hit a horse. He was also a keen boatie, and Commodore of the Whangaparaoa Yacht Club. Fred died on 15 July 1995.

7 **CECILIA DOROTHY** born 11 June 1907 at Coromandel, went with Vera to school on 10 May 1915. She married CUTHBERT DUDLEY MARGAN (a butcher) in 1929. Sadly Dorothy died within a year of her marriage, on 15 Nov 1930, of a kidney problem.

8 **PATRICK CHARLES** (Young Pat) born 20 Feb 1912 at Coromandel, started school 26 March 1917 but soon attended the Mangere Bridge School, in Auckland. He died 21 Nov 1972 at Mourea. Young Pat spent some time in the Navy, then became a director of Lines Bros NZ Ltd, then managed a shop in Rotorua selling farm equipment. Later he had a dairy on the Tauranga side of Rotorua. (GB & RW)

(1) Young Pat married RENE ELEANOR GEORGE (born 2 April 1916) a daughter of Sydney Douglas George & Floris Hilda Knuckie. Pat and Rene had one child they named ANTHONY WAYNE PETLEY born in 1939 and who died 3 March 1984 in a car crash near Tauranga.

Wayne, a pharmacist in Te Puke married Mary Baker also a pharmacist and who also had a shop selling plants next to the Pharmacy. Wayne and Mary had 3 children ...

CLAIR, MEGAN and LOGAN.

Pat and Rene divorced.
Rene married Alexander Creighton Lobbin.

(2) Pat married NANCY JOYCE HARRIS in 1946 and had 2 children... **KAREN** 1948 and **WILLIAM** 1952.

--oo00oo--

AGNES and PAT M PETLEY'S family tree follows ...

We are very grateful to Arthur's son Ken, who helped our researcher Gwyneth with family history facts and the following Family Tree, gathered about 2000.

AGNES WOODS married PATRICK McLEOD PETLEY .... FAMILY TREE
they had 8 children .... Lila, Arthur, Nellie, Jenny, Winnie, Vera, Dorothy & Pat

AUGUSTA MARY PETLEY
known as Larley and Lila
born 15 June 1892, Tairua, NZ
died 30 August 1972 (80)
married 25 January 1916
THOMAS HENRY MULVIHILL
born 1887
died 25 Oct 1968 (81)
bur at Te Aroha Cemetery.

1 child named ... Elizabeth

ELIZABETH (BETTY) LEON MULVIHILL
born 5 July 1917
died 8 July 1987 (70)
married in 1948
FRANK CRIST
then married in 1954
THOMAS EDMUND FOLEY
born 1915
died 11 Dec 1973 (59)
buried at Te Aroha, NZ
no children

ARTHUR GLADWYN PETLEY
born 12 July 1894, Whitianga, NZ
died 9 April 1976 (81)
married 1917
ALICE MAUD BOWATER
born 23 March 1894
died 2 June 1970 (76)
Buried at Karori Cemetery, NZ

8 children ... Joyce, Velda, Phyllis, Colin, Ken, Rita, Raymond & Barry.

JOYCE PETLEY
born 25 March 1917
died
married
WALLACE GILLIAND
born 25 March 1917
died
buried
no children

VELDA NGAIRE PETLEY
born 10 October 1919
died
married
HOWARD HENRY TATTON
born 1919
died
buried
2 children ... Neville & Leslie

NEVILLE TATTON
born

LESLIE TATTON
born

PHYLLIS PETLEY
born 5 December 1920
died 1 March 1993
married
JAMES ANDERSON
born
died
buried
3 children ... Patricia, Anthony and David.

PATRICIA ANDERSON
born

ANTHONY ANDERSON
born

DAVID ANDERSON
born

ARTHUR COLIN PETLEY
born 1 February 1922
died
married
KATHLEEN BAYLIE
see next page

RAEWYN PETLEY
born

WARWICK PETLEY
born

Arthur & Alice continued	Colin & Kathleen continued KATHLEEN BAYLIE born 3 children ... Raewyn, Warwick and Julie	JULIE PETLEY born
	PATRICK <u>KENNETH</u> PETLEY born 7 May 1923 (Ken) died married 22 January 1946 BEVERLEY CORBETT born died 5 children ... Susan, Jocelyn, Alison, Robyn, Adrienne.	SUSAN MARION PETLEY born 7 February 1948 married RODNEY SOMERVILLE born 2 children ... TONY SOMERVILLE born 7 February 1970 BLAIR SOMERVILLE born 14 December 1971
		JOCELYN CLARICE PETLEY born 30 December 1950 married ALBERT KEAN SHERMAN born 3 children ... BEVERLEY stillborn ELIZABETH ANN SHERMAN born 4 May 1977 WILLIAM ALBERT SHERMAN born 30 July 1979
		ALISON DIANNE PETLEY born 16 April 1952 married ERIC WAGEMAKER born 2 children ... BENTON JACOB WAGEMAKER born 22 January 1982 RYAN KEN WAGEMAKER born 4 July 1987
		ROBYN LESLIE PETLEY born 16 April 1957 married LINDSAY HARPER born 3 children ... DAVID LINDSAY HARPER born 24 March 1978

Arthur & Alice continue

Ken & Beverley continue

Robyn & Lindsay's children

JENNY HARPER
born 1 November 1979

BRIAN HARPER
born 1 December 1981

Robyn (Div) & married 1999
GORDON REID
born

ADRIENNE JOYCE PETLEY
born 18 December 1958
married
RALPH HAWKE
born
2 children ...

ALANA JOAN HAWKE
born 9 February 1990

BRADLEY PETER HAWKE
born 23 Feb 1993

RITA PETLEY
born 15 August 1924
died 1 October 1996
married
ALLAN GILLIES
born
3 children ... Russell, Nigel and Brent.

RUSSELL GILLIES
born

NIGEL GILLIES
born

BRENT GILLIES
born

RAYMOND PETLEY
born 16 August 1925
died 27 Oct 1993
married
DAWN ....
born

BARRY FRANCIS PETLEY
born 27 April 1927
died 11 April 1930 (3)
buried Westport Cemetery

NELLY PETLEY
born 11 August 1897
died 24 January 1898 (5 mths)
buried at Coromandel Cemetery. (C of E section)

Jenny next page

JEAN ALMA PETLEY (Jenny)
born 21 April 1899 Coromandel
married 19 September 1918
WILLIAM HALL SCHOLFIELD
born

no children

secondly Jenny married
ART DRUMMOND
born

adopted VALMAI …………

ELSIE WINIFRED PETLEY
b 9 March 1902 Coromandel
died 20 August 1960 (58)
married 1920
ERNEST PARKER GRAY
born
3 children …

daughter born 1921

son born 1929

son born 1932

VERA PETLEY
born 8 April 1904
died 3 November 1989 (85)
married 19 December 1923
INGLIS IVAN LITTLEWOOD
born 20 October 1903 Taupiri
died 23 April 1955
buried Waikumete Cemetery

5 children … Norma, Ivan, Peggy, Desmond & Rex

NORMA LITTLEWOOD
born 8 July 1924
died 31 August 1993 (69)
married 14 September 1946
RON WILLIAMSON
born

3 children … Marilyn, Ivan and Kenneth.

MARILYN WILLIAMSON
born
married
WAYNE STOKES
born
3 children …

DAWN STOKES
born
married
RICHARD BISHOP
born
1 child …

JONATHON BISHOP
born

CHERIE STOKES
born
married
JAMIE HARTLEY
born
1 child …

ADAM HARTLEY
born

MARK STOKES
born

IVAN WILLIAMSON
born
married
SANDRA HIGGS
born
3 children …

STACEY WILLIAMSON
born

Vera and Ivan continued	Norma and Ron continued	Ivan & Sandra's children KELLY WILLIAMSON born BRETT WILLIAMSON born KENNETH WILLIAMSON born married DONNA ..... 1 child ... KENDRA WILLIAMSON born
	Norma secondly married 22 July 1966 at Christchurch ALEX COPELAND HAY born	
	IVAN WALKER LITTLEWOOD born 11 August 1925 died 30 May 1991 (60) married 22 November 1952 SHIRLEY HELEN HAYR born 2 children ... Ivan & Shirley	IVAN ROSS LITTLEWOOD born 13 September 1953 married 14 April 1984 SHERREE MAY GOORD born 28 December 1959 2 children ... MICHELLE E LITTLEWOOD born 10 March 1986 DARREN R LITTLEWOOD born 1 September 1988 SHIRLEY JOY LITTLEWOOD born 16 December 1956 married 11 June 1976 RUSSELL JOHN TAYLOR born 10 February 1954 2 children ... KELLY JOHN TAYLOR born 7 November 1976 CORYN MAREE TAYLOR born 1 October 1979
	PEGGY LITTLEWOOD born 19 February 1927 married 3 July 1948 REGINALD CHARLES FREDERICK SPOONER born 27 May 1926 3 children ... Reginald, Peggyanne, and Carolyn.	REGINALD STEVEN SPOONER born 2 January 1949 married AILEEN BARBARA BROWN born 1 child ... LUKE CAMERON SPOONER born 26 November 1980 PEGGYANNE FAY SPOONER born 9 January 1950 married PETER ROBERT REID born 2 children ... NICOLA JANE REID born 8 October 1974

Vera and Ivan continued

Peggy & Reginald continue

Peggyanne & Peter's children

STEPHEN ROBERT REID
born 28 April 1976

CAROLYN JEAN SPOONER
born 28 August 1957
married
GRAHAM LEONARD PLUCK
born
4 children ...

KELLY ANNE PLUCK
born 29 July ....

NICOLE FAY PLUCK
born 25 October 1983

HAYLEY JEAN PLUCK
born 18 October 1985

MATTHEW LEONARD PLUCK
born 8 February 1989

Vera secondly
married 7 April 1943
FREDERICK CHARLES BARKER
born
died 15 July 1995

DESMOND LITTLEWOOD
born 2 April 1929

REX LITTLEWOOD
born
died at 1 years old

CECILIA DOROTHY PETLEY
born 11 June 1907
died 15 November 1930 (23)
married 11 December 1929
CUTHBERT DUDLEY MARGAN
born
died

no children

PATRICK CHARLES PETLEY
born 20 February 1912
died 21 November 1972 (60)
married 1937
RENE ELEANOR GEORGE
born 2 April 1916
died 9 February 1989 (72)
1 child ... Anthony.

ANTHONY WAYNE PETLEY
born 1939
died 3 March 1984 (45)
married
MARY BAKER
born

3 children ... Clair, Megan & Logan

CLAIR JEAN PETLEY
born 10 May 1965

MEGAN ELINOR PETLEY
born 12 February 1968

LOGAN DOUGLAS PETLEY
born 9 October 19[illegible]

Pat and Rene separated
PAT married in 1946
NANCY JOYCE HARRIS
born
2 children ...

KAREN JUDITH PETLEY
born 17 February 1948

WILLIAM HARRIS PETLEY
born 16 June 1952

8..... WILLIAM MORRIS WOODS was born 10 April 1868 in Auckland and was baptised 12 May 1868 by the Rev W J Dean of the Primitive Methodist Church.
On this same day William's mother's half-sister Jane Thomas (nee Morris) baptised her son John Thomas at the same church.

1893 & 1894 Electoral Rolls, William M Woods (moulder) was listed living at Lower Vincent St.

WILLIAM (25) married (Becky) **REBECCA JANE DUNN** in 1893. They had 3 children **Mary, William, & Hugh** (more below). The family lived at 24 Disreali St, Ponsonby, Auckland.

1900 & 1902 Auckland Directory lists William Woods, moulder, living 2 houses north of brother Edward at Lower Vincent St.

1919 William senior (a moulder) died 18 May 1919 aged 51 of cancer. The undertakers Watney Siburn buried William at Purewa Cemetery, Auckland. Block A, Row 017, plot 030.
His last residence was 17 Lower Vincent St, Auckland.

1941 Becky was born in 1871 and died aged 70, on 24 July 1941. She was cremated at Purewa Cemetery, Auckland. Her last residence was 15 Ligar Place, Grafton, Auckland.

--oo00oo—

William and Becky's CHILDREN

Daughter **IRENE ILMA MARY** (known as May) born in 1894 and was married in 1926 to Harold (Harry) Louis Possenniske, a pharmacist at Otahuhu, Auckland. He died while on holiday in London, England aged 72 during June 1967. There were no children. (CW, BDM)

Son **WILLIAM MORRIS WOODS** born 1896, had attended Nelson Street School, Auckland, then served an apprenticeship with Mr J K Alexander, as sign-writer, until mobilised for duty at Garrison Artillery at Fort Cautley, Devonport, NZ where he served 3 months.

On 14 Dec 1915 aged 19, he volunteered for active WW1 service in the 11th Reinforcements, 5th Battery, NZ Field Artillery.
On 2 April 1916, he was sent overseas to serve in Egypt and France. He was first wounded at Messines 7 June 1917, he returned to the fight to be gassed in March 1918 and after 3 months recovering joined his battery again, to be killed at Bapaume, in France, aged 22, *'on 26 August 1918 in the field'*, William was buried at the Achiet-le-Grand Communal Cemetery Extension, Pas-de-Calais, France, grave plot IV.U.11. (CW+MM)
The Army misspelt middle-name Morris, as Maurice.

William's medals were sent to his wife Becky ... The British War Medal and the Victory Medal.
Photos of cousins William M Woods, and of Charles E Thomas, sat on RW's sitting room mantelpiece for many years. (RW)

The page 301 photo is of a part of the **MEMORIAL CROSSES** (one each) in The Field of Remembrance at the Auckland Museum on Armistice Day 2018 in memory of the 18,277 New Zealanders who lost their lives 100 years ago, during the Great War. (WW1) **The second cross up reads ......**
"2/3128 Gunner W M Woods (CW)

--oo0oo—

Son HUGH GEORGE WOODS was born 1898 and died 22 November 1968 aged 71. Hugh was buried at Hamilton Park Cemetery by Reece Ashby & Co. His last address was 10 Adam St, Waihi and he seems to have remained single.

--oo0oo—

9..... EDWARD WOODS was born in the Chapel St home, Auckland on 2nd December 1870. His birth was registered by Moses Crocker of Elliott St, Auckland.

He was known mostly as Edward but some knew him as 'Ted'.

1893 & 1894 Electoral Roll aged 21, & 22 Edward was at Lower Vincent St, a labourer.

1896 EDWARD (26) married **MAY LOVATT MARSH** (19) on 24 Dec 1896, at the Registrar's Office, Auckland.
Edward's occupation ... 'Machinist'. (Cert CW & AStar 21 Jan)

EDWARD, MAY and EDDIE

Relatives who witnessed the wedding included Arthur Henry Marsh and Richard John Marsh both Miners of Kuatonu.
May was the fourth daughter of Richard John Marsh.
All of the first eight Woods children had by this time left the Lower Vincent St home but Edward remained with his

wife May, and supported his mother Mary Ann and younger brother Harry for some time.

1898 SON: Their only child **EDWARD HENRY WOODS** was born 2 February 1898 at the Lower Vincent St house.
In **1899** Edward's mother and brother left Lower Vincent St to live in Canada St with Mary Ann's brother William.

1900 Auckland Directory ... Edward (30) was living in Lower Vincent St, 2 doors south from his brother William M Woods.

1902 Electoral Roll.
Edward, 32, was a 'mill-hand', living at Lower Vincent St.

1906 A postcard addressed to son Eddie (aged 8) shows his parents address as ... **34 Lower Vincent St.** Celina Freeman (May's Aunt) was advising the family she would arrive on the midday train. We do not know when Auckland's houses first received numbers but this is the earliest we have found of a number for the Woods' family's Lower Vincent St home. (CW)

EDWARD & MAY'S HOMES:
The Auckland Street Directory and Electoral Rolls, show Edward and May continued to live at 34 Lower Vincent St until about 1909 ... and then shifted to Emma St (later became Marlborough St) Mt Eden.
They lived in two houses here ... 1909 to 1916 at number 22, then moved to number 18 and shifted from here in 1918. The electoral rolls show in 1919 they lived at 29 Rocklands Ave, Mt Eden, home of May's sister (Maybella Goodman nee Marsh) while their new home was erected. They moved into 15 Ewington Ave, about 1920, where they lived the rest of their lives. (CW)

15 Ewington Ave home.

During these 30 or so years, Edward and May's son Eddie bought the house next door and he and Edna became their neighbours in Ewington Ave, Auckland. (CW)

Photo of EDWARD aged 76 and MAY 69 at son Edward Henry's wedding in 1946

"Uncle Ted became a foreman at Goldies Timber Mill and later he and Eddie had a stationery shop opposite RW's pharmacy at the junction of New North and Dominion Roads." (RW)

1938 Electoral. Edward and May, and son Eddie were both living at 15 Ewington Ave.

1946 Electoral. At 15 Ewington Ave were Edward (foreman) and May, plus son Edward (joiner). Later this year Eddie married.

1954 Electoral. 15 Ewington Ave was occupied by Edward and May Woods. Son Edward Henry Woods and wife Ann.

1958 EDWARD WOODS (87) died on 12 October in Auckland.

1960 MAY LOVATT WOODS (82) died 28 December.

They are buried together at Waikaraka Park Auckland, (Area 5, Block B, Lot 405)

MAY'S WILL:
On 7 Nov 1960 May signed her Will and added a codicil the same day. Basically she left gifts to the Methodists & the Lepers Trust and generous sums to her son's widow Annie and niece Myrtle Smith. Her three grandchildren also received the balance.

--oo0Ooo--

Son ... EDWARD HENRY WOODS

1898 Born 2 February, only child to Edward & May Woods In early years he was known as Eddie, but later used Edward.

1918 Aged 20, on 8 April, Edward Henry enlisted in the **NZ Army**. He was given number 85513. WW1 Service Records show he lived at 18 Emma St, Mt Albert, was on that date employed by the Union Steam Ship Company as a joiner, had had experience in the NZ Field Artillery Corp, and was willing to serve overseas in the NZ Expeditionary Forces. WW1 officially ended on 11 Nov 1918, so we do not think he was sent overseas.

1919 Electoral Roll (ER) Edward Henry (21) was living with his parents at 29 Rocklands Avenue, Mt Eden ... a joiner.

1926 EDWARD HENRY WOODS (28) married EDNA HILL on 3 November at the Methodist Church in Dominion Rd, Mt Eden and son EDWARD KEITH WOODS was born 24 Nov 1928.
May and her daughter in law Edna, had a cake shop in Mt Albert for a while when Keith was a small child. (CW)
EDNA died 14 February 1998 at Glamis Hospital, Mt Albert, Auckland, and was buried at Eden Gardens Memorial Park.

> **1980 Son Keith married** 1 May 1980 in Auckland ... DOREEN SNEH PRABHA who was born 6 March 1951 in Fiji. They had one child they named GITA SNEH KALAPRAJI WOODS born 16 October 1980 at National Women's Hospital, Auckland.
> Keith became a technician with the Auckland Hospital making intra-venous solutions, and had an article on this subject published in the Pharmacy Journal about 1962 or 1963. (RW)

1928 ER. shows Edward H (a joiner) and Edna living at Seaview Terrace, Mt Roskill, Auckland.
1935 ER. Edward H (joiner) was living with his parents at 15 Ewington Ave, Mt Roskill, Auckland.
1938 ER. Edward H (joiner) now living with his parents Edward and May Woods at 51 Ewington Ave.

1946 MARRIAGE: Edward Henry's first marriage was dissolved in 1940 and aged 48 he married ANNIE (Ann) EVELYN VAGUE (33) on 1 August 1946 at the Baptist Church, Shackleton Rd, Mt Eden. Ann was born 28 March 1913 in Auckland.

Edward Henry Woods and Ann had two children ...
Ann Christine Woods (born 8 September 1947) and
Ralph Graeme Woods (born 13 July 1949) in Auckland.

Ralph married SUSAN ELIZABETH BEEVER on 9 December 1972 at St Aiden's Church, Remuera. They had 2 sons ...Nigel Scott Woods b1980 and Matthew James Woods b1991.

Edward Henry Woods and wife Ann

1946 ER. Edward Henry was recorded twice ... wrongly, a joiner at 15 Ewington Ave ... and correctly with Ann at 223 New North Road, Arch Hill at the residence over his shop.

STORES: Edward Henry operated two businesses, side by side, at 223 New North Road, Auckland and lived above them.

A Lending Library and a Stationery Shop.

The photo below shows the stamp inside one of their books.

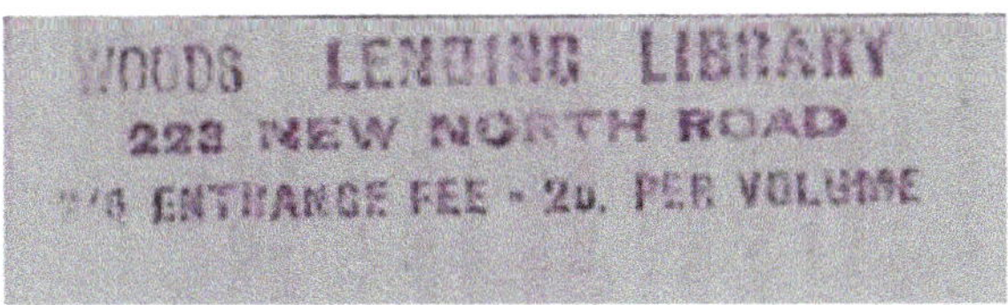

1949 ER. Edward H, shop keeper, Ann, and son Keith (student) now living at 21 Ewington Avenue, next to his parents.

Edward Henry Woods' stationery shop. **(CW)**

Ronald Woods writes ... *"Uncle Ted and Eddie had a Stationery Shop right opposite my Pharmacy at the junction of New North and Dominion Roads".* (in 2018 now under a huge interchange.) The photo, taken by P J Rodgers, Professional Photographer of Morningside, Auckland, shows the interior of the shop with many varieties of stationery plus tobacco items and kiddies toys. Standing behind the counter is Edward Henry's father Edward and at 76 he seems to have helped his son out from time to time. Edward Henry operated his Stationery Shop from about 1946 until he died in 1956. (photo colourised by 'myheritage') (CW)

1951 Jane Haslett left her *'nephew Edward Henry Woods, a New North Rd Stationer',* 200 pounds in her Will.

1954 ER. Edward H and Ann lived at 21 Ewington Ave and he was described as a Shop Keeper.

1956 EDWARD HENRY WOODS died 21 August at Greenlane Hospital aged 58 ... when his children were aged 28, 9 and 7.

His Will simply states ... *"all to my wife Annie Evelyn Woods, absolutely"* which he signed on 26 August 1947.

1957 ER. and **1963 ER.**
Ann Woods ... Widow, living at 21 Ewington Ave.

1960 Widow Ann Woods received a generous sum from the Will of her mother-in-law May Woods.

37 years after her husband died ....
1993 ANN EVELYN WOODS died 9 May aged 80.
Edward Henry and Ann were buried together.
(Area 5 Block B plot 337) Waikaraka Park, Auckland. (CW)

Harry and Ann's headstone at Waikaraka Park Cemetery, Auckland.

--oo0oo—

The VAGUE family.

Ann Evelyn Vague (born 1913 NZ, registered as Annie) was a daughter of WALTER VAGUE (born 11 February 1879 at Creswick, Victoria, Australia) and OLIVE MAUD GOYEN.

Ann had 3 siblings named ... Leslie John born 1911, Phyllis Eliza 1915, and Cyril Walter Vague born 1917.

1911 ER. Walter Vague lived Vauxhall Rd, Devonport, Auckland

1916 NZ ARMY RESERVE: Walter employed as Sanitary Drainer of Orakei Road, Remuera, married with two children.

1928 ER. Walter Vague (City Council employee) and wife Olive lived at 81 Orakei Rd, Remuera.

1938 ER. Olive and daughter Ann (single) lived at 111 Orakei Rd, Remuera. (Ann's father Walter died in 1937)

--oo0oo--

The MARSH family.

1877 **MAY** was born 3 June a daughter of RICHARD JOHN MARSH (settler) 1840-1911 and ELLEN ELIZABETH KNAGGS 1843-1931, at the township of Wade, (now Silverdale) Whangaparaoa, Auckland.

There were nine children for Richard and Ellen ...
Frances (Fanny) born 1864, Elizabeth (Cissie) 1865, Arthur 1866, Mabelle 1868, Richard 1870, Edward (Ted) 1872, Frank 1874, May Lovatt 1877, and Daisy 1879.

Richard John Marsh and Ellen Elizabeth Knaggs (CW)

1911, *July 16, Richard John Marsh late of Pine Island* (now Herald Island) *and eldest son of Captain Marsh, Royal Navy and director of the Isle of Man Bank, died aged 71 at his son-in-law's* (Edward Woods) *Emma St home, Mt Eden.* (Auckland Star 17 July)

Richard and Ellen Marsh were both born at Kilham, Yorkshire, England. Richard & Ellen were buried at Waikumete Cemetery … Plot 14, Row 5, Division E, Presbyterian section. (CW)

Edward Henry's daughter Christine Woods (noted here as CW) has more extensive information of all her families.

We also thank Christine for her willing assistance in researching all of John and Mary Ann Woods' children's families, and the Woods' families in Norfolk, England.

--oo0Ooo—

EDWARD WOODS married MAY LOVATT MARSH ……… FAMILY TREE
they had one child … known in early years as Eddie and later as Edward

EDWARD HENRY WOODS b 2 Feb 1898 d 21 Aug 1956 (58) married 3 Nov 1826 EDNA HILL b 16 Aug 1902 England d 14 Feb 1998 m disolved 1940 1 child …	EDWARD KEITH WOODS b 24 Nov 1928 d 13 Feb 1997 married 1 May 1980 NZ DOREEN SNEH PRABHA b 6 March 1951 Fiji 1 child …	GITA SNEH KALAPRAJI WOODS b 16 Oct 1980 2 children …	KYRA WINTER KALAPRAJI WOODS b 29 Dec 2001 Auckland KASPIAN HUNTER EDWARD WOODS-PERESE b 29 Aug 2015 Auckland
Edward remarried m 1 Aug 1946 ANN EVELYN VAGUE b 28 March 1913 d 9 May 1993 (80) buried Waikaraka Park, with Edward. 2 children …	ANNE CHRISTINE WOODS b 8 Sep 1947 Auckland, NZ		
	RALPH GRAEME WOODS b 13 July 1949 m 9 Dec 1972 SUSAN ELIZABETH BEEVER b 3 Sep 1949 2 children …	NIGEL SCOTT WOODS b 10 Jan 1980 m 5 Oct 2018 NICOLA RENNIE b	
		MATTHEW JAMES WOODS b 4 Sep 1991 partner JESSICA JOY WATERS b 17 May 1995	RILEY JAMES WOODS b 13 May 2016 CONNOR ANTHONY WOODS b 14 Dec 2018

10..... HENRY JOSEPH WOODS

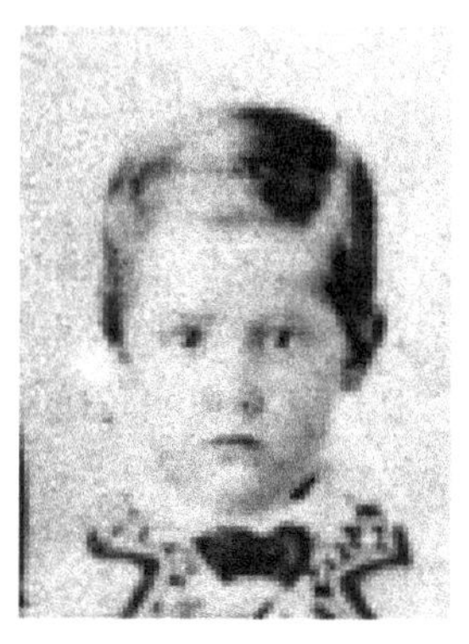

1875 Known as **Harry** he was John and Mary Ann Woods' 10th child, born 11 Jan 1875 at the Chapel St home.

Harry was baptised 13 April 1875 by the Rev Harris of the Primitive Methodist Church. He became a tailor.

Photos ...
Harry aged about 5 and as a young man.

1899 Aged 24, Harry went with his mother Mary Ann when she shifted to her brother William's Canada St home. He continued to support Mary Ann and William until it became necessary for his sisters to take care of Mary Ann. (RW)

1905 Electoral Roll. Harry, a tailor, lived at Canada Street.

1910 ... Harry's Uncle William (Lowe) Morris died 4 July 1910 and from his Will, Harry inherited the property of 8 Canada St, Mt Eden .... *"the whole of my real and personal property whatsoever and wherever absolutely"* other than two bequeaths of money to his mother and sister Jane Thomas now a widow.

Harry finally received the Deed of ownership of the home on 18 March 1911. When Harry died in 1964 the Public Trustee took control and the house left the Woods family on 18 March 1965. (Title CT92/12 ... transfers 58488 & 65056)

1912 Harry 37, married on 29 April 1912 to ETHEL JANE BEACH 34 at the residence of the Reverend White, Mt Roskill, Auckland. Harry and Jane had known each other for 20 years before their marriage. (RW)

Jane was born 2 November 1878. (also see page 319)

Harry and Jane had three children they named ...

RONALD b1913, ILA b1915 and JACK b1918.

1917 NZ ARMY RESERVE ROLL

Second Division. Harry listed as reservist with two children.

1914 & 1928 ER.

Harry and Jane were living at 8 Canada St.

1938 photo.

HARRY, JANE and granddaughter GWYNETH (CW)

1938 ER. Harry, Jane and Ila (single) living at Canada St.

Son Ronald now married and living at 43 View Road, Mt Eden.

1949 ER. Harry and Jane were living at 8 Kawaka St.

(Same house but street renamed.) (Jane died in 1949.)

1957 & 1963 ER. Harry living at 8 Kawaka St ... retired.

Son Ronald writes that his father Harry lived his first 24 years at Lower Vincent Street, then continuously for 65 years at Canada St (name was changed to Kawaka St) .... from 1899 until he died in 1964. (RW)

Harry spent fifty years working for the same person ... George Tutt... a Men's outfitter and tailor. Harry himself was a tailor although in later years of his business life he did not do much actual sewing. (RW)

Ronald notes the dates of his uncles and aunts came from an old bible that was in Aunty Jinnie Hazlett's possession when she died. This bible in 1999 was with R Paul Woods in Tauranga ... a grandson of Harry and Jane's. (RW)

In recent years this bible was possessed by granddaughter Gwyneth *Woods* Broadbent.

Photo of **HARRY and his mother MARY ANN WOODS**

This photo is estimated taken when Harry was about 5 ... so that's around 1880 when Mary Ann was aged 45/46.

JANE died aged 71, 12 December 1949.

HARRY died aged 89 on 26 September 1964.
They are buried together at Waikaraka Park, Auckland.
(Area A, Block EXT, Lots 269 and 269A)

Harry's Will: Wife Jane died before Harry, and son Jack died many years before Harry, so the will left ... *"the whole of my estate whatsoever nature and whatsoever situate"* to be divided equally between his son Ronald and daughter Ila. (signed 31 Jan 1950)

--oo0Ooo--

BROTHERS ... Edward and Harry Woods
Estimated taken mid 1950s. (CW)

--oo0Ooo--

Harry and Jane Woods' 3 children ....

A 1913 Son RONALD WOODS was born in 1913.
He has supplied a lot of detail of these Woods families and his initials (RW) show at the end of each section he provided.
1936 Ronald married and raised 7 children. (more detail p 322)
1951 Ronald was the recipient of a 250 pounds bequeath from his Aunt Jane Haslett's estate.
He became a Pharmacist in 1934 and in 1841 started his own shop on New North Road, near the corner of Dominion Road.

--oo0Ooo—

B 1915 Daughter ILA WOODS was born in 1915.
1951 Ila was the recipient of a bequeath of 250 pounds from the estate of her Aunt Jane Haslett.
She married in 1942 but had no children. Ila and husband Harry, after WW2 managed various stores in Kaitaia, Helensville and Moerewa. She wished her parents had spelt her name in the usual manner ... Isla.

--oo0Ooo—

C 1918 Son JACK WOODS, born 1918, died whilst a back seat passenger in a car that hit a tree in Jervois Road, Auckland, at 11pm the evening 17 Nov 1939. Jack was an apprentice printer, single, 21 years old and was buried at Waikaraka Cemetery, Auckland. The Auckland Star (18 Nov 1939) named him John but he was registered as Jack, and they advise his 2 friends escaped injury. His death certificate states that at this time the family lived at 8 Kawaka Street, Auckland and his father Harry was employed as a salesman. (RW)

--oo0Ooo--

Harry, Jane and son Jack's headstone at Waikaraka Park Cemetery, Auckland.

The BEACH family:

ETHEL JANE BEACH was the daughter of THOMAS BEACH and CHARLOTTE BURGESS who married in NZ, 26 Aug 1872. Jane was one of 6 children .... Charlotte Annie 1873, Margaret Kate (Katie) 1875, Mary Matilda 1877, Jane 1878, Winifred Mable 1881 and Thomas William 1887 who died 1888 (aged 1y10mth).

Thomas Beach was born in 1826 and died 26 Sept 1911.
At the time of their marriage Thomas was 40 and a widower and Charlotte was aged 16. They married at Residence of Rev C W Rigy, Karangahape Rd, Auckland. Thomas signed by 'X'. (cert)

Thomas' parents are unknown at present.

Thomas (the father) b1826 and d1911 (86) was buried at Waikumete Cemetery Nonconformist section A Row 2, plot 16, with his son Thomas William Beach.
Charlotte (the mother) b1856 and d1899 (43) was buried with daughter Katie (14) and buried in Plot 18, next to Thomas.

--oo0oo—

The BURGESS family:

CHARLOTTE BURGESS was born 1868 in New Zealand, the daughter of THOMAS BURGESS and his wife JANE KIMBER. who married in 1862 and had a total of 14 children ......

Thomas James 1863-1915; Stephen 1864-1865; William Charles 1865-1966; Esther Jane 1867-1914; Charlotte 1868-1943; John Henry 1869-1955; Henry and Robert (twins) b1871. Henry d1958 & Robert d1931; Frances 1873-1898; Sarah Helen 1875-1931; Albert 1877-1953; Edith Maud 1879-1966; Frank 1881-1970; and Edgar 1883-1959:

Thomas (the father) and wife Jane are buried with daughter Frances at St Augustine's Anglican Church in Clarkville, (just south of Kaiapoi) Canterbury, NZ.

--oo0oo—

The KIMBER family:

JANE KIMBER, born 13 Oct 1839, was the second child of STEPHEN KIMBER and HESTER GLASS. The other three children were James b1837; Charles b1842 and Henry b1845.

--oo0oo—

The BROADBENT family:

Granddaughter Gwyneth Broadbent has further research of this family.

PHOTO ...
L to R ... Gwyneth, and Arnold's parents Winston and Grace Broadbent, and Arnold, with children Stephen, Michelle and baby.

—oo0oo—

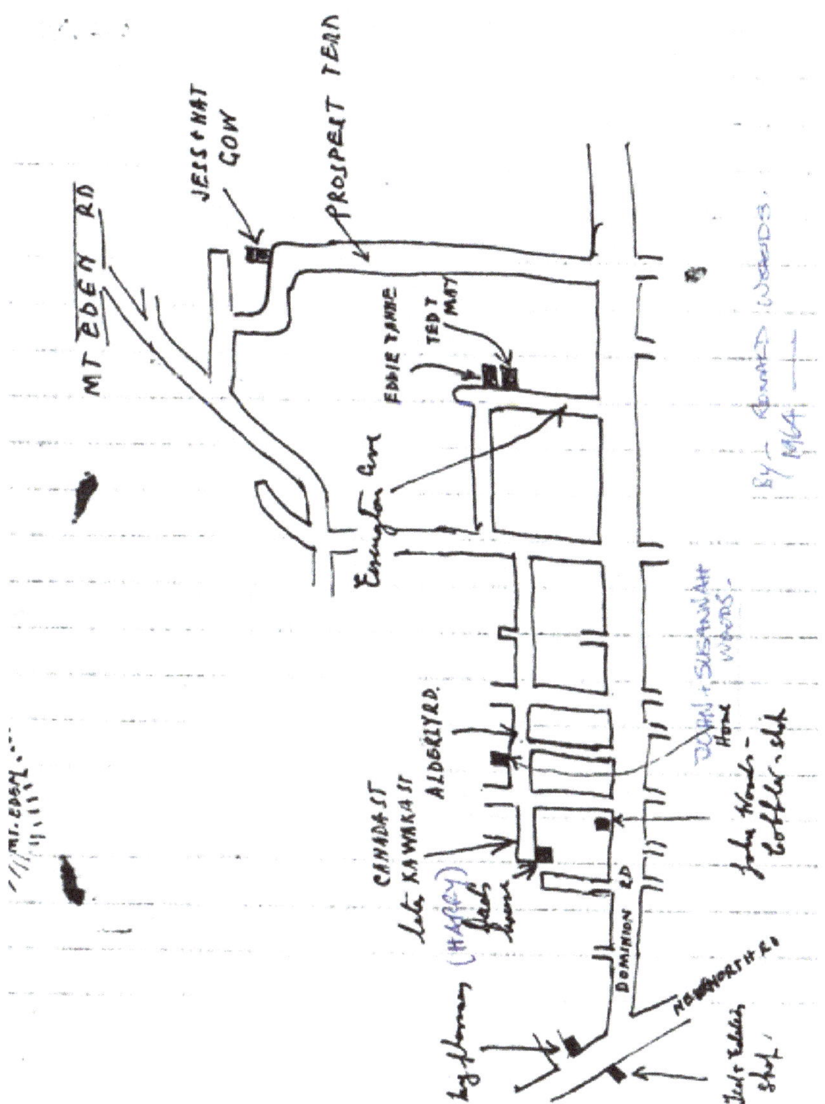

Ronald Woods, drew this map showing how close the homes and businesses for most of the family, were to each other.

--oo0Ooo—

HENRY (HARRY) JOSEPH WOODS married ETHEL JANE BEACH .... FAMILY TREE
they had 3 children .... Ronald, Ila, and Jack

RONALD WOODS
born 14 Feb 1913
died 20 May 1982 (69)
married 30 Nov 1936
MARY LILIAN UTTING
born 20 July 1913
died 2007 (94)
bur Waikumete. Auckland

7 children named ...
Gwyneth, Gordon, Lynette, Ian, Paul, Elizabeth and Alan

GWYNETH ISLA WOODS
b 21 May 1938
died
married 21 Dec 1960
ARNOLD WILLIAM ...
BROADBENT b23 Oct 1936
d 5 April 1997 (60)
bur Paeroa, NZ
Arnold was son of Winstone George Broadbent b1918 and Grace Edith Yoeman b1911 NZ

4 children ... Stephen
Gavin, Michelle, Suzanne

STEPHEN GEORGE BROADBENT
born 9 May 1962
died
married 21 May 1983
JANET FOSBERRY
born 15 Dec 1961 in England.
died

2 children

REBECCA LOUISE BROADBENT
b 7 Oct 1991

AMY SAMANTHA BROADBENT
b 21 July 1994

GAVIN DEANE BROADBENT
born 23 Sept 1964
died
married 28 April 1989
KAREN AUDAIR GIBBONS
born 27 Nov 1963 (divorced)

MICHELLE GRACE BROADBENT
born 22 April 1968
died
married 29 June 1991
ERNIE JOSEPH PENE
born 4 May 1961
died

2 children

DANIEL WILLIAM PENE
b 1 Dec 1995

ALIX HINEWAI PENE
b 25 Sept 1998

SUZANNE MARY BROADBENT
born 25 June 1969
died
partner
DAVID FRANCIS ROONEY
born 21 Nov 1971
died

2 children see next page

Ronald & Mary continue

Gwyneth & Arnold continue

Suzanne & David continue

TAYLOR ARNOLD ... BROADBENT ROONEY
born 28 Dec 1997

THERSA CORAL ROONEY ... BROADBENT
born 17 March 1999

GORDON JACK WOODS
b 23 Aug 1940
married 6 Oct 1962
ANN WELTON
b 8 Feb 1940 England

4 children ... Janine
David, Christine, Mark

JANINE MARY WOODS
b 22 Mar 1964

DAVID GORDON WOODS a
b 31 July 1969
m
YVONNE TOLSON
b
3 children

DANIEL SHAUN WOODS
b 25 Sep 1989

ALANNAH JANE WOODS
b 14 Jan 1991

KYLE STEPHEN WOODS
b 18 Jan 1994

David 2nd marriage ...
on 16 Apr 1998
ROCHELLE
b

CHRISTINE ANN WOODS a
b 2 April 1970
partner
NIGEL MILLER
b
2 children

JORDAN MARIA WOODS
b 16 Apr 1993

HOLLY ANN WOODS
b 6 Oct 1995

MARK WOODS a
b 6 Mar 1973

GORDON 2nd marriage ...
on 25 Sep 1982
BARBARA SHIRLEY ARNOLD
b 26 Oct 1945

Ronald & Mary continue

Child	Grandchildren
LYNETTE MARY WOODS b 21 Nov 1942 married 15 Jan 1965 RUSSELL JAMES HILTON b 13 Feb 1943 3 children ... Craig, Andrew, Kaylene	CRAIG JAMES HILTON b 28 Apr 1968 married 26 Aug 1995 New York, USA REBEKAH SUZANNE ARMAO b 4 Mar 1976 USA 1 child — ALEXANDER MICHAEL HILTON b 24 Apr 1999 USA ANDREW GRANT HILTON b 20 June 1970 married 28 May 1994 DE-ANNE THRUSH b Feb 1976 Andrew's 2nd marriage on 4 July 1998 NZ LAURA SHIRLEY b 4 March 1976 Canada KAYLENE MAREE HILTON b 14 May 1974 NZ
IAN HARRY WOODS b 24 May 1945 married 22 March 1969 GLENYS RUTH COMPTON b 12 Sep 1948 3 children ... Nicola, Rochelle, Gareth	NICOLA RUTH WOODS b 26 March 1971 married 7 Dec 1996 WYN RAY WARNER b 13 Sep 1975 ROCHELLE JOY WOODS b 29 July 1974 GARETH IAN WOODS b 26 Aug 1977
RONALD PAUL WOODS b 27 May 1951 married 2 Jan 1973 GAYNOR PAULINA TITIHUIA PAUL b 7 June 1953 3 children ... Rhonda, Huia, Paula	RHONDA MOANA WOODS b 22 June 1973 HUIA ROSEMARY WOODS b 28 July 1975 PAULA RETIHIA LILLIAN WOODS b 26 July 1986
Elizabeth see next page	

Ronald & Mary continue		
	ELIZABETH (Liz) JEAN WOODS b 21 June 1952 married 28 Nov 1981 WILLIAM ESPERSON b 28 April 1950 4 children ... Rachel, Hannah, Sarah and Deborah	RACHEL ELIZABETH ESPERSON b 20 Oct 1982 HANNAH MARIE ESPERSON b 1 Jan 1984 SARAH LYN ESPERSON b 2 Aug 1986 DEBORAH LAURA ESPERSON (Debby) b 13 Jan 1992
	ALAN DENIS WOODS b 10 Oct 1958 married 12 Aug 1978 KATHRYN FAE CONNOR b 7 March 1958 2 children ... Matthew and Odette	MATTHEW ALAN WOODS b 12 Oct 1978 ODETTE ROSE WOODS b 8 Oct 1983

ILA WOODS
b 3 Feb 1915
d 25 April 1997 (82)
buried Kaitaia with Harry
married 21 May 1942
HENRY ARTHUR FINCH FINDLAY (Harry)
b 1 July 1915
d 25 Oct 1998 (73)

JOHN (Jack) WOODS
b 5 Sep 1918
d 17 Nov 1939 (21)
buried Waikaraka Cemetery, Auckland.

Harry's Family Tree compiled by his eldest Granddaughter GWYNETH about 2000.
Unless nominated the event happened in New Zealand.
b = born, m = married, d = death

ACKNOWLEDGEMENTS

OTHER WRITINGS and SOURCES.

(A) Auckland: City of the Seas x A W Reed 1955
(BC) Birth of a City, Wellington x A H Carman 1840
(CA) The City of Auckland x John Barr 1922
Beauties of England & Wales by Rev J Evans 1812
'The Bolton' ships Register of Emigrant Labourers. 1840
(EW) Early Wellington by Louise Ward 1928
Earliest New Zealand x John Butler 1927
England, House of Commons Poor Laws 1834
Gleanings of the Histories of Flint by J Poole 1831
Gazetteer of the British Isles. 1887
Pioneers of Port Nicholson x David McGill 1984
Primitive Methodism in Auckland 1849-1913
Fifty years of Primitive Methodists in NZ
(SNZ) The Story of New Zealand
(SS) Settlement by Sail x G W Jackson 1991
Te Aro by E Menzies
Topographical Dictionary of Wales by S Lewis 1834
Tours of Wales by T Pennant 1778.
White Wings by Henry Brett
INTERNET SITES included: Ancestry, FamilySearch, PapersPast NZ, UK BDM, NZ BDM, Genuki, Wikipedia, Timespanner, MyHeritage, UK Census, NZSocG, Google, plus Auckland Library.

SPECIAL THANKS to descendants ....

BE	Brenda Emus	Adam Turner == Lancaster family
CW	Christine Woods	Barry Stringer == GWD Morris family
GB	Gwyneth Broadbent	Leslie Walter == Reynolds family
GF	Gordon Fraser	Lisa Ryan == Turner family
JP	Jill Price	Maureen Garces == Everard family
MM	Murray Meikle	Patricia Bridgeland == Perry family
PM	Peggy Meikle	Rachel Tranter == Ivory family
RW	Ronald Woods	NZH ...The Herald, Auckland
T	Trevor Price	BofPT ... Bay of Plenty Times

INDEX

GENERAL INDEX NEW ZEALAND

--oo00oo--

SHIPS from ENGLAND to NZ

--oo00oo--

INDEX of FAMILY MEMBERS mentioned in TREES and in HISTORIES.

Married females are recorded under their MAIDEN names

... NOTE ...
Woods in bold caps are parents John & Mary Ann. Woods in bold small letters are their 10 children.

FAMILY HISTORIES

THE FOLLOWING PAGES CAN BE USED TO RECORD NEW INFORMATION AND NEW BIRTHS, MARRIAGES AND DEATHS.

www.ingramcontent.com/pod-product-compliance
Ingram Content Group UK Ltd.
Pitfield, Milton Keynes, MK11 3LW, UK
UKHW021827270726
14058UKWH00001B/19

9 780473 531089